What Happened

TO THE

Roman Catholic Church? *What Now?*

*An Institutional
and Personal Memoir*

GABRIEL MORAN

ISBN: 978-1-09838-758-7

Library of Congress Control Number:

CONTENTS

INTRODUCTION

This book is a memoir of what has happened in the Roman Catholic Church during the last seventy-five years and some of what should be done as a result. This church memoir includes a personal memoir of my participation in the story. I make no pretense that I was a major figure in the institutional story, but I was on the scene as some of the story unfolded. The personal anecdotes are intended to illustrate what was going on in the institution.

The Roman Catholic Church has been slowly breaking up for the past seventy years. It is now less Roman and its claim to catholicity is questionable, but it is not likely to disappear. It is in its worst crisis since the sixteenth century, but a changed institution will surely emerge from the crisis.

If one were to pinpoint when this crisis began, a good choice would be November 1, 1950. On that day, Pope Pius XII declared that it was a "defined doctrine" of the Roman Catholic Church that Mary, the mother of Jesus, was bodily assumed into heaven. Millions of Roman Catholics rejoiced at this announcement, which supported popular devotion to the "mother of God." For example, on August 15, the Feast of the Assumption, millions of Catholics flocked to the ocean because of a belief that on that day there was a cure in the water for whatever ailed you.

The world of scholarship, however, was stunned. The pope's declaration initiated a ten-year debate between Protestant and Roman Catholic scholars. And within that debate was an intramural debate among Catholic scholars. The Protestant-Catholic argument was mainly between biblical scholars who had been cooperating in their scholarship and were largely in agreement on what the Bible says. Protestant-Catholic cooperation on *the New Testament* was relatively recent when the pope made his 1950 declaration. Protestants cried foul. They complained that Catholic scholars had not been honest in assuring them that the church's teaching was rooted in the Bible. Here was a blatant disregard of scholarship. The story of the Assumption has no basis in the New Testament or in church tradition before the fourth century.

Catholic New Testament scholars had little to offer in response. They handed the problem to theologians to come up with an explanation. That led to a debate among Catholic theologians. One group of them had been deeply affected by biblical research and critical study of early church history. On the other side were theologians who started with church doctrines and looked for a way to defend them. There followed a debate of ten years that led up to the first document at the Second Vatican Council on "the sources of revelation."

I had a small part in reporting the 1950s debate. What follows is an example of my personal history that I include in this book because it might throw some light on what was occurring in the institution. In this case, it happens that I wrote a master's thesis in 1962 that was published with the title *Scripture and Tradition: A Survey of the Controversy.* The book started out as my first term paper in graduate school. I was surprised and fascinated to learn of a debate about "sources of revelation," having assumed that such a basic question in the church had been resolved centuries ago.

After I diligently prepared what I hoped to be the manuscript of my thesis, I showed the work to my advisor. He took one look at it and dismissed it. "You can't do it," he said, "you missed all the main sources that are in German." I was crestfallen but I refused to give up. While I studied German every day I tracked down the German cast of characters and the theological journals in which they published the relevant essays. I was able to rewrite the thesis with appropriate citations in German to satisfy my advisor.

At issue here was not just my limited linguistic skills. Looking back at this moment, one can see that the emergence of "vernacular" languages within seminary teaching, theological discussions, and demands for liturgical change set in motion all the changes that followed in the church. It would no longer be the "Latin church" and while the adjective "Roman" still applies, Rome is now playing a changing role that is still in flux.

Until the middle of the twentieth century the Roman Catholic Church officially existed in the Latin language. The seminary manuals were in Latin, the professors supposedly taught in Latin, and the seminarians were examined in Latin. Furthermore, Latin was a dead language, and so the meanings of words were the same in the twentieth century as they had been in the sixteenth century. The Bible was not written in Latin but St. Jerome's Latin translation in the third century (the *Vulgate*) was taken to be the official word of the Lord.

When scholars went back to the original text of the New Testament in Aramaic and Greek, they found numerous errors and infelicities in the *Vulgate*. That was the beginning of what would rock the Roman Catholic Church in the second half of the twentieth century. The brilliant scholars of the Bible were not trying to change the church. Just the contrary. Every biblical scholar I encountered in the early 1960s was conservative if not reactionary in their theology. They wanted to quietly do their historical and linguistic work for exegeting ancient texts. They wanted no part of the doctrinal flare-ups, which resulted from their studies.

I had no awareness of how wide sweeping would be the effect of the debate that I was summarizing in 1962. The existence of a debate between the Protestant and the Catholic scholars in the 1950s was something new.

The Catholic and the Protestant scholars had barely talked with each other since the sixteenth century. Even a serious debate among Catholic scholars was unusual.

The loosening of the Latin language in the 1950s made possible the debate among scholars that led to a volcano of change a decade later. My 1963 book was written in English with a sprinkling of French, German, Spanish, Italian and, of course, Latin. In the debate, there was an agreement among all parties that the Latin text from the Council of Trent had primacy. But how that text was translated into many living languages could produce shades of difference. The debate could not have taken place seventy years earlier, and seventy years later the debate sounds slightly ridiculous.

The Council of Trent had said, "divine revelation is contained partly in scripture and partly in tradition." At least, that would have been the standard translation into English. What became the center of debate was the meaning of "partly." Could the words *partim ... partim* (partly in scripture, partly in tradition) be imagined other than two faucets, two buckets, two containers, or a similar metaphor? Could one imagine a single "source" that is available either in one outlet or the other?

The first position seemed to be the obvious meaning that the Council of Trent had intended, and which had centuries of support behind it. But some modern scholars were trying to move away from the assumption that the Bible is a bucket of truths supplemented by other truths that constituted "tradition." Could the direction these scholars wished to move in be reconciled with the Council of Trent's formula.

My book could only conclude with a summary of the two sides of the argument. In later years, I would tell people that the only thing worth reading in the book is footnote number one, which says that this is the wrong problem. What that footnote reflects is what I concluded after immersing myself in the debate. It seemed to me that the problem was not whether there are one or two sources of revelation. The question that seemed to get lost was the meaning of "revelation."

Church members had been assured that no matter what was going on in the world outside the church, the doctrines of the church were as stable as a rock. There was room for debate about individual doctrines, but the basis of all doctrine was ancient, unchanging, and beyond debate. It was this assumption about the solidity of the church's teaching that made the change of the 1960s so unsettling.

The liturgy became the place where the change of language came home to every Roman Catholic. The Latin Mass was a fixture of many centuries. Little boys aspiring to be altar boys had to learn the Latin responses to the priest's introductory prayers. The congregation listened to the familiar sounds of "Kyrie eleison," "Agnus Dei" and "Ite missa est." The Latin language, far from being thought of as a barrier, was a protection of what philosopher Gabriel Marcel called a mystery, a term which signifies not a problem to be solved but an experience that can always be deepened.

The march of the vernacular languages, however, was unstoppable. Sunday Mass would be more appreciated, it was argued, when the congregation understood everything that was said. Everybody in the congregation was now expected to participate in all aspects of this new liturgy. Instead of listening to a choir that might draw from beautiful Gregorian chant, which is based on the rhythm of the Latin language, the congregants were now supposed to sing, something for which they had no preparation and no appropriate music at hand. The result was, and in some places still is, torturous musical renditions. Few parishes thought it worthwhile to invest in a music program or a music teacher.

The great hope was that English was the solution to the church's problems. I was present at the first (officially approved) Mass in English. I remember some enthusiastic singing of the great Lutheran hymn, "A Mighty Fortress is Our God." There was excitement and expectation that the church had finally arrived where it belonged. What I especially remember from that evening was a warning from Episcopalian and Lutheran visitors. "Don't think your problems will be solved by translating every-thing into English."

There remained a significant part of the church, and there still is, that wanted no part of destroying the mystery of the Latin Mass. Change was called for, but church officials might have moved slowly by starting with the translation of the readings that are addressed to the congregation. The music might have been something other than 1960s popular music that quickly went out of style.

It would probably have been better for the church if the Second Vatican Council had taken place decades before the 1960s. Reforms might have been slowly introduced. Instead, the bishops and their advisors at the Council tried to take giant steps while their language still trailed behind them. They did make some initial reforms, but in the atmosphere of the 1960s their every move seemed to be revolutionary. The Council might have been the beginning of a reform movement that would have contin-ued in the following decades. A Third Vatican Council and perhaps sev-eral more councils should have occurred by now. Instead, a reaction began in the 1970s. Revolutions that start and then promptly stop do not turn out well.

There are many fine church histories of the Council period. But I am not aware of anyone who has identified the main engine of change in the same way as I do. My contention is that the activity itself of the Second Vatican Council, as covered by television and press reporters, showed a church that was not based on the unchanging truths that it had previously made claim to. The official teaching of the Roman Catholic Church was and is the result of a political process, which includes lobbying, debate, and voting. And even though Latin was still the official language at the Council, the real debates were not taking place in Latin.

There is nothing wrong with a political process but in this case it conflicted with a meaning of divine revelation as God's own truth that had been transmitted from the apostles to the bishops. The Second Vatican

Council tried to get some distance from the Council of Trent's version of divine revelation. It commissioned the writing of a document by biblical scholars who used New Testament language and imagery to avoid directly confronting what had been taught by Trent.

The result was a Vatican II document with beautiful biblical imagery that avoided asking if there is such a thing as divine revelation, and if so, what is it and where is it? The pope and the bishops continue to speak of revealed truth as if the year were 1950. Catholic theologians have not been willing to probe the consequences of the fact that church officials do not possess a divine revelation on which to base their teaching.

Who This Book Is For?

Every author has an intended readership in writing a book. The potential readers for whom the book is intended might be a small group. But if what is in the book is well written and relevant for the intended group, the book is likely to find a wider readership.

This book is directly intended for Roman Catholic readers who wish to understand what is going on in their church. Because it is a book especially concerned with language, the reader needs to be willing to read reflectively. Like the great philosopher, Ludwig Wittgenstein, I am interested in slow readers. The book is about the big changes that have taken place in the Roman Catholic Church together with changes that I or others are proposing in the present. I am interested in Roman Catholics, not only those who are classified as liberals but also those who consider themselves conservative. I try to be respectful of the church's past, its tradition and history.

This book, however, is not neutral reporting. It is a book of advocacy, but the advocacy is mainly linguistic. I concentrate on language because it structures an institution, even though that fact is usually hidden in plain sight. One virtue of linguistic advocacy is that there is always room for disagreement. Words are ambiguous; the simpler and more important the words are, the more ambiguous they are. What I primarily hope for from a reader is not agreement with my conclusions but attention to the questions.

In addition to Roman Catholics, I hope for some readers who were formerly church members. That group is about thirty million people in the United States, many of whom understandably have no interest in the church. Many others, however, retain some connection, whether an appreciation of some activities by church members or anger at the influence of the church on their lives and the life of the nation. I share some of their feelings, for example, about the horror of the clergy sex-abuse scandal. For former Roman Catholics, I can only promise that my arguments are open to scrutiny and are not obscured by ecclesiastical jargon.

Finally, this book might interest Protestants, Jews, Muslims, and others who are fascinated or puzzled by the survival and success of the Roman Catholic Church. Although this church may be in its most serious crisis since the Protestant Reformation, the Roman Catholic Church and other Christian Churches are not likely to disappear soon; they retain a powerful place in the life of the nation. Whatever one's attitude to the Christian churches, every citizen has a stake in the shape and influence of these institutions. This book examines Roman Catholicism in that context.

This book, like my previous books, follows the words to get at the foundational ideas of the institution. If one goes looking for the ideas of revelation or natural law, it may not be clear whether or not one has found them. If one looks for the words "revelation" or "natural law" there is no ambiguity when one finds them.

Following the words may no longer seem important when politicians today, and even some professors, routinely say about a dispute that, "it doesn't matter what you call it." One of the marks of Catholic tradition has been an attention to words. Its beliefs are precisely stated. I have claimed that the beginning of the church's crisis was linguistic. Can the church survive a translation from Latin?

Getting the words right is still an urgent concern in the most serious matters. In a court of law, swearing to tell the truth means using words accurately. A physician writing a prescription needs to get each word right. Professional reporters know how important it is to quote a source exactly. Even between friends, the right word can be of inestimable value and the wrong word can destroy trust.

Dictionaries that give a definition of a word by citing a few other words do not provide an understanding of how several meanings of a word are related. One must be aware of a word's history and the present meaning or meanings of a word. The whole inquiry is a messy and illogical business, but language is the best instrument we human beings have. We agree or disagree in our words.

PART ONE

CHAPTER ONE:

The Calm 1945–1960

The Roman Catholic Church is in danger of complete collapse. It is large enough and powerful enough to go on indefinitely while continually making repairs and circling the wagons. But it could use a better analysis of how and when this church stopped being a stable institution in society's sea of change.

In the early part of the twentieth century, the church's members were utterly loyal to the institution and its every teaching. Today things are different. What brought about such major changes in a short time, short at least in the history of the Christian churches? I tell the tale from inside the experience of that period but with a critical view of what is needed to understand the church's failure and some of what a radical reform would require.

This chapter on the period of 1945–1960 describes what was happening on the surfaces of the United States of America and the Roman Catholic Church. In both cases, the calm hid rumblings below the surface. Cracks appeared in the foundation of both institutions. Both country and church conveyed the appearance of extraordinary stability in the face of a common enemy, the threat of worldwide communism. That opponent also gave the appearance of a mighty power but eventually it simply dissolved.

The hidden problems of the United States of America and the Roman Catholic Church would surface in the 1960s and the struggle with these problems left permanent effects in both institutions.

The World War II was not only a horrible slaughter of human beings. It was a crisis in the foundations of the political and social order. The World War I had awakened the European thinkers to their naiveté in assuming the continuing spread of democratic ideals and scientific enlightenment. The brief period between the wars was hardly one of peace. The resumption and spread of war raised even more fundamental questions about whether there was any basis on which to rebuild a modern civilization that had lost its way. The crisis was obviously moral and for many people religious.

The United States of America had from its beginning been a peculiar combination of scientific enlightenment and evangelical Christianity. The early part of the twentieth century was characterized by doubts about the place of religion in the public life of the country. The World War II raised new questions. Alan Jacobs in his book, *The Year of Our Lord 1943*, traces the writing of thinkers who were preparing the way for a humanistic revival of Christianity. "The war raised for each of the thinkers … a pressing set of questions about the relationship between Christianity and the Western democratic social order, and especially about whether Christianity was uniquely suited to the moral underpinning of that order."[1]

The end of the war ushered in a period of religious fervor in the United States. Religious leaders were greatly admired, and politicians were attentive to those leaders and their institutions. Surprisingly, the Roman Catholic Church occupied a prominent role in this national religious renewal. The country was looking for a strong institution and a powerful ideology to counter the secular ideologies of the age. The Roman Catholic Church seemed to be the rock of stability that many people were looking for.

The Roman Catholic Church had not previously drawn strong support from outsiders. In 1933, Franklin Roosevelt said to two of his most trusted advisers, Henry Morgenthau, Jr., a Jew, and Leo Crowley, a Catholic: "You know that this is a Protestant country. Jews and Catholics are here only by sufferance."[2] It is not surprising that Roosevelt thought that way. It was a common view among Protestants. It is surprising, however, that Roosevelt would say that to his Catholic and Jewish advisors. Religious bigotry was usually veiled in those days.

The opposition to the Roman Catholic Church was based upon a suspicion of Catholics having "dual loyalties," referring to church and country. But friends and foes were curious and even fascinated by this ancient institution and its legions of dedicated workers. Two people at the time who illustrate the interest in the Roman Catholic Church were Thomas Merton and Fulton Sheen, figures who represented contrasting aspects of the church's popularity.

Thomas Merton's book, *The Seven Storey Mountain*, was an autobiographical account of the author's conversion to the church and his entrance into the severe Trappist order. The book sold six-hundred-thousand copies when it was published in 1948.[3] The Trappists suddenly seemed attractive to many men who perhaps did not fully grasp what life would be like in a contemplative religious order. People flocked to Gethsemane monastery in Kentucky with the hope of conversing with Merton or at least getting a glimpse of the celebrity monk.

Fulton Sheen was a New York monsignor who became one of the earliest television celebrities. Television suited him better than the classroom did. A famous story at Catholic University concerned a student who raised his hand to ask a question in Sheen's class. There was a tremor of disbelief; the monsignor was not to be interrupted. Sheen was given a slot on the Dupont network at eight o'clock on Tuesday evenings. The time was considered a TV death wish because it was opposite Milton Berle, the biggest draw on television. In the late 1940s and early 1950s, most of the citizenry gathered in their living rooms to watch one of the three or four television channels.

Sheen surprised everyone by offering real competition to Berle in the years 1951 to 1957. He reached an audience of thirty million people. I can remember in the Methodist household, where I spent many hours of my youth, the family enthusiastically embraced Sheen's sermons. That was not an attitude that Methodists were previously known for. Sheen became known for his conversions. He was able to bring into the Roman Catholic Church some rich and famous people.

When I was in a Catholic novitiate in the early 1950s the novice director intercepted the copy of Merton's autobiography, which my mother had sent to me. It was considered too racy for my innocent soul. Fulton Sheen's books, however, were readily available. I avidly read his history of modern philosophy. Although he claimed to show how every modern philosopher was wrong, his books gave me a catalog of the philosophers whom I wanted to read in the future.

My earliest memories are completely dominated by the war. I was six-years old at the time of Pearl Harbor, but I remember that Sunday and what immediately followed. The war touched every family, some profoundly. I can picture my father coming home and telling my mother that he would not be drafted. He was thirty-seven years old at the war's beginning and the draft age was set just below that age. One of my uncles was on the front line in Europe, although it was never spoken about. He simply came home and drank himself to an early death.

Everything about World War II remains imprinted in my memory. I can picture my nine-year old self standing outside the church discussing the "battle of the bulge" that was occurring in Europe. I think back with horror and shame at celebrating the dropping of the atomic bombs. I heard no contrary voices. Soon after those bombings, I was at a baseball game with my father when the end of the war was announced.

The changes after the war were less dramatic than I had expected. A war mentality continued; only the name of the enemy changed. Everything was suddenly about the menace of "godless communism" and that it might represent the final battle between Christ and the anti-Christ. When the Soviet Union acquired atomic bombs there was palpable fear that a war was inevitable in which hundreds of millions would be killed. The church presented a protective shell against these horrors while at the same time the church was stoking fears.

I vividly remember Sunday, June 25, 1950 when war began in Korea. I did not understand why my mother was so distressed about a war in a place that I had never heard of. But she knew exactly what the news meant. She had been down this road twice before and she was worried about the safety of her sons.

Before the war, the United States had indicated that South Korea was not an important part of its stand against communism. But when an invasion of South Korea occurred, General Douglas McArthur wrote to one of his congressional supporters: "… if we lose the war to communism in Asia, the fall of Europe is inevitable. Win it and Europe would probably avoid war and yet preserve freedom." McArthur, who was in charge of the U.S. troops, was constantly pushing to widen the war. He was miffed when he was told not to bomb within five miles of the Chinese border.

Eventually, President Truman relieved McArthur of his command. He came home to a hero's welcome that included a ticker-tape parade, which drew seven million people. I remember the classroom being turned over to listening on the radio to McArthur's speech before Congress.

The Chinese did not like the United States army on its border and helped the North Koreans to fight to a standstill against the coalition of U.S. troops and the South Korean army. An armistice finally stopped the military conflict but a half century later the Korean peninsula was still not at peace. An historian of that war wrote: "A new Korean War could break out tomorrow morning, and Americans would still be in their original state of overwhelming might and unfathomable cluelessness; armies ignorant of each other would clash again and the outcome would again yield its central truth: there is no military solution in Korea (and there never was.)"[4]

Thirty years later, when I was teaching many Korean and Korean American students, I had to admit that I was ignorant of the United States war on the Korean peninsula. My ignorance included not knowing what name Koreans used for the war. I was too embarrassed to ask Koreans for help, so I went to the university library. I found no books on the subject. I thought at first that I was looking in the wrong section, but I eventually realized that there were few histories of that war. That lack has been partially corrected in recent years but citizens and leaders of the United States seem to have amnesia about most of the wars that the United States has been in.

During the 1950s the United States government employed religion in its contrast between freedom and communism. The Roman Catholic Church, which was eager to prove its patriotism, became known as fiercely anti-communist. It was on the side of America and freedom. It supported characters such as Senator Joseph McCarthy and other political leaders who were "anti-communist."

The Boston Post, a rabidly right-wing newspaper, came into my home every day and I read it avidly. Throughout the 1950s, I was caught up in the pseudo-patriotism of right-wing politics. Even when the Roman Catholic Church had its first U.S. president in John Kennedy, the rhetoric of anti-communism continued to dominate policy decisions of the country.

The placid surface of the United States between 1945 and 1960 hid issues of justice that simmered just below the surface. Television sitcoms of that era are sometimes cited for evidence that family life was stable. Each household had a white father and mother presiding over their two or three children. There were problems on the home front but none that could not be solved with all parties satisfied in the end.

There is a question, however, whether those idyllic pictures of the family portrayed reality or were a longed-for ideal. There were marginalized groups that were not much seen on television or elsewhere in public images. Women, blacks, and gays were expected to return to their pre-war invisibility, but things had permanently changed during the war even though it took more than a decade for this changed world to become evident.

There were plenty of signals that many women were ready for a different arrangement than the one that confined them to taking care of the suburban home. Television and popular novels portrayed women as the ones who were really in charge. The men left home in the morning to work at an office and arrived home for dinner. Men brought home the paycheck, but women ran the home and most other things.

Society had a male problem more than a woman's problem, but it would be the women who eventually rebelled. What is surprising is how long women put up with their status before middle-class women organized a protest. As had happened in the nineteenth century, white women were inspired by black protests for justice and equality.

The Black movement for civil rights, which would explode in the 1960s, had already begun in the 1950s. Like most white people I was barely aware of this movement in the far away south. The movement is dated from December 1955, when Rosa Parks, a woman in Montgomery, Alabama, refused to give up her seat to a white man on a city bus.

Parks's arrest touched off a protest that led to a boycott of the city buses. Blacks constituted 75 percent of the ridership, so the year-long boycott had a significant impact. A federal court ruled in favor of Parks and her backers. The Supreme Court reaffirmed the lower court's ruling that the segregation laws in Alabama violated the U.S. Constitution's fourteen amendment that forbids racial discrimination.

The leader of the protest was a twenty-six-year-old Baptist pastor named Martin Luther King, Jr. whose name will forever be identified with the uprisings of the 1960s. Under King's leadership the movement appealed to moral and religious principles, as well as to political rights. He was continuing the nineteenth-century movements that were concerned with abolition and protests against Jim Crow laws. Evangelicals were the leaders in movements for social justice. The main Protestant churches and the Roman Catholic Church were not prominent. Most northerners were fine with protests in Alabama, but they would later express skepticism and opposition when King brought his poor peoples' army north.

Garry Wills writes that in this era, "many Catholic intellectuals turned from commercialism toward eternity, or to the thirteenth century as a plausible substitute for eternity. They took up Gregorian chant, St. Thomas Aquinas and the work of French Catholic literary stars, such as Francois Mauriac, Georges Bernanos, Pierre Teilhard de Chardin and Jacques Maritain."[5] The United States failed to produce its own literary stars. The historian John Tracy Ellis indicted the U.S. church of that period for its lack of a Catholic intellectual culture.[6]

The Roman Catholic Church in the United States was a formidable institution that seemed not subject to change. That was its strength but ultimately it was also its weakness. The church had acquired political influence by reason of its size and by its members who were loyal to what the church leaders taught. Until the Second Vatican Council in the 1960s, there was absent not only dissent but also debate about policies.

Internally, the church had not developed the mechanisms of political give and take, something that every large institution needs. When politics is thought to be beneath the dignity of an institution, its authority pattern can easily become corrupted. A bishop who had experienced those years described to me the annual meeting of U.S. bishops when Cardinal Francis Spellman was in charge. The bishops would file into a conference room and be handed a document that had been prepared before the meeting. The Cardinal would ask whether there were any objections; if not (there never were) the statement was approved unanimously and made public as what the bishops had agreed upon at the meeting.

The cultural and political arrival of the Roman Catholic Church was indicated by a series of Supreme Court rulings in the 1940s. Some of the rulings also showed a fear of the rising power of the Roman Catholic

Church. For the first time the Court put the metaphor of "church and state" into the legal language of the country.[7] The language is often said to be in the U.S. Constitution, but it was introduced by Thomas Jefferson in a letter to Connecticut Baptists in 1804.

There was little doubt about what "church" referred to in the 1940s. Some of the Irish immigrants who found their way into politics became powers in the big cities. Their influence raised new questions about government services for parochial schools. The Supreme Court's wall to separate government and church called into question any services that aided Catholic schools. Direct financial aid would not be forthcoming, although some services for children, such as busing, were allowed.

The Court's rulings against religious practices in the state schools would later be specified and included reading from the Bible and saying state-mandated prayers. Protestant groups were shocked to have these decisions applied to their practices. They had not thought that decisions about the church applied to them. There was resistance, especially in the South where many schools disregarded prohibitions of Christian expressions.

A sign of the moral influence that the Roman Catholic Church exercised was the "Hayes code," which controlled all the movies made in Hollywood.[8] Catholics took a pledge each year to follow the classification of movies according to the Legion of Decency. That was fair enough but until the end of the 1950s the church effectively censored what everyone in the country could see in their local movie theaters.

Hollywood would later see the benefit in a rating system to help parents judge the suitability of movies for their children. But the censorship in place for more than two decades was rigid, especially on anything concerning sexual matters. During the 1950s, Cardinal Spellman got himself into ridiculous fights over a series of movies that he thought were too frank about sex.

Growing Up Catholic

I have sometimes said with only slight exaggeration that as a child I knew of only three kinds of people: Irish Catholics, French Catholics, and Yankees. In the town of my youth, the Irish dominated the east side of the river, the French the west side, and the rich Yankees who ran the town lived in the north end. The city was almost two-thirds Roman Catholic. There were more children in the Catholic school system than in the public system. The neighborhood, however, was ethnically diverse. Differences of nationality or religion were not a big topic among the children, but the parents were no doubt keenly aware of such things.

New Hampshire during this decade was 99 percent white. I do not remember a single encounter with a black person in my childhood. The only ocean resort in the state had unwritten rules that kept out blacks (and Jews). I was shocked to discover that fact when I was an adult. I did not think of my parents or anyone else I knew as racist. If the term racism is limited to hatred of people whom one knows, then neither my relatives nor I would be included in the term. Nevertheless, it has been a lifelong struggle to root out the ignorance and wrong assumptions that were part of my upbringing in an all-white world.

My experience growing up in that small New England city was very different from the Catholics I later came to know who grew up in New York City. They would identify themselves by the parish that they belonged to, something I would never have thought to do. They knew about Ireland, immigration, and the difficult experience of Catholics in the history of the United States; I knew almost nothing about those topics. Their lives revolved around the parish and the Irish or Italian experiences that were foreign to me.

It was only much later that I came to appreciate that my parents' generation had to struggle against discrimination. I was unaware of how recently the sign "Catholics need not apply" was common in the city.

My mother was born in the dormitory of the textile mill where she went to work at age thirteen. She said that the Yankee owners took delight in making the girls work on Christmas day, a main Irish Catholic holy day. She was always proud that she had "got her education," eight years of school with German nuns. That was superior to the French girls who worked in the mill; they usually had only a few years of schooling. My father was fortunate to finish high school. Both parents were determined to see their children through college. All five children finished college and four of us went on for graduate degrees.

By the middle of the twentieth century the Roman Catholic Church was an institution to be reckoned with. The church at that time was compared favorably with General Motors for its organizational efficiency.

Within that large and powerful institution Roman Catholics were able to find an alternative to the strongly individualistic character of the United States. Today, older Roman Catholics look back nostalgically to the church before the Second Vatican Council. There is no going back to the 1950s, but those Catholics have a legitimate point who think that the experience of community needs to be revived for the church to have a vibrant future.

Before the Second Vatican Council there was an ethnic bias to the church's communities. Irish immigrants had arrived in great numbers before other Catholic immigrants from Germany, Italy, Poland, and other countries. The Irish Americans not only had numbers but also the English language. The Roman Catholic Church in the United States became for many outsiders and some insiders the Irish Catholic Church.

Other church members formed ethnic parishes that generally lacked much power in church matters. Priesthood was a much-praised vocation in Irish American families. The Roman Catholic episcopacy reflected a dominance of Irish Americans and reinforced that dominance.

Beneath the outer covering of men speaking for the church it was women who were the lynchpin of community life. The nuns ran the gigantic school system with little help, especially financial aid, from the clergy. The pastor of the parish of my childhood said with seeming pride that each of the nuns in the parish school cost him one dollar a day. The nuns also provided a major part of the country's hospital system as well as serving in other social work. The sisters were sometimes ridiculed by outsiders but often they were grudgingly admired.

Catholic mothers did not have an easy road. They took care of a large family and a husband who typically was not in a high paying job. They found support in the church and especially "the faith." They often were the leaders in the parish or other church organizations. For example, the Catholic Family Movement that was founded in the 1940s included extraordinary women who understood the need for liturgical change, ecumenical involvement, and social action. The usual role offered to these women in the parish was as a volunteer for the Confraternity of Christian Doctrine (CCD). This teaching of the catechism to the children who were not in Catholic schools was given little support and almost no money.

As the fourth child in the family, I had my route in school set for me. I attended eight years of elementary school with the Sisters of Mercy, and then four years of high school under the stern guidance of a religious order of men, the Christian Brothers. I was aware, even as a child, that the nuns did not have any advanced educational credentials but that was not thought to be the main requirement for dealing with a room full of children.

I look back with admiration and gratitude for the Sisters of Mercy who were a major part of my childhood. Sister Mary Carmel in the first grade managed sixty children, something she did daily for decades. She provided the basics of learning through her care and dedication rather than by any educational theory. The eight years of school were pleasant, although somewhat boring because I was easily able to master what was needed for being considered a good student. That meant maintaining the reputation for good conduct and high grades that had been set by my older siblings.

Religion teaching consisted of questions and answers that were in *The Baltimore Catechism.* The book was a product of the nineteenth century with a content that was established by the sixteenth-century Council of Trent. Some of the questions and answers had words or phrases that did not make any sense to me but overall it seemed a marvelous book that gave answers to everything important in life. My mother had studied from the same book more than thirty years earlier. She vouched for the book as the main guide that one needed in life.

Confession of one's sins every two weeks and holy communion each Sunday kept one on the straight path of virtue. The main problem with confession was trying to come up with a sin or two for the regular cleansing of the soul.

High school was a different experience. The school lessons became secondary to the contest of trying to run with the popular crowd. I received high grades, but I learned very little. Like many boys of the time, I was determined to be an athlete although I was hopelessly lacking in talent. I spent endless hours on the basketball court for three years before admitting to myself that I was not going to succeed.

At the end of high school, I followed my brother to the state university although I had no idea of what I wished to do in life. At the end of a year in college I made a sudden decision to join the Christian Brothers while having little knowledge of what I was in for. I am surprised that I never had a moment of regret for what I did. I have always been grateful to the brothers for the years I lived as one of them and I have continued to be in close touch with them.

The Roman Catholic Church of the 1950s had firm principles of morality that provided a certainty that other organizations lacked. But its officials drew conclusions and applications that were far less certain than the principles. Church officials conflated principles with precepts or rules of conduct. That lack of distinction did not seem to matter because the system came as a single package.

The moral system was accepted as part of "the faith." But there is a problem if moral principles are not reexamined in the light of changing situations. A fixed system of moral precepts does not prepare people to enter the give and take of political, economic, and cultural debates. The tendency of church leaders was to claim that they stood above the fray from where they could proclaim universal truths.

The religious order of the 1950s exemplified the conflation of principles and precepts. Life was regulated down to the smallest detail. There was required an obedience to the rule of the order and to the commands of the superior. To an outsider that might seem gruesome. But at the time, with the air of certainty that the church breathed, the burden seemed light.

As I prepared to enter the brothers, I had no idea what to expect. The vocation director who drove me to the novitiate gave me one piece of advice: "Some strange things will be required of you. Just remember that the system has been in existence for centuries. Everything has passed the test of trial and error." It was good advice even if it was not entirely accurate. I enjoyed the discipline in the novitiate, but it was evident that some practices had long outlived their usefulness and should have been retired.

After the novitiate, I received the three years of college that I needed to finish my bachelor's degree. The brothers ran their own college as part of Catholic University in Washington, D.C. That part of the training was called the scholasticate. It was comprised of several hundred young men living in one building who studied in one hall. The time for study in the "common room" was limited. Those times were the most intense atmosphere of study I have ever encountered. Brothers who were academically weaker got help from others. Failure was not an option. I loved the atmosphere and developed a great interest in studies, something I had never previously had.

In 1958 I began teaching in a high school that was a powerhouse of academic excellence. The school had been built for a capacity of a thousand students; by the time I arrived, it housed fifteen hundred. That kind of crowding of teenage boys was not a good atmosphere for teaching. The brothers' residence that could comfortably house twenty men had thirty-two. My yearning for a room of my own had to be postponed.

The work was grueling because the system was to require homework and a written quiz every day. I confronted about two-hundred and fifty boys each day and followed that by working in other school activities. I was not highly effective in the classroom. I thought I would be able to teach well in a different setting but managing a room with fifty teenage boys was beyond me. Several brothers not much older than myself helped me. A few years ago, I said to one of those men who was still a brother: "You don't know it, but you got me through my first year of teaching. I want to thank you even though I am sixty years late."

The Christian Brothers were known for running good schools, well-organized and academically demanding. The men were dedicated to teaching and they were determined that their graduates would be well prepared for whatever followed in life. They were proud of the work they did even though it was not appreciated in many ecclesiastical quarters. During the 1950s, a famous Cardinal got rid of the brothers in their one school in his diocese. He said that the brothers were "an unnecessary luxury" because he was paying fifty dollars a month for each of the men. He did not want the nuns to hear about that and demand a pay raise for themselves.

The Catholic schools were known for their discipline, a word whose root meaning is not punishment but teaching. Parents who were not Catholic sometimes sent their children to Catholic schools because they were assured that the schools were orderly places in which teaching could occur. In the brothers' schools, corporal punishment was not as common as is often rumored. However, there was some physical punishment that, when looked back upon from today, must be called shameful. Very few of the men were inclined to be violent but sometimes they gave in to the pressure of situations they were in. One older brother told me about his experience in an institution to which delinquent boys were sent by the New

York courts. He was put in a yard with several hundred boys and told to keep order. He was given a stick along with the sole instruction, "don't let anyone get behind you."

During my third year of teaching, the provincial superior, Brother Charles Henry, visited the community and interviewed each of us. He was a fine scholar who was aware of rumblings in the European Catholic Church that foreshadowed big changes in education. He made an extraordinary offer to me. He said that he would like me to study religious education and become an expert for the province. For that purpose, he said I could go anywhere in the world and study as long as I needed in order to prepare myself. That was an offer that I could not refuse. The organization's leaders seemed to think that I had academic promise; I also think they were just mercifully getting me out of the high school classroom.

The church was soon to be hit with an avalanche of change. I was fortunate enough to have the leisure of stepping back to study what was happening.

Like so many people, I had lived through the decade of the 1950s oblivious of anything except the calm operation of the church that was finding a more secure position in the country's positive attitude to religion. The only threat seemed to be the shadow of Communism's might, which was always to be feared, but the country and its military power quickly put down any nearby disturbances in South America and the Caribbean. The Roman Catholic Church in the United States was the source of a con- tinually expanding missionary group. At home, the Catholic schools were educating a larger percentage of Catholic children than ever before. The future looked placid. What could go wrong?

CHAPTER TWO:

The Storm: 1960–1968

The Roman Catholic Church entered the 1960s seemingly at the pinnacle of success in its United States journey. Being a Catholic was no longer an impediment to any position, including president of the country. There was still discrimination against Catholics in some professions, but that problem did not often surface. Pope Pius XII ruled the universal church from 1939 to 1958 and his man in the United States, Cardinal Francis Spellman, used a firm hand in his position as Archbishop of New York from 1939 to 1967. The system was formidable.

When people refer to the decade of the 1960s the reference is almost mythical. Every decade of history has its ups and downs but for those of us who were adolescents or young adults at that time, the 1960s were of such intensity that almost everything after that time has had an anti-climactic feeling. Passion can have both good and bad effects. The cliché applies to the 1960s: "It was the best of times; it was the worst of times."

People born after the 1960s often seem to take a condescending attitude toward a decade that is easy to ridicule. It was a time of funny clothes as both men and women experimented with new ways of interacting. Conservative commentators, including many church officials, see the 1960s as the time when human passions were unleashed, and civilization collapsed. It was a decade of assassinations, wars, and the undermining of all social mores.

These attacks on the decade of the 1960s have a basis. But for people who lived through the changes that occurred in that decade, it was a time of great hope. People were experiencing the pangs of a new world being born. Those people were naïve although the world did experience monumental changes; it is just that the results were not what had been hoped for. Nevertheless, nearly all the movements for justice in today's world emerged in the 1960s.

The movement for racial equality led the way for most of the other movements. The glacially slow progress of the preceding century toward equality for blacks was influenced by the experience of black soldiers who had fought for their country during World War II. They proved to anyone who needed proof that they were equal to their white counterparts in competence, courage, and loyalty. Having seen other parts of the world, they were aware of how things could be and should be different in the United States, both in the rural south and in the big cities of the north.

Protests for racial equality that had begun in the 1950s accelerated at the beginning of the 1960s. Several impressive leaders emerged who could get the attention of the country. As has been true throughout U.S. history, there were black preachers who drew upon the Bible as well as the history of the country in demanding justice. It must be admitted that the churches did not lead the way. Martin Luther King, Jr. used to say that "Eleven o'clock on Sunday morning" is still the most segregated hour of the week.[1]

Something that did emerge at the time was cooperation among Catholic, Protestant and Jewish activists for the extension of human and civil rights. Ecumenical conferences were made realistic by these ventures of cooperation on the street. Those of us who grew up ignorant of the history of our country suddenly awoke to the discrimination against our fellow citizens. We marched in protests that were of limited value. I remember going with a group of brothers to a Maryland town that was in the news for its nightly conflicts over race. The military officer in charge of keeping the peace told us to go back to Washington and lobby our representatives for a public park that would achieve more good than our presence could. I was shocked to hear him say that he had heard more gunfire during the conflict in that small town than he had heard in Vietnam.

Martin Luther King, Jr. was a much more controversial character than he is remembered today by the white people. He was approved by northerners when he held demonstrations in southern states. When he came north to Chicago and linked race and poverty, he was accused of getting into questions of economics for which he was not professionally qualified. But it did not require a master's degree to see the connection between racial discrimination and poverty. What caused an even bigger reaction was when King linked race and the United States war in Vietnam. I can still picture the evening at Riverside Church one year to the day before he was assassinated. King, despite warnings from many of his supporters, indicted the government for its foolish and costly war that especially burdened black people.

King's most famous speech on the steps of the capitol in 1963 is invariably referred to as the "I have a dream" speech.[2] That title allows the white people to remember the speech as fitting in nicely with the standard U.S. rhetoric. The speech does end on a hopeful note symbolized by a dream of how things will someday be. But most of that speech is a searing indictment of the history of race relations in this country. By 1963 King was not far removed from the more radical voices of Malcolm X, James Baldwin, or Rap Brown. Martin Luther King, Jr. was cut down at the age of thirty-nine, having accomplished more in his lifetime than those of us who have twice that much time on earth. In the 1960s there seemed to be actual progress on race, whatever had been the horrors of the past. President Lyndon Johnson, who had shown little leadership on race during his time in Congress, as president was dedicated to passing legislation that would complete what John Kennedy had begun. The Civil Rights Bill of 1964 and the Voting Rights Act of 1965 seemed to finally put the country on a path that would right the racial disgraces of the past.

When I now reread literature from that period or listen to King's speeches, it can be difficult to see that we have made progress at all. Certainly, there is more awareness of the problems. Black people are visible in the entertainment industry and black politicians are no longer a rare phenomenon. But poverty remains extensive with high unemployment among young black men. The rate of incarceration of black men is a national scandal. Police forces across the country, with few exceptions, have remained white. The conflicts between cops and black men are a terrible legacy of the past, something that great numbers of white people seem finally to have grasped in the protests of 2020.

Martin Luther King, Jr. was intent on bringing the Christian churches to leadership in opposing racism. Since the work of Quakers in the seventeenth century, some of the churches have been at the forefront of opposition to slavery and to supporting equality for black citizens. The Roman Catholic Church's record is not distinguished. It is true that the Catholic immigrants had their own struggle and lacked political power. By the twentieth century, however, the Roman Catholic Church had acquired significant political power but remained on the sidelines of the black movement for equality.

It is amazing that black citizens continued to believe in the promise of the United States. The religion of black people is sometimes dismissed as otherworldly. Some of it may have been but even the slave literature was realistic about the failures of church and government to live up to the ideals on which the country is supposedly built. Black people relied on the Bible as their basis of hope; they were intent on changing conditions in this world as well as looking to a better world in the future.

The Roman Catholic Church during the last seventy-five years has struggled to overcome its past attitudes on race but progress has been slow. Church leadership shows little racial diversity, only slightly better than its monolith of gender. There are some parish churches that are predominantly black. In those churches the liturgy usually has a liveliness that is absent in the typical white suburban parish. Preaching in black churches has a passion to it, and the whole congregation is likely to be involved in the music.

The movement for black civil and human rights spearheaded the other social movements of the 1960s, many of which are still with us. The women's movement, a renewal of efforts that began in the nineteenth century, was entwined with the struggle for racial justice throughout history but also in tension with it. I will comment in the next chapter on the magnitude of change represented by the women's movement and its continuing significance for the Roman Catholic Church.

The gay rights movement was not directly related to the black movement, but it is not just a coincidence that the movement emerged in the late 1960s. The cry for justice had spread from black leadership to other people who had long been excluded from having a public presence. In this case, also, the Roman Catholic Church has struggled with the extraordinary changes in social attitudes to homosexuality since the 1960s. I will discuss the gay/lesbian revolution in Chapter Eight.

Old people joined in the cry to be heard by political leaders. A group of older women called "the Grey Panthers" were at first patronized by the news media but they were a serious group that achieved some success in calling attention to the plight of older citizens. They started with a group of fewer than a dozen women and no financial resources. They learned how to play the news media to their own advantage.[3] Old people, like other groups, were looking for respect and the chance to contribute their talents to society. Since the 1960s the older population has achieved great economic improvement. I will comment in Chapter Nine on the situation of the old today.

The indigenous people decided that it was time for white people to stop calling them Indians (a name imposed on them by a lost Italian).

"Native American" as a name was not enthusiastically received. After all, if white people were serious about that name, they would start calling themselves foreigners or hyphenated Americans. The "Native Americans" could simply be called "the Americans." Still, white people were at least becoming aware of the damage done by the U.S. government policies and the Hollywood movie images of "the Indian." Many young people in the 1960s were attracted by (native) American spirituality.[4]

The awareness of the (native) Americans' way of life was an aspect of the environmental movement. Concern for the environment seemed to sum up all the other movements at the end of the 1960s. "Ecology" was a new word for most people although it had been around since the beginning of the twentieth century. There had been a concern with the environment among many scientists and writers in previous decades.

At the end of the 1960s environmental awareness suddenly blossomed in the public's consciousness. There seemed to be a remarkable consensus on Earth Day 1970.[5] After the conflicts of the preceding decade, there was relief at a celebration in which everyone could join. It was a pleasant but misleading experience. The environmental movement seemed to be politically nonpartisan. But the issue quickly became part of the political division in the country.

One reason why political and social change was so intense in the 1960s was because for the first time in history there was a genuine worldwide communication system led by television. Combined with that development was a sudden jump in the number of young people in universities. A protest at a Paris university would immediately spark a similar protest in New York and Tokyo. By today's standards the means of communication were still primitive, but the effect of television was electrifying. At a time when most families in the country gathered around the TV set for the 6:30 p.m. network news, there was a potential for uniting people even though television's immediate effect was more often divisive.

The several movements for social change might not have coalesced if they had not been brought together in opposing an unpopular war. For the first time in history, war was brought into the living room on television. As with many of the movements then and now, the division in the country was mainly by age. The old trusted the country's leaders and were intensely loyal to the country that had accepted them or their ancestors. The young were fed up with war generally and this war in particular.

It is astounding to look back at that period and see that the United States had seemingly learned nothing from its intervention in Korea. Another civil war in a small Asian country became the next place that had to be defended lest communism overrun the world. John Kennedy had already involved the country in Vietnam. Historians have speculated that Kennedy might not have taken the country into full-scale war. But his successor, Lyndon Johnson, was determined not to be accused of losing a war.

Guided by his advisors, especially his defense secretary, Robert McNamara, Johnson kept sending more troops and more bombs. As the war escalated, the country became split; the young people were decidedly on the anti-war side. What spread from an opposition to the war was a distrust of all authority.

The Roman Catholic Church, like every large institution in the United States, was affected by a threat to its authority. The protests for black civil rights and the call by women for social and economic equality were part of the mix. The church was not a leader in either the black or the women's movements. Historically, it had lagged behind in attracting black members and in lending support for the black struggle for equality. Although women made up the majority of the church's members, the male clerical leaders were skeptical of a women's movement for equality.

The more powerful force for change came from the pressures that arose within the church. Church members were better educated than in the past and many of them did not see their education reflected in the way that they were treated by the clergy. There were new studies of church history, the Bible, moral theology, and other aspects of church life. The scholarship created a more critical attitude on the part of many members to the current church leadership.

What seemed evident to many scholars was that church officials were just reacting against the big changes all around them. Their attitude was that we have the truth, so why should we listen. There were aspects of popular culture, including music, film, books, and clothes, that church officials often condemned without understanding the forces propelling these changes.

The death of Pope Pius XII in 1958, who had reigned over the church during and after World War II, inevitably raised questions of whether a new pope might see the need to change some church policies. Pope Pius XII was not as rigidly conservative as many people assume. But he was the top man in a system that ruled a worldwide empire. The papacy had become a position of regal powers.

An uncertainty of what and who should follow Pius led the College of Cardinals to elect a kindly seventy-nine-year-old man to be a caretaker pope. The man who took the name of John XXIII surprised everyone by raising big questions of where the church stood. His encyclicals on social justice and peace were meant for the whole world. He was not speaking in ecclesiastical dialect but seeking to engage contemporary people.[6]

What was shocking was the Pope's announcement that there would be an ecumenical council, something that had not occurred in a century. Many people wondered what the point of such a meeting of the world's bishops would be. Had not the doctrinal questions of the church been settled by the Council of Trent in the sixteenth century and the Vatican Council in the nineteenth century? Why was there a need for a council in a church that had affirmed the infallibility of the pope?

Pope John's brief answer to the need for a council was the word *aggiornamento*, which translates as "bringing up to date." The intention to bring the church up to date was questioned then and ever since. The church was supposed to bring a timeless view to the problems of the world and stand as a monument of stability in a quick changing world.

The (First) Vatican Council had never officially ended, having been interrupted by political events. That Council had begun by describing the role of the pope in the church. It had intended to then take up a description of the bishop's role, but the council was dispersed before it could do so. The infallibility of the pope that it had proclaimed was seldom exercised but there was a kind of spillover to all the dealings of the pope and even the bishops. It seemed that many things without being infallible were to be accepted as all but infallible.

A Roman Catholic would have been unwise to disagree with anything that the pope or a bishop said. I remember a case at Catholic University involving a seminarian who was taking his final oral exam. He was told that the answer he gave to one question differed from the church teachings. He said he knew that was so, but he still thought his answer was correct. He was immediately dismissed from the seminary.

For several decades before the Council there were great scholars whose work was in tension with the fixed system of the Roman Catholic doctrine. I am fascinated that so many of them went about their study of history, scripture, theology, and canon law even as they surely recognized that their church had many failings in the past, and that the present leaders were not receptive to the scholarship that they were offering. They somehow managed to hold on to both their scholarship and a church that was led by people who at best tolerated them.

Some of these scholars did live to find vindication at the Second Vatican Council. The Council fathers realized the need for these scholars. Each bishop had his "expert" (*peritus*). Even with that help, however, the bishops were not capable of assimilating all the new material put before them. To their credit, many of the bishops did listen but they could not do more than point to the need in the future for church leaders to be receptive to the works of historians, exegetes, philosophers, and scholars of religion.

I began graduate study in the field of religious education in 1961 at the Catholic University. Although the mission of the department was to improve education in the Roman Catholic Church, most of the courses were on the Bible, theology, and liturgy. The main reason for the department's name, "Religious Education," which went back to the 1930s, was to differentiate it from the school of theology for seminarians. What evolved during the time of the Second Vatican Council was an undeclared competition between a new view of Catholic theology in the religious education department and a largely unchanged view of theology in the school of theology.

What I most appreciated about the department was that I was encouraged to follow my interests wherever they led. I became interested in the nature of divine revelation. My master's thesis, *Scripture and Tradition*, published in 1963, might have become irrelevant if the Second Vatican Council had immediately settled the question. At the first meeting of the Council, the bishops were presented with a document on the "sources of revelation" that repeated what the Council of Trent had said. If the bishops had ratified the document with few or no changes, the Council might have quickly gone through a series of documents and the participants would have gone home.

Surprisingly, a few bishops at the first session protested that they needed time not only to consider the document, but also to get to know the other bishops. The document on sources of revelation was returned to the committee. According to historian John O'Malley, that was "the decisive moment for the direction [the council] would take."[7] Instead of the Council wrapping up its work in a few months, it became a major world event of more than three years' duration.

What I thought I had learned from writing Scripture and Tradition was that there was a need for an examination of revelation itself. I chose for a dissertation topic an understanding of divine revelation in relation to religious education. In the Fall of 1964, I wrote the first half of my dissertation on divine revelation. I did not know what my advisor's reaction would be when I showed him the challenge that I was raising to the church's understanding of revelation.

He gave me his full support and I wrote the remainder of the work in about six weeks. The second half appears to be an almost paragraph by paragraph application of the first half of the work. Actually, the process was more the reverse. I worked from the premise that an idea of divine revelation had to make sense educationally. From there I worked back to what the theology had to be. That was a premise that I could not admit at the time.

I finished the dissertation in April 1965 and took doctoral orals shortly afterward. The doctoral panel of four professors consisted of three people from my own department who were enthusiastic about the work. The fourth person was a priest from the philosophy department who spent all his time insulting me. I did not know whether one negative vote would sink me, so I remained deferential but all the time I was thinking "someday I will get you in a fair fight" (I never did). I passed the examination, on what might have been a three to one vote.

I was unusually fortunate in having a publisher waiting to publish the dissertation. But when their editorial staff looked at the 550 pages, they proposed publishing it as two books. I was disappointed because the two parts were so integrally related. But the publisher was no doubt wiser than I. Few people would have read a five-hundred-page book.

The first half of the dissertation was published in January 1966, as *Theology of Revelation*.[8] The timing could not have been better because the Council had just concluded its work in the previous month. Many theologians were no doubt skeptical about my book, but the reaction did not seem especially negative. Scripture scholars were not much interested in the work. What surprised me was that people in religious education were the main readers even without the education part, which was dealt with in a separate book that followed in the summer of 1966.

I was inundated with invitations to speak to church groups through-out the United States and beyond. I could take only a few of these invita-tions because I was teaching six days a week in a program at Manhattan College. The program had been established by my mentor and friend, Brother Luke Salm. He graciously welcomed me into the program and gave me his full support. Luke was one of the great men I have met in my life. I am embarrassed by the fact that I did not sufficiently appreciate his kind-ness and his support at the time.

I am aware that the effect of the books was largely a matter of tim-ing. If the books had been published ten years earlier or ten years later, they might have had little impact. Apparently, many people in the Roman Catholic Church were at a point in their lives where they were ready to consider a big change. That was especially true of members of religious orders, including those who came to study at Manhattan College. I was sometimes accused of running a marriage bureau for nuns and brothers. I remember a mother superior in Kentucky phoning me and saying that she had sent sisters up there to study but they never came back. I insisted to her and to others with similar complaints that I was not encouraging people to make major changes in their lives. The combination of living in New York and encountering heady new ideas were more important than anything I was doing. Several women over the years have thanked me for my presence being the occasion for meeting their future husband.

The Second Vatican Council

The most surprising thing about the Second Vatican Council is that it hap-pened. The result of the Council is that it initiated major changes in this worldwide organization of over a billion people governed by an "infallible" leader. No one alive had ever experienced an ecumenical council and no one could predict its outcome. The Council produced sixteen documents on all aspects of the church life. The first document, and in some ways the one with the most discernible impact, was on the liturgy.

The changes in the liturgy got the attention of every Roman Catholic. The liberal wing of the church had been advocating changes for decades without much success. The conservative side assumed that the Mass and other sacramental practices were unchangeable. The first tiny change in the prayer called the canon caused an uproar. Adding the name of St. Joseph revealed that the text of the Mass could be changed, something that had been unthinkable to many church goers.

The translation of the Mass from Latin to English seemed to many people the most obvious thing to do if participation in the Sunday ritual was to be encouraged. Changes that included the priest facing the people and the people receiving communion in their hands made the mystery of Holy Communion disappear for many people.

I think that the liberals were right that the church's liturgy was hampered by outdated elements. But I think it can be argued that the changes were too fast and too sweeping. It is the nature of ritual to be unchanging from one generation to the next. There are always voices complaining that a ritual is outdated. The legitimate question is whether some accretions over the years are obscuring the main meaning of the ritual. Some of the Latin prayers and hymns that had been part of the liturgy for centuries could have been retained at least until more study had been made of what people were ready for. Participation in the new liturgy was exciting for a while but enthusiasm soon tailed off.

Changes in the liturgy cannot be blamed for the crisis in today's church. The bigger problem was in the Council's attempt to rethink the structure of the church in its document *Lumen Gentium*. The document was praised at the time and the bishops perhaps did the best that could be expected. In fact, the bishops surprised knowledgeable insiders by starting the document with a consideration of the people who make up the church. What had been expected was that they would begin where The First

Vatican Council had been interrupted and take up the role of the bishops. Unfortunately, the Second Vatican Council's document as a whole did little to create a structure with accountability for every office of the church. The clergy-abuse scandal reveals this lack of accountability.

The document known as the church in the modern world is one of the Council's best documents. It oriented the church to dealing with the problems in today's world. The projects that it spells out for the church are hampered by a lack of fundamental changes in the church itself that is supposed to carry out these tasks.

The Council did open dialogue with other religious groups, starting with Protestant Christians, some of whom had an official role as observers. They helped to keep the Council honest, and they provided some excellent commentaries. The willingness of the official Roman Catholic Church to enter dialogue with Protestants was a big step. Theologians and scripture scholars had been cooperating for decades but seldom with official endorsement and encouragement.

There had been an "ecumenical movement" since early in the twentieth century, but the Roman Catholic Church had distanced itself from it. The Council document on "ecumenism" that welcomed dialogue with the "separated brethren" was a sharp change, which took some adjusting on both sides. Toward the end of the Council, I attended a board meeting of the Religious Education Association, which was planning its 1966 conference on "the ecumenical movement." The first question raised at the meeting was why I was in the room given that the ecumenical movement had nothing to do with Catholics. At the subsequent conference in Chicago, which had the theme of the ecumenical movement, the Catholic participation almost overwhelmed the organization.

The Second Vatican Council endorsed the idea of freedom of religion. To people in the United States this change seemed long overdue. The document was the personal project of the U.S. Jesuit, John Courtney Murray. Throughout the 1950s Murray's views on "church and state" had been censured by bishops and conservative theologians. The Council's adoption of his views on religious freedom was a deserved vindication of his long- fought struggle.

The Council was covered by news media – newspapers, magazines, and television – in the restrained way that big events were covered in those days. There were interviews, television commentaries, and regular reports in the press. Major news magazines, especially *Time* and *Newsweek*, were fascinated by this new openness of the Roman Catholic Church. The inner workings of the Council were regularly featured in the secular press.

What would not be a surprise today but was something new then was a series of articles in *The New Yorker* that were gathered into a book, *Letters from Vatican City*, published under the pseudonym, Xavier Rynne.[9] The book had gossip and private discussions that could only have come from insiders. There was nothing scandalous in this reporting, but it shined a light on factions and lobbying efforts that the bishops would have preferred to be kept private.

It was this process, I believe, that produced the Council's most profound effect. What was evident for the whole world to see was that the teachings of the Roman Catholic Church were the result of a political process, including factions, debates, lobbying, and voting. Some people in the past were aware that the doctrines were the conclusion of arguments. The Council, however, had thrown open the whole messy process from which teachings emerged.

The Council fathers thought that the sixteen documents that they published were the main product of the Council, but the most important result was an upending of the church's basis of authority by the revelation of how church doctrines come to be.

Experts on the Bible had long ago concluded that every word of the Bible is a human word. The words might be inspired by a divine influence, but the words were not spoken from heaven. It was hardly a radical move to acknowledge that this idea from biblical criticism applied to every church doctrine. Even more obviously than in the case of the Bible, church teachings are formulated by human beings in human words. The delay in extending that biblical understanding to church doctrines made the effect earth-shaking when the Council did so by its actions. The fact that church teachings are the result of an historical process and are subject to change does not mean that the teachings are false.

The basis of authority in the Roman Catholic Church needed to be rethought after the Council. But the bishops did not or could not acknowledge a shift in how the authority of the institution had to be built on something other than the claim to have authority directly from God. Since the Council, the doctrine of divine revelation has received very little attention. The assumption is that the Council document on revelation provided a definitive statement on the issue.

I will examine, in Chapter Four, the idea of divine revelation and the Second Vatican Council's Constitution on Divine Revelation. I only note here an irony. While the idea of revelation was undermined by the debates of the bishops, the resulting problem can only be solved by more debate. But instead of the bishops talking to each other, the church needs a conversation involving the whole church. The Second Vatican Council initiated a revolution, but when the disorder and confusion of radical change began to surface, the bishops tried to stop the revolution.

The Second Vatican Council closed on December 8, 1965, which Bernard Häring pronounced was "the day the Council begins." I remember at the time saying, only half-jokingly, that the last action of the Council should have been to burn their sixteen documents. What was needed after the Council was not the application of documents but for every bishop to go home and replicate the conciliar experience that he had had in Rome.

These local councils, unlike the one in Rome, should have been composed of men and women with a wide variety of experiences to share. Those councils should have continued until the Third Vatican Council was held. That council should have been composed so as to realistically deserve the description "ecumenical." Other religious groups could have been invited. They would undoubtedly be suspicious and perhaps unwilling to participate. But if the Roman Catholic Church were clearly trying to be catholic, some other religious groups might be interested. The Third Vatican Council, or one with a more suitable name, is long overdue.

One of the Council's great challenges was to finally accept the history of the church's relation to the Jews. The persecution of Jews, in which the Roman Catholic Church undeniably played a major role, is the worst scandal in church history. The debates at the Council under headings such as "deicide" and "God's rejection of the Jews" were often embarrassing, but the Council finally passed a document that Jewish leaders generally praised.[10]

Many Roman Catholics might not understand the profundity of this problem and what still needs to be repaired. It was probably inevitable at its origin that the Christian movement would become a tradition distinct from the Jewish tradition. But the uprooting of Christianity from its original soil left the church with a limited understanding of its own foundational documents. Christianity needs the help of Jews to understand biblical history, including the life and teachings of Jesus of Nazareth.

Throughout most of history, Christianity has viewed itself as obviously superior to Judaism. The Christians took over all the best ideas of the Jews while claiming to bring those ideas to fulfillment. In that view, Jewish religion became irrelevant or false. Christian scholars in the last century have tried to find a way to soften their triumphalist claims to be the final religious truth. That has not yet been entirely successful.

One possibility for having a mutual and cooperative relation is found in the writing of a medieval Jew named Judah ah-Levi and revived by one of the great writers of the twentieth century, Franz Rosenzweig. Both writers viewed Christianity as a tree that grew from the seed of Judaism and has cast its shadow across the whole world. Christianity, in Rosenzweig's words, is the "readying and preparation of the Messiah for whom we wait." Instead of history perceived as Jewish promise and Christian fulfillment, history is the preparation for the revelation in the last age. Christianity is the missionary of God's speaking to all people as interpreted through Jewish and Christian traditions.[11]

Could Christianity see itself that way? It would require Christians to place divine revelation where it was originally located at the end of history not in the past. And related to that change, Christians would need to stop referring to Jesus of Nazareth as the Messiah. That is not as drastic a change as it may seem. Christians could continue to affirm Jesus as the Christ with the philosophical and theological connotations they have given to that term. "Messiah" is a Jewish term, and the Jews have a right to say what the term means. Jesus the Christ, it seems fair to say, did not bring on the messianic age. The fullness of Christ is still awaited. Christians could join Jews in working for the peace and justice of a messianic era.

Other changes of language should and would follow. Christian scholars have tried to avoid the claim of Christianity's superseding Judaism by referring to the "Hebrew scriptures" instead of the Old Testament. But Hebrew scriptures/New Testament does not make logical sense and hides the problem. A proper contrast would be Jewish scriptures/Christian scriptures. Christians need the Jewish scriptures to understand their own Christian scriptures. Christians and Jews should be able to work for realistic progress based on faith and sustained by hope.

A great weakness in the church's organization had been the education of the clergy. Seminary education before the Second Vatican Council was an induction into a system that the individual was expected to accept and apply. The instruction was to be in Latin and the student's success depended upon memorizing orthodox doctrines. Some intellectually curious clergy did their best to fill out what was lacking in seminary education. But once priests were immersed in the duties of a parish, they often had little time for continuing their education.

Cardinal Spellman, during the Second Vatican Council, recognized that his pastors needed reeducation in what was going on. He made a requirement for appointment as a pastor in the Archdiocese of New York that the priest take courses that were conducted at the chancery in Manhattan. The Cardinal asked Manhattan College for someone to teach a course on the Catholic doctrine. I was called in by the Academic Vice President of the college and told that I was the chosen teacher. In those days when you were told to go you went.

The class consisted of about forty men who were about to become pastors in the Archdiocese. Each Wednesday afternoon for a semester they took courses on scripture, psychology, and the Catholic doctrine. They had been out of the seminary for over thirty years and were not accustomed to academic courses. I came last on the Wednesday menu after they had been blitzed by the seminary's expert on the New Testament and by a well-known psychologist. I was an unknown.

I approached my task with trepidation. I was thirty-years old; each of the students was fifty-six. What I prepared for was a clash between the new theology, which I had to offer, and their old theology, which they probably treasured. What I was not prepared for was an absence of any fight. They had very little to say; in fact, my problem was trying to get them to open up at all as to what they believed. They were more frightened of me than I was of them. But their reticence stemmed more from a fear of each other. They were fearful of revealing what they did not know.

I could best get their attention by bringing in a copy of *Time* or *Newsweek*, both of which had recently discovered the Roman Catholic Church as a lively source for news. My message was that they needed to know what their parishioners might be asking them about that week. We ultimately got along but it was the most difficult course I have ever taught. They could never relax and be open about what they knew and what they didn't know. I felt bad for them. Their plight reflected the system in which they were operating. They deserved better preparation for the tidal wave of change that was about to hit.

Bishops who were selected from priests such as these men obviously needed some continuing education of their own. I can recall being involved only one evening at the Fordham University for a series that was presented for bishops. Such a program was a good idea that needed expansion.

The role of bishop was seen mainly to be an administrator rather than a pastor or a theologian. The bishop was cast as the guardian of orthodoxy. The bishop's job was to run a smooth organization and see that none of the priests got out of line. It was expected, of course, that "the faithful," that is the non-official members of the church, would follow the lead of the clergy and would not be disloyal to the church in any words or actions. But the Council had unintentionally changed what the loyalty of "the faithful" would mean in the future.

CHAPTER THREE:
The Fateful Years

The year 1968 was the culmination of what had been happening in big institutions for more than a decade. Something seemed to happen in 1968 that caused a permanent rift in everything that followed. Both the Roman Catholic Church and the United States of America underwent big changes. The intersection of the changes in country and church was stunning. And for some of us, the personal changes that were happening in our lives heightened the effects of the changes happening in the big institutions.

The political crisis in the United States severely tested the existence of the country. The civil war in Vietnam that the United States had stumbled into, starting in the 1950s, reached a crisis point in 1968. President Lyndon Johnson, a genius of domestic politics but inexperienced in international affairs, had listened to the wrong advisers who kept insisting on a greater involvement in the war.

A draft was needed to supply the 500,000 young men who would be sent to fight in a war, which many of them did not believe in. In 1968 alone, 300,000 men faced the draft. The existence of a lottery to choose winners and losers in the draft selection was an attempt at fairness, but it gave a further bizarre twist to the whole business of the government's control of the life and death of these young men. The men who were lucky to be left behind, along with a newly assertive generation of young women, protested loudly from the universities.

The year 1968 was the moment when President Johnson admitted that the situation was beyond his control. He announced that he would not run for re-election. Then, the hope that was put in Robert Kennedy to become president was quickly and brutally ended by his assassination in June of that year. The country turned to Richard Nixon who said that he had a plan to end the war. It became evident after his election that no such plan existed. There is even evidence that he interfered in attempts at peace in 1968 so that he could be the country's savior.[1]

The war continued to its inglorious end during the Nixon presidency, which was abruptly ended by his resignation in 1974. The war's effects spilled over into every aspect of national life. It created a cynical attitude toward all authority. All the institutions suffered from what seemed to be the confusion and weakness of their leaders.

Whether the Second Vatican Council just coincidently happened as society was undergoing all these changes is impossible to measure. What seems clear in looking back at that time was that there was a window for major structural change in the church that opened in the mid-1960s. By the mid-1970s, the window had closed. What had been established by then was a deep division in the church that has never been healed.

The 1968 Encyclical

Some people trace the division in the church to the birth control encyclical, Humanae vitae, in 1968. I think the encyclical was the end of a process not the beginning of the crisis. Pope Paul VI had been worried that if he proposed a change in church teachings, it would undermine his authority. He was right. But his attempt to shore up that authority by asserting that there would be no change in the church's teaching on "artificial contraception" also undermined church teachings. He was wrong if he did; wrong if he didn't because the process of undermining church authority had already occurred before 1968. The Pope's dilemma merely made it obvious. I used to jokingly say that the pope was a double agent. The only way to get Catholics to think for themselves on the issue was to write a document that was indefensible.

Church officials had already accepted birth control in one form called the rhythm method. Defenders of "natural family planning" make torturous distinctions to sustain a claim that this practice is not birth control.[2] In addition, Pope Pius XII had given official approval to the "rhythm method" in 1951 for reasons of a "medical, eugenic, economic and social nature."[3] The pill was another form of birth control that did not interfere in sexual intercourse. Even with the strange obsession that church officials had with not allowing anything "artificial" in birth control, the pill would allow the Roman Catholic Church to join the rest of the world in facing up to the need for effective birth control.

Shortly before 1968 I was present at a meeting of moral theologians from across the country. The conversation got more interesting after they had had a few drinks. Some of them were obviously agonizing over whether they could continue to represent the church's position on sexual matters. I remember one prominent professor at the Catholic University saying: "I have spent my life defending the indefensible." That was a sad thing to hear from a man who had been a scholarly and popular teacher for decades.

Most of these men were not willing to join in any rebellion. In fact, the most common view seemed to be that the condemnation of birth control had to be maintained because if that failed the church's condemnation of abortion would be the next to fall. I was not part of the conversation, but I thought that an inextricable linking of the teachings on birth control and abortion was inaccurate and dangerous. The Catholic bishops seemed to share the same fear that the theologians had expressed. When it became obvious that the teachings on birth control was widely rejected, the bishops decided to make an absolute stand on abortion. No debate would be entertained; no compromises were possible. Abortion became the unforgiveable sin.

Pope John XXIII had established a commission on birth control that was to advise the Second Vatican Council. But the Council was thought to be incapable of handling the issue. Pope Paul VI inherited the commission that would advise him. The Pope stacked the commission with people who seemed likely to support the ban on contraceptives. The commission continued to meet after the Council ended.

At its first meeting, the commission was a small group, all of whom were in favor of continuing past teachings. It was several years before the commission was enlarged to include Catholic couples whose experience was invaluable. One of the few women on the commission described to me her exchanges with Cardinal Ottaviani about sex. I doubt that the Cardinal was accustomed to having his wisdom so thoroughly rebuked. At the end of the commission's discussion in 1967, the vote was 52-4 for change. But the minority were not about to give up. That groups included Cardinal Alfredo Ottaviani, head of the Congregation for the Doctrine of the Faith and John Ford, a Jesuit moralist from the United States. Together they put together a minority report, which was leaked to the press along with the majority's report.[4]

The Pope was under intense pressure from both sides of the issue. The highly respected Cardinal Leo Joseph Suenens encouraged the Pope to accept the majority report. So also did the outstanding moral theologian, Bernard Häring. In the end, Cardinal Ottaviani, the guardian of orthodoxy, prevailed. The pope overruled the commission's finding and published the encyclical *Humanae vitae* on July 29, 1968.

Pope Paul VI tried to present a positive view of the human person in line with Catholic tradition. He was rightly concerned that sex should not be turned into a commodity that is degrading to person and society. Much of the encyclical would have been praised if it were not for the fateful passage in which Pope Paul asserted that every act of sexual intercourse must be directed toward procreation.

In a 2020 interview Pope Francis said of *Humanae vitae*, "the great controversy at the time was over the [contraceptive] pill, but what people didn't realize was the prophetic force of the encyclical, which foresaw the Neo-Malthusianism that was just getting underway across the world. Paul VI sounded the alarm over that wave of Neo-Malthusianism."[5] Pope Francis has a legitimate point here. But his reference to the pill as a "controversy of the time" is disingenuous. He fails to acknowledge the disastrous response of the church at that time and ever since that time to the question of birth control. On the fiftieth anniversary of the encyclical's publication there were thoughtful defenses of it.[6] Its reputation as a document may not be fair but its undeniable effect was calamitous.

The lobbying and pressures on the pope that had led up to the publication of *Humanae vitae* did not become widely known until years later.[7] But enough was known by enough people that the publication of the document could not possibly lead to the conclusion that "Rome has spoken, the case is ended." The pope's agonizing over which direction to go had made it evident that no absolute moral precept would emerge. The very existence of a commission to determine church teachings raised a question of the kind of certainty that could be claimed. Discussion of whether this teaching is "infallible" seems to me preposterous.

The acceptance of the encyclical became a litmus test for conservative Roman Catholics. Their view was that if some people wanted to abandon the faith, that was their choice. But the bigger danger was the presence of people who were called "cafeteria Catholics," who would decide which teachings of the church are or are not acceptable. However, many people who rejected the encyclical said that it was only this one point on which they were challenging church teaching. They believed that Pope Paul VI had made a serious mistake and that one's conscience had to take precedence.[8]

I vividly recall the morning that *Humanae vitae* was published. Charles Curran, a moral theologian at Catholic University, was already collecting signatures on a statement of refusal to accept the document. The movement spread rapidly to other leading theologians in the country; six hundred of them eventually signed the document. The Vatican could hardly excommunicate most of its leading lights. Charles Curran took the brunt of the reaction. He survived an early attack on his academic post at Catholic University, but Cardinal Ratzinger later succeeded in getting him fired. Amazingly, Curran remained a priest in good standing and went on to a career at Southern Methodist University. The Roman Catholic Church was the poorer for not having in one of its universities an excellent and dedicated teacher of Catholic morality.[9]

The Crisis of the Religious Order

The religious order had ancient roots in the church, and it supplied hundreds of thousands of men and women who were dedicated to the works of the church, including schools, hospitals, and foreign missions. There had been changes throughout the centuries, but the basic form had remained intact: communities of women and communities of men who took vows of poverty, chastity, and obedience.

In the 1960s, the religious order was the canary in the coal mine whose upheaval signaled what was to occur in the whole church. A vow of obedience meant following a rule of life and the commands of a superior. From its earliest existence, the motto was: "The voice of the prior is the voice of God." The questioning of the church's authority would eventually affect every Roman Catholic, but it hit the religious order immediately. The pope's wish to bring the church up to date applied most obviously to people who were dressed in seventeenth-century clothing. They were called "the religious," people who "left the world" and lived the "religious life."

The nun's habit became a symbol of what was to happen with the Roman Catholic Church. The conservative or reactionary part of the church was vocal in criticizing any change in the appearance of religious sisters. Many of these women, however, thought that they could do a better job if their dress was simplified. What was perhaps not admitted on either side was that the purpose of the habit was to cover up the fact that a nun was a woman. The attempt to admit small changes, a modified habit, was an improvement in some ways, but for many people it only made obvious the need for a more radical change. The liberals said that eliminating the habit would be liberating for the women. They were right but the conservatives' fears also proved to be accurate when many of the women felt free enough to leave convent life.

The whole process played out in a short period of time. At the end of the Council, in 1965, the number of young men and women entering novitiates was still on the rise. Novitiates and scholasticates were being expanded to keep up with the growing numbers. Then, suddenly, the effect of the Council, together with changes in the surrounding society, caused a collapse of the religious orders.

These communities that were shaped by prayer and by dedication to help others were a great feature of the Roman Catholic Church, but like the rest of the church there was a need to rethink the basis and the form of such special communities. That did not happen immediately after the Council and the existing organizations were hit by a mass exodus of members in the decade that followed the Council.

The first change that was needed was a change of language that described the organizations of women and men who dedicated themselves to the work of the church. The language of "entering religion" and "leaving the world" was never accurate but in the middle ages it indicated the radical attempt to follow what was said to be "the evangelical counsels of poverty, chastity and obedience." The word "religion" that had referred to practices of worship changed its meaning in the sixteenth century to refer primarily to institutions. In neither the earlier meaning of "religion" as practices nor its later meaning as an institution did it make sense to call some people "the religious" or to describe them entering the "religious life." That language raised an obvious question about what kind of life other church members lived. Assigning the term "religious community" to these specialized communities excluded everyone else from living in a religious community.

I was convinced that this language obstructed not only reform of the orders but also reform of the church. I took on what proved to be a quixotic task of changing this language. I admit that I had few allies who saw any problem here. And even at the present time the language remains what it has always been except for the invention of a few terms, such as "women religious" and "men religious," that are even more illogical than the traditional language (the adjective and the noun having been reversed). The language continues to obstruct dialogue between members of these special communities and the other communities in the church. The language is also confusing for other religious groups in their dealings with the Roman Catholic Church.

I remember writing to the religion editor of the *New York Times* in the late 1960s about a front-page article on a prominent nun who was leaving her order. The headline of the article was: "Sister X leaving the religious life." I wrote to the editor, who happened to be a Protestant minister, pointing out that there was no evidence that she was leaving the Roman Catholic Church, let alone the religious life. I asked if he would join me in trying to get the church to change its language. I received back a friendly letter but in it the editor said it was too bad that the Catholic Church speaks that way. He had missed my point. I was proposing that if the Times, CBS, PBS, the U.S. government, and other powerful institutions used more accurate language, the Roman Catholic Church would be forced to reflect on itself.

In pursuit of my hopeless project, I wrote a brief essay in 1970 that was probably the worst thing that I ever published.[10] I do not think I was wrong, but I only succeeded in infuriating a lot of people. The essay was mainly on the language of the religious order. I said that the religious order had suffered a fatal blow at the Second Vatican Council. I was calling for action not attacking nuns. Some people blamed me for the exodus from the orders in the early 1970s, but the exodus had already begun before 1970. I came across to some observers as encouraging people to leave, and they blamed me when great numbers did leave. I hardly think my eight hundred words were that influential, but I admit that my words were not helpful.

I thought that I had credibility to write such criticism because I had recently been elected as a provincial superior of the Christian Brothers. That fact, I discovered, provided me no cover at all. I also thought that I had gained the trust of readers because of a best-selling book, *Experiences in Community*, that I had co-authored in 1968 proposing reforms of the religious order.[11] My co-author was Maria Harris who was a Sister of St. Joseph; it was the first cooperative work we did; after that, we regularly worked together.

Maria Harris became a more popular and effective speaker than I was. She knew how to say quite radical things in a way that did not upset people. That population included a few bishops who were so taken by her personality that they did not realize she was proposing radical changes. She never got banned from speaking except when we were working together. We used to call our act good cop/bad cop. She knew much better than I did how to handle a crowd.

Maria and I later worked widely as a married couple until her death in 2005. Her books *Dance of the Spirit* and *Jubilee Time* on spirituality reached a wide audience in the secular world.[12] She wrote powerfully on Jewish-Christian relations, art and education, old age, and feminism. Maria's books continue to sell, and she is remembered fondly by a great many people.[13]

I naively believed that instead of getting married we could create a new kind of community with a new context for marriage and family life. I delayed our getting married for many years which she agreed to, but I think

I was very unfair to her. She tried to work with me on my hopelessly naïve project, but she was much more realistic about what was then possible.

My belief at the time was that the existing religious order could evolve into an organization with concentric circles of membership. The orders still had large numbers of people who could provide a base for some radical experiments in community. Eventually, the religious order and parishes could coalesce. Instead of a few people being said to have a religious vocation and living in a religious community, baptism would be the calling of a religious vocation, and every member of the church would have some form of a religious community.

At a 1968 national meeting ("chapter") of the Christian Brothers, I suggested that our discussion start from one obvious fact: eventually, most of the men leave the order. Instead of thinking of that fact as failure, we could think of the men's time with us as a successful preparation for their future in another vocation. I said only half-jokingly that in my province of Long Island and New England part of our mission had become providing well-trained teachers for the public schools of Long Island. Those schools were very happy with the arrangement. One man told me that when he went to be interviewed for a job in one of the schools, the interviewer said: Am I correct that you were a Christian Brother? He replied: Yes. The interviewer said: You're hired.

One intriguing practice of the religious order was that the members took vows for one year at a time, and then for three years, and only then did they take "perpetual vows." That kind of sequence makes sense. What was unrealistic was the compressing of the sequence into the years before age twenty-five. Perhaps in the past most people were certain about the future course of their lives at the age of twenty-five. That does not seem to be true today. As I later suggest with reference to marriage, people must grow into permanence; it is not accomplished by saying that one intends to do something permanently.

The Roman Catholic religious orders could have learned from Buddhism. Invite people for six months, a year, or whatever length of time they wish to share in this kind of life. Some people would constitute a core of permanent members, other people would move on to a different vocation. In an informal way that is actually what happened for many individuals who spent time as a religious sister or religious brother. They have remained supporters of both the work of the order and their friends in the order. Nearly all the hundreds of people I know who were brothers (and the smaller number of former sisters that I know) have a positive attitude about the time that they spent in a religious order and are grateful for the preparation they received there for their subsequent life and work.

The tragic aspect of this development is that the orders themselves are on the verge of disappearing. Many of them are experimenting with attracting young associates for a year or a few years. If they had tried these experiments when the orders had large numbers, they might be leaving an impressive successor instead of small and struggling programs in most places. I have nothing but admiration for the people in religious orders, as well as their young associates. But the Roman Catholic Church missed a chance to create an imaginative new institution.

The Clergy Problem

At the time when I said that the religious order had suffered a fatal blow at the Second Vatican Council, I said that the clergy did not have the same problem. The priests would likely go on for now with little change. But when they did have a crisis it would be worse than the crisis that had hit the religious orders. The religious orders continued to go on with declining numbers and an aging population. The communal nature of the institution has made its ending gentle and admirable.

I take no pleasure in having predicted that the clergy would eventually have its own crisis and, lacking a sense of community, that they would not have the resources to respond effectively. The recent scandals of the Roman Catholic clergy exemplify what goes wrong with partial revolutions. Sex-abuse among the clergy has been coming to light since the 1980s, and especially in a 1995 *New York Times* exposé and in a detailed study by the *Boston Globe* in 2001, but the problem has deep roots.[14]

At the 2018 meeting of U.S. bishops, Bishops Barry Knestout and Thomas Olmstead cited the rejection of the encyclical *Humanae vitae* as the source of the problem.[15] The comment seemed weird to journalists, but in a way the two bishops were right. If one takes that encyclical as the line where the collapse of the church's authority became evident, the encyclical publication and its rejection was the moment when the clergy and bishops found themselves in a different church without the supports and safeguards that they were accustomed to.

Catholic priests since the middle ages have been required to promise "celibacy," which explicitly excludes marriage but implicitly forbids all sexual activity. The promise of celibacy is often confused with the monk's vow of chastity. The "secular" priest was to be like a monk but without the protections and support of the monastic life. The chief characteristic of brotherhoods is community. The vows that the monk takes are aspects of community life. As a life-long commitment, a vow of chastity is meant for very few people but as a temporary discipline of life it could be a valuable experience for many people. It was never a proper model for the lives of secular clergy.

The life of the "secular priest" was always very demanding. He had status and respect from the "laity," and when he became a pastor, he seemingly had great power in his small kingdom. Although he was always in danger of going astray, the rigid system in which he operated exercised a tight control. It was not a practice for "father" to shed his collar and hang out at the local bar. Since the priests were men, there were no doubt sexual failures, but full-blown scandals did not frequently emerge.

In the 1960s, the Second Vatican Council began an overdue reform of the Roman Catholic Church. But hardly had the church opened to the contemporary world when a reaction set in. The result was that the clergy still had all the power, but now many of the restraints were missing. That happened at a time when a sexual revolution was underway in society. Not much was done to improve the training of the priests nor to provide institutional support for them.

The result was predictable; although, the horrific details of what some men have done were beyond imagining. A man could now have a secret life alongside one's public life as a man of God. The sexual inclinations that had been repressed now found a range of expression, some of which were appalling. The priest still had power, especially over young people who were told that priests were trustworthy.[16]

The Roman Catholic Church is not alone in having this problem but the promise of celibacy, an assumption of holiness, and a bureaucratic pyramid of authority, gave the sex problem of the Roman Catholic clergy a distinctive and sometimes frightful aspect. The bishops did not help themselves by their attempts to cover up the problem. They often moved men from one parish to another who should have been removed from active ministry. Some bishops did the best they could but that did not prove to be enough.

Not having dealt with the problem earlier, church officials are now faced with a cascade of data that often lacks a context. One of the most voluminous reports from a Pennsylvania grand jury embodies the problem and some of the unfairness of how it is reported. Peter Steinfels, who is as knowledgeable about this scandal as any individual, wrote a detailed and pointed criticism of the Pennsylvania report.[17] The main problem with the report, Steinfels showed, is a lack of any historical sense. Also, a grand jury is a strange author for any such report; it only receives data from a prosecutor. Some priests and bishops have been unfairly treated by the way that the story has unfolded.

The story is nowhere finished. The church having failed to police its own problem is now being investigated by states' attorney generals throughout the United States and by secular governments in other countries. The financial costs are devastating but that is not the main problem. For many people, the Roman Church has lost all credibility. Sexual crimes are the responsibility of individuals but in this case there is also a failure of the institution.

Thomas Doyle sounded the alarm on this crisis beginning in the 1980s, but he received little response. He has said: "Proposals of reform have to deal with the structure of the church. The history of sexual abuse, denial, and cover-up has been embedded in the clerical culture that has not only protected but enabled it, and this culture is no longer capable of hiding, controlling, minimizing, or eradicating it. Nor is it capable of continuing to sustain the myth of clerical superiority based on the magical thinking about the nature of sacred orders."[18]

The Church's Sex Problem

The clergy sex-scandal is symptomatic of the official church's failure to understand the sexual upheaval of recent decades and the centuries of misdirection that led up to the widespread rejection of official teaching on sexual matters. There are many church teachings that flow from how sex is understood. There is not much point in church leaders discussing gay marriage or communion for divorced Catholics when the underlying question is the official teaching on sex.

Augustine of Hippo, who provided direction for the whole Western church, is blamed for having had a distorted view of sexuality. He and many other church officials were wrong in thinking they understood human sexuality. However, Augustine was not wrong in realizing that the sexual drive in a human being is powerful and that it takes a disciplined life to direct this drive. Augustine describes the inability of a person to simply say yes or no to the sexual drive to be a result of "original sin."

I think he meant by that misnamed doctrine that human beings have been making the same sexual (and other) mistakes from time immemorial. He was more realistic than people who think that it is simply a matter of being reasonable or having "will power." A human being cannot just choose whatever he or she desires. When faced with several possibilities, a person can only negate all the possibilities except one, thereby allowing the body to follow this one remaining inclination. Looking back at a person's life it can appear that a person never had a choice. The choice consisted in the ability to say "no."

For centuries, the Roman Catholic Church taught that sexual behavior was not only to be restricted to marriage but even within marriage it had to be directed toward procreation. It seems safe to say that this teaching on sex could never work. Only an extraordinary individual could healthily direct all his or her sexual energy into other outlets. Preaching this sexual code of abstinence for all people was unrealistic.

Why did western society generally agree with this Catholic code until the middle of the twentieth century? Lawmakers were concerned with what men would otherwise do. (They lacked imagination about women). Church and society feared what would happen if men's sexual desires, sexual imagination, and sexual behavior were unleashed? Women, children, and every institution would be under threat.

An unrealistic code of behavior could not survive the twentieth century. Unfortunately, the rejection of what is unrealistic does not automatically produce a realistic alternative. In the 1960s, society decided that control of sexual behavior should be left to the individual. Without institutional help an individual man is almost helpless to deal with the forces of his own body. Better sexual education that begins in infancy is indispensable. But in the teenage years, when a boy's body all but explodes, he desperately needs to develop healthy controls and outlets. Instead, he is met by an avalanche of sexual imagery, hypocrisy among public officials, and few models of adult sexuality to guide him.[19]

One surprising thing that the women's revolt of the last few years has shown is the pathetic sex lives of powerful men. A surprising number of these men are not out on wild sexual escapades. They seem driven by the need for a human contact (tactile, aural, or visual), something that they apparently can't find in straightforward human encounters.

The Roman Catholic Church's official view of sex is widely treated today as a guilt-inducing scold or as material for late-night comedians. However, what is still on the books and is insisted upon by church leaders for over a billion people deserves serious treatment. Perhaps most older people have made up their own minds about these teachings and most younger people have never bought into church teaching on the subject. But even the fact that the teaching is ridiculed is a sign that there is something important still there. After seeing a play that consisted of altar boys telling tales of clerical misconduct, I said to my companion: "I can't decide whether the enthusiastic reception of this play means that the Catholic Church is in its death throes or that the Catholic Church is one of the few institutions that is still powerful enough to generate passionate attacks."

For dealing with sexual themes, film makers had to use their imagination to circumvent the Hays Code, which had the powerful backing of the Roman Catholic Church. An example of the code's long list of rules was, "Passion should be so treated that these scenes do not stimulate the lower and base element."[20]

When practically all censorship disappeared, pornographers were let loose to show anything they wanted but that was not good news for the quality of movies. It is estimated that almost one third of all Internet activity is pornography. The large quantity suggests that most of the products are boring. The repressed world of the 1950s is no model for eroticism. But pity the young people of today who are overwhelmed by a sea of sex talk and crude imagery before they can begin to figure out their own interests and imaginations.

Pornography is closely connected to the practice called "masturbation." That word was invented in the nineteenth century as a pseudo-scientific term for something that was condemned as a horrible practice. Boys were warned that the practice would have dire physical and mental consequences. The obsession with condemning this practice continued well into the twentieth century.[21]

I never actually heard the word masturbation throughout my childhood although its condemnation was the center piece of every church retreat and mission for boys. After a few days of drowsy response to the preacher, all ears were attentive when the big topic arrived. Everyone knew what the preacher was roundly condemning as a grievous sin although the preacher never quite said what he was talking about. Every adolescent boy in the congregation could have supplied one of a dozen names for the activity in question.

In the Vatican's 1975 document on homosexuality, masturbation is named as a violation of natural law because it "contradicts the finality of the faculty." Every act of masturbation is said to be a mortal sin.[22] That statement is just plain cruel to every adolescent trying to figure out what is happening in his or her body. The statement is a painful example of the inability of the Roman Catholic Church leaders to come to terms with the fact that sexual activity has a range of human meanings that are separate from generating babies.

For human beings, sex is not ultimately about biology but about the relations between women and men, women and women, men and men. All these relations can be called sexual although the term "sexual relations" has taken on a much narrower meaning. A revolutionary movement among women has been coming into existence around the globe during the past century. It has been upsetting a power arrangement that had existed for several millennia. The relation between women and men is the center of the story although questions about the other two relations, women-women, men-men, have accompanied that central change. These relations between human beings are in a context of changes in the human-nonhuman relation.

A half-century ago a newly fashioned word, gender, borrowed from the world of grammar, was introduced to distinguish biological sex from a social role. I doubt that at the time anyone foresaw that a distinction between sex and gender would later generate a debate about such things as public bathrooms. People who have unimaginative views on sex get impatient with such discussions, but these new questions reveal how much the human race still does not understand about sexual diversity and the existing range of sexual practices.

The distinction between sex as a biological characteristic and gender as a social category has been so helpful that it seems incredible that the distinction had not previously been made. The term sex would best be used only for the restricted purposes of biology. "Sexual" describes characteristics that are primarily attributed to either the male or the female, but which characteristics are exclusive to either sex is a subject that requires study and human testimony. Comments by church officials on these matters do not inspire confidence that they are open to learning anything new about sex and gender.

The "woman's movement" in the United States began in the middle of the nineteenth century. Ever since the country was founded on a claim to universal rights, there had been women who saw clearly that the proposition "all men are created equal" excluded women, not only linguistically, but also intentionally and in practice. It took some time for a movement to get going and the term "woman's movement" in the nineteenth century still suggested a gathering of individual women asking for equality. The twentieth-century's term "women's movement" indicated a more unified political movement in which women were ready to act.

The long struggle for the vote was finally completed in 1920 with the passage of the nineteenth amendment. There were some immediate effects, especially in the "lifestyle" of many women but equality of opportunity for most women was not achieved. The great depression of the 1930s and the war in the 1940s posed obstacles to social progress. However, an unintended change was brought on during the war years when women were left to run the country.

At the beginning of the 1960s, dissatisfaction among women reached a critical mass.[23] The Roman Catholic Church was not well prepared for this uprising among women. Women had come to feel that they now had control of their own bodies and their own lives. The availability of effective birth control, which was at the center of the movement, placed the Roman Catholic Church in direct conflict with the women's movement. The birth control pill changed sexual practices during the decade of the 1960s and gave women a sense of freedom that had not been possible before.

I remember the morning in my undergraduate ethics class when the professor announced that the FDA had approved a pill that would act as a contraceptive. He asked us whether we thought that such a pill would be considered morally acceptable by church officials. While most of our professors simply told us what they thought to be so, this professor wanted us to do our own thinking about ethical questions. He was obviously conflicted himself how to think about this new pill.

I cannot remember how I initially responded to the existence of the pill but as I later reflected on the question it seemed to me (and still does) that here was a way out of the dilemma that the church officials had created for themselves. I did not know at the time, but it seems to clinch the argument that Pope Pius XII had already said that the pill in question was acceptable for regulating a woman's cycle.[24] If birth control is acceptable and if the pill was safe, why wouldn't church officials approve it? Women could plan pregnancies as integral to their lives. They could finally exercise "responsible family planning."

Church officials could have expressed some reservations about the pill's safety for women. The Roman Catholic Church could have been aligned with women when health concerns were later raised about the pill. Instead, church officials simply pronounced that the pill was morally unacceptable.

The legalization of abortion in 1973 was for many women the final step in the process that had begun decades earlier. The legality and accessibility of contraception and abortion made possible the rise of women in business, politics, the arts, and technology. New generations of women have gladly jumped at the new opportunities.

Men and women have experienced difficult adjustments in this new world. A smoothing out of problems will take several more generations. The change in relations, however, is irreversible. Even if governments try to reverse what has happened there is no world to go back to.

The permanence of change in the relation between men and women was signaled by changes of language. I remember the day I picked up the *New York Times* and read that they had decided to use Ms. as a title for women. The conservative *Times* had until then continued to call women Miss or Mrs. That day the world changed. Soon after "he and she" became the standard way to refer to individuals instead of assuming that "man" could include "men and women," and that "he" could cover both "he and she." Fifty years later these changes sound obvious but at the time there was fierce opposition. Today, even the most conservative men in business or politics are careful about their gender inclusiveness.

One effect of not identifying a woman by her marital status was that women were able to decide how to identify themselves sexually. The nineteenth-century woman's movement was careful not to attack society's pieties about family life. The acknowledgment of lesbianism was slow in coming. Even in the 1960s many straight women thought that lesbians should not be welcome because it would cast the women's movement as an attack on the family. Today most people seem to accept that gay and lesbian people simply provide a variation on sexual life and that they support and sometimes include a family.

What should church officials do about this seismic change in women's lives? The first thing would be to acknowledge the existence of this change throughout the world. The church's officials are all men, which is a characteristic that is ultimately untenable. For the present, they could try to avoid condescending pronouncements and instead invite the participation of women.

One of the first pronouncements of Pope Francis was: "With regard to the ordination of women, the church has spoken and says no. Pope John Paul II has said so with a formula that was definitive."[25] It was a strange way for the pope to begin his tenure in office. The pronouncement signaled that he was not very attuned to what was going on among women around the world. The word "definitive" had meant in the past that the pope has spoken, the case is closed. Pope Francis has found that that is no longer true.

Women in the church should have power equal to men. An open discussion of how to do that is needed. The ordination of women might or might not be a help in that direction. When the question of women deacons confronted Pope Francis, he reluctantly appointed a commission to study the matter. How widespread is the interest of women in the deaconate is unclear. I suspect it depends on one's view of how change in institutions happen. Are deacons a first step in a series of steps to achieve equality for women, or would women deacons be an attempt to shore up the current structure?

One of the U.S. bishops' clumsy attempts to respond to women was to announce that the bishops would produce an encyclical on women. The announcement was met with some ridicule by women and accompanied by their advice that it was not a good idea. The bishops, nevertheless, appointed one of their own to go around the country and listen to what women had to say.

On the Sunday afternoon when this bishop held a "town meeting" in New York, Maria was invited to join a small group of women who would have dinner with the bishop after the forum. Maria could not attend, so she sent me. The meeting in the old cathedral of Brooklyn was interesting to me but I think a shock to the bishop who seemed to be a nice enough churchman. I do not think he was ready for what a group of women in Brooklyn would have to say about the proposed document on women. Several women described the abortion they had had; all of them were skeptical of a document on women that the bishops would produce.

The dinner afterward with the bishop included about eight women and me. They continued to speak their mind to him. One woman asked him about the ordination of women. He said that the Pope had told the bishops that they could not speak about women's ordination. At this point, he turned to me and asked: "Can the Pope tell us to do that?" I had not intended to say anything but since he asked me a question, I replied: "I suppose the Pope can tell you to do anything. The question is whether you will follow that." The opinion-gathering that afternoon, and perhaps other similar outings for this beleaguered bishop, killed the project.

I am not of the right sex/gender to pronounce on what women want. I learned a long time ago to keep quiet on that question. I did learn some things from my forty-year relation with Maria and from fifty years of teaching courses that were predominantly attended by women. I also learned from my three sisters about the intelligence and competence that women can bring to society's problems.

After my oldest sister had raised four children, she thought it was time to return to work outside the home. She enrolled in a community college, but she was worried that she would not be able to keep up with the young people. I had seen dozens of women like her at NYU, middle-aged women who had taken care of families. They were nervous about whether they could handle the studies. They usually turned out to be the best students in the course. As I suspected would happen, my sister was shocked at the backward state of many of the younger set. Within a few months she was teaching them. She went to work for a small company, which discovered after a short while that they could not get along without her.

There are millions of women – especially black women – who still do not have the opportunity to use their talents for the country and for the church. Both the country and the church are the poorer for this deficiency. But the times have been changing for fifty years and the change is accelerating. Men have good reason to be anxious. Their comfortable spot at the top of most institutions is being eroded. They can fight against the rise of women or they can welcome a world of healthy and cooperative relations.

Control of Speech

One important aspect of episcopal control that collapsed in the period of 1968–74 was the control of speech, both oral and written. Up to the 1950s the Vatican and the local bishops were able to control the flow of ideas and to cut off any tendencies to unorthodox ideas. The clergy and the religious orders were directly under the control of the guardians of orthodoxy.

An "Index of Forbidden Books" included most of the works of modern philosophy. A funny thing happened to me regarding the "Index." I came upon a separate section in the scholasticate library in 1961 that contained most of the books in philosophy that I was interested in. I happily worked my way through most of them before discovering that this section of the library was for the Index of Forbidden Books. I had a brief crisis of conscience but by that time the whole business of condemning books was collapsing.

Anything that individuals published had to receive an imprimatur – a permission to print. There may originally have been a valid idea for this practice. Writing could be evaluated by one's peers and if something was wrong it could be corrected before the work reached a wider public. But by the middle of the twentieth century what existed was an arbitrary system of censorship and the silencing of some of the best minds of the church.

When someone published a book, he (and occasionally she) could apply for an imprimatur where the book was written, published, or printed.

Some bishops became known for approving everything that was submitted to them. Naturally, they were popular places to apply for permission to publish.

In 1968, a book known as the *Dutch Catechism* became one of the best publications for explaining to Catholic adults what was going on in the church and theology.[26] Before the book was published, the U.S. publisher had called me. He was upset because the book had been refused an imprimatur by the easiest of the bishops. The idea of publishing a catechism that had been refused an imprimatur was unheard of. I said that I thought the book would still sell despite that fact. I was later relieved when my hopeful assurance turned out to be accurate. The book became a best-seller and probably helped to sink the imprimatur.

Without my knowledge or wish, the publisher submitted my book *The Present Revelation* to that same bishop.[27] I doubt that he read the book, but he refused the imprimatur. By that time, I did not care. I did write to him, however, and said that if he had found something heretical in this book, he should have refused an imprimatur to my previous book on the topic.

My experience in those years was like many other Roman Catholics who were trying to be loyal to the church while exploring new ways of church organization and education. I tried to avoid verbally attacking the bishops. I sympathized with their struggle to do what they thought their job entailed. But often their efforts were clumsy and self-defeating. The following example is probably typical of what happened in many places.

When I was the head of the province of brothers, the principal of our largest high school was summarily dismissed. The school had been doing marvelous things especially in integrating boys from the lower economic ranks. The Christian Brothers had established whatever standards for school administration that the diocese possessed. I knew the principal to be a superb teacher, an excellent administrator, and a fine human being.

I went to a meeting with the bishop of the diocese. I was accompanied by two brothers who knew far more than I did about administrating schools and about that school in particular. The bishop was accompanied by his director of education. Before the meeting, the bishop pulled me aside and said: "We won't have any trouble here, will we?" I said truthfully: "I don't know."

At the beginning of the meeting, I asked the diocesan director of education why the principal had been fired. He replied that it was because the principal had lost the support of the community. I said that to my knowledge the faculty supported him, the students supported him, and the parents supported him. "What community are you talking about?" He replied: "Local pastors do not like the way some of the students speak." I replied: "At least I know now what the word community means here."

The meeting revealed that the director of education had never visited the school, had no documents or other evidence, and lacked any knowledge of school administration. I had known going into the meeting that it was a foregone conclusion that the principal would not get his job back. He and the assistant principal, who had resigned in protest, went on to do greater things with their manifest talents. I hoped that the meeting at least got the director of education fired by an obviously embarrassed bishop. Unfortunately, the intrusion of bishops and their clerical appointees into schools to exercise control over what they do not understand was common then and still occurs today.

I was banned from speaking in most U.S. dioceses and a few dioceses on other continents. It was impossible to know how many dioceses because the process was usually one of getting your name crossed off from a list of speakers. Seldom did a bishop confront you directly. There was then, and I assume there still is, a right-wing group that circulated warnings around the world. I was banned by bishops who knew nothing about me except that they had received a warning that I was trouble. I probably did bring trouble on myself by saying some provocative things. Still, the idea that

I was dangerous seemed ludicrous at the time and even more ludicrous in hindsight.

My most dramatic banning was in Kenya. The Archbishop of Nairobi met me at the airport to tell me that I was not welcome in his diocese. I did not have a plane reservation to take me elsewhere, so I went to my motel room. I was followed there by the archbishop. He was waiting for me to say that I would obey him. I had immediately decided that I wouldn't speak at the university where the talk was scheduled. I did not like this situation: black African leader in a conflict with smart-aleck white guy from New York. Nevertheless, I stubbornly refused to say that I would obey him. We sat in silence for several hours. I had nothing to say and nowhere to go; I knew he eventually had to leave, which he did. I had several pleasant days in that beautiful country and talked with some of the people who had come to Nairobi for the talk that had been canceled.

Some years later the Archbishop told the superior of the Christian Brothers in Rome, Charles Henry, that I had used an African tactic of silence with him. Actually, I was silent because I had nothing to say. I later wrote to him, respectfully disagreeing with him. I did admire his forthrightness, which contrasted with the usual practice of being banned from behind closed doors.

PART TWO

The story that I am recounting of what happened in the Roman Catholic Church makes a change of direction in this section. The account in the three previous chapters traces the church's problem in chronological order up to the 1970s. By that time, all the major problems had surfaced that are still with the church.

The following chapters of this book examine the individual problems and the pressing issues that would be involved in a reform of the church. Chapters Four and Five, which constitute Part Two of the book, are the hinges on which all the remaining chapters depend. Chapter Four examines the intellectual crisis of the church; Chapter Five is a similar examination of the moral crisis affecting the church.

When bishops are asked about the acceptability of some practice, for example, gay marriage, they routinely reply that it is unacceptable because it is opposed to divine revelation and natural law. Both terms seem to them almost self-evident. A Catholic accepts the guidance of these two sources of truth, both of which go back to the beginning of Christianity. I doubt that most bishops have ever explored in depth the origin, history, and contemporary problems associated with each term.

The format of these two chapters in Part Two is also radically different from the chapters that have preceded. The form of each chapter is unsatisfying, but it is the best that I can offer. My attempts to present a complete exposition of the two topics proved unworkable. Each topic deserves not only a book but many books. Rather than try to guide the reader through a very complex story, I supply a series of bullet points that I hope are clear. The story line that follows these points in each chapter is to invite the reader to think along with me on a journey that for me has lasted sixty years.

CHAPTER FOUR:
The Intellectual Crisis of Catholicism

The Roman Catholic Church's intellectual crisis lies in the foundation of its teaching. The crisis is centered on the term and idea of revelation, but this problem is seldom investigated. Since the Second Vatican Council, the assumption has been that divine revelation was rethought and that any previous problem was solved. I would argue, however, that the Second Vatican Council did not even address the problem and essentially left the issue where the Council of Trent had placed it in the sixteenth century. Bishops and theologians still make assumptions about the existence and nature of divine revelation as if this were 1950 or 1850.

The complexity of this problem – historically, linguistically, philosophically – requires me to admit that I cannot present an adequate examination of this question in one chapter of a book. It is doubtful that any individual could provide a complete answer. A team of people, including philosophers, historians, linguists, and others would be needed. The story takes place both within and outside the boundaries of the Roman Catholic Church. Catholic theologians can make only a very limited contribution on this question because revelation functions as a presupposition of theology. The following list of bullet points, which are mostly just facts, need to be explored.

1. "Revelation," the Greek *apokalypsis*, originated in middle eastern religions and it conflicted with the biblical tradition. The religious use of the term revelation was the idea that at the end of history a veil will be raised, and everyone will see the truth. Until then, only a few people have a key to that truth.

2. The biblical metaphor was that God speaks. The first words of the Book of Genesis are, "God said … " The biblical image is interactive: God speaks, humans listen, and then they respond. The metaphor of revelation was that God reveals or "unveils" the truth and that humans can do nothing but accept the truth that has been revealed.

3. God speaking was within history; revelation signaled the end of history.

4. Revelation entered the Bible by way of the last book of the New Testament, the *Book of Revelation*. There was considerable resistance to its inclusion in the biblical canon because it conflicted with the content and style of the other books. But it claimed – inaccurately – the authority of the apostle John.

5. The idea of revelation was attractive to many people and was a threat to the church. What can be called the domestication of revelation to bring it under the control of the church's official teachers was achieved through translation of the Greek *apokalypsis* by two different Latin words, *revelatio* and *apocalypsis*.

6. Revelation, as *revelatio*, was used for references to the past. Revelation, as *apocalypsis*, continued to refer to the end of history. The *Book of Revelation* became known as The Apocalypse, which people who were not Greek speaking did not usually associate with the meaning of revelation.

7. Augustine of Hippo was a key figure in interpreting the Book of Revelation's description of a "thousand year" reign. According to Augustine, the thousand years that follows the apocalypse/

revelation refers not to the end of history but to the history of the church. Revelation was said to have been concluded by the death/ resurrection of the Christ.

8. Revelation, or what has been revealed by God, was now said to be "transmitted" from apostolic times to the present under the guidance of the bishops. The main doctrines of the church are not the product of human invention. Instead, God is their source in the teachings of Jesus and his apostles.

9. The idea that God revealed the truth to the human race by about the year 30 C.E. and then ceased to reveal anything further has always been a problem for the credibility of Christianity. A resistance to this belief within the church has been offered by the liturgy's language that God is speaking now to the congregation.

10. A second resistance to the claim that revelation ended with "the death of the last apostle" has been by the church's mystics who might be described as people who listen and respond to the Holy Spirit. The great mystics, such as Hildegard of Bingen and Meister Eckhart drew on the *Book of Revelation* for their reflections on revelation. They did not reject the past, but they listened for the divine word in the present with the interpretive help of the past.

11. Revelation was not an especially prominent term in Christian writing. The Council of Trent fixed the meaning of revelation as the basis of Catholic Church teachings. It pronounced that revelation is contained in two sources: scripture and tradition. The image of revelation, which was conveyed by that formula, was an object that could be divided into two collections of material.

12. Scriptural study in the nineteenth and twentieth centuries raised questions about divine revelation as contained in the *Bible*. Biblical scholars avoided conflicts with church authorities by distinguishing between inspiration and revelation. The entire text of the *Bible* is inspired or guided by the Spirit; not every word of

the *Bible* is revealed by God. The *Bible* is clearly the product of human authorship, including mistakes that affect human documents. In addition to biblical studies, historical research showed that there is no second source of revealed truths that were handed down from apostolic times.

13. The Second Vatican Council's *Constitution on Divine Revelation* was the work of scripture scholars who were given the task after an initial document was rejected. The authors presented revelation in biblical imagery while they avoided contradicting the Council of Trent. The document surprisingly makes no references to the *Book of Revelation/Apocalypse*, which is the main source of "revelation" in the *Bible*.

14. The second chapter of the *Constitution*, which is on the "transmission of divine revelation," is the sure sign that the document does not face the problem of the nature of a divine revelation. The document does not ask: What is divine revelation and where is it? There is no object or thing that can be transmitted. The only intelligible way that "divine revelation" could be used today is as a verb.

15. The Second Vatican Council by its actions undermined the idea of revelation. The whole world could see that the Catholic Church teachings are not directly from God by way of transmission from the apostles, Instead, church doctrines are the product of argument, lobbying, and voting, something that also happened in earlier councils. Textbooks covered over this fact of legitimate debate by presenting previous church councils as defending true doctrine and declaring other views to be heretical.

16. The church has a "deposit of faith" not a deposit of revelation. Statements of Catholic doctrine are not divinely revealed truths but statements of faith, which have been formulated by the

church. God speaks/reveals; humans believe/trust. Catholic theology is reflection on articles of faith.

17. The church must now rethink the foundation of its teachings, which are based on the consensus that emerges from a tradition of study and debate. Paradoxically, the solution to the problem of revelation is to have more of what brought on the problem, that is, more debate by more members of the church. Any solution requires a structural change in the church so that all the members who are sufficiently knowledgeable about the church's mission and history can contribute to the church's teaching.

The Story Line

The points listed above can form the spine of an argument about how the idea of revelation originated, how it entered Christian history, how it rose to a central place in church teachings, and how it has been undermined in recent centuries. I have neither the time nor the scholarship to fill out this story. The story needs to be told by a team of scholars in a series of books that would be linked together.

Until that happens, the Roman Catholic Church's teaching will continue to be weakened or rejected because its official teachers are defending what has been undermined by scholarship from within the church and from outside the church. Most Roman Catholics cannot pinpoint the weakness of the church's teaching, but they strongly suspect that something is wrong in the way that Roman Catholic bishops still try to pronounce the truth and treat disagreements as "dissent" instead of an indication of the need for debating formulas of belief.[1] The idea of the "development of doctrine" is now almost universally accepted in the church and can answer many questions about changes in church teachings. But the *basis* of all church teachings, the concept of divine revelation, is the main reason for the intellectual crisis of the church today.

I first became interested in the question of divine revelation in 1961 when I was introduced to the argument concerning "sources of revelation." From my first encounter with that question, I sensed that something was missing or else that the debate was obscuring a deeper problem. I often told people that the only thing worth reading in my book Scripture and Tradition, which summarized that debate, was footnote number one in which I wrote that revelation itself is the problem: "Revelation is never really an object that can be divided or contained. The invitation of the God revealed in Christ can only be proclaimed by the Church and answered in faith."[2]

My conclusion to that book led me to attempt a study of divine revelation. I had no idea how difficult and puzzling such a study would be. An examination of divine revelation would quickly lead outside the boundaries of Catholic theology. At that time, when I was writing a dissertation at the Catholic University of America, that fact was a problem which I could not address. I was aware that my title "Theology of Revelation" was illogical. Catholic theology presupposes a divine revelation; no field can study the presupposition of its own existence.

I was also writing the work while the Second Vatican Council was taking place. The Council began by rejecting a document on the sources of revelation that simply reaffirmed the Council of Trent's two sources of revelation: scripture and tradition. When a new document was mandated by the Council, the task was turned over to biblical scholars. They did not question the existence of a divine revelation but instead concentrated on stating the belief in biblical imagery.

I obtained a copy of the document, which was to be debated at the final session of the Council. I trusted that no major changes would be made, and I left space in my manuscript to insert quotations. My book, which was published a little more than a month after the Council's approval of the Constitution on Divine Revelation, appeared to be a commentary on the conciliar document.[3]

The *Constitution* was received with great enthusiasm and has never received serious criticism. I was disappointed with the document, which seemed to me to miss the main point. The question was not how to describe revelation but whether the claim to possess a revelation from God makes sense. Biblical experts were not the group to raise such a question.

I had tried to address the question starting from education, that is, from what is occurring in the present. My book became popular among educators in the church. The idea that divine revelation is occurring now made sense educationally.[4] Theologians, exegetes and church officials were less enthusiastic about the thesis. I constructed an elaborate argument to sustain my claim that one could be orthodox in saying that divine revelation occurs in the present. The book followed the format of a theology book, but it concluded by pointing beyond Catholic theology to an ecumenical or universal meaning of divine revelation.

My book tended to be reduced to a slogan, "continuing revelation," as books often are. I unwisely tried to write a follow-up book that would clarify what I meant, and which started from where *Theology of Revelation* ended. That book, *Present Revelation*, was not well received, deservedly so.[5] It lacked discipline and historical grounding for its claims. In the years that followed, I was sometimes allowed to speak on the topic of revelation, although I was relegated in official circles to a writer on catechetics.

When I was teaching a course at Boston College in the 1970s I outlined what I had to offer about the nature of revelation. An evangelical student asked me how my explanation was related to the *Book of Revelation*. I dismissed his question as irrelevant, but it bothered me. Twenty-five years later, I finally tried to answer his question in a book entitled *Both Sides: The Story of Revelation*.[6] That book was the closest I came to getting the story straight. Although much of the material was there to tell the story, I still missed the main story line. I separated the story into two tracks. What I imagined as the minor track was actually the key to the story. What I called the two sides of the story could not be separated.

I devoted more time to *Both Sides* than anything I have ever written. Much of the time was spent laboriously trying to find what all the "fathers of the church" said about revelation. It was a frustrating experience because I could find so little material, either among the Greek fathers' use of *apokalpsis* or its translation in Latin literature. I thought I must somehow be missing what was there. I missed the real story that in fact there is little there. Revelation was not a central doctrine in the early church fathers. Only where the *Book of Revelation* had its influence did the term revelation show up. I was still assuming that the *Book of Revelation* was a side story instead of the main story line.

Classical Latin had the term *revelatio* that went back as far as Ovid. One would expect that *revelatio* would have been used as the translation of *apokalypsis*; sometimes it was. But in the late second century Tertullian used *apocalypsis* as a Latin term. What might seem to be a minor technical blip of translations opened the possibility to the split that occurred in the Latin church. When Jerome translated the New Testament into Latin, he had two terms for translating the one Greek term. Jerome chose to use *revelatio* for translating the six times that Paul uses *apokalypsis*[7] while he used *apocalypsis* for the *Book of Revelation*. This use of two different Latin words was probably not just random. Jerome was highly critical of the prophecies in John's Revelation.

Jerome's translation of the Latin *Vulgate* paved the way for Augustine of Hippo who is the central figure in the story of revelation. He associated the two terms for revelation with two very different meanings that were radically split in time. The *Book of Revelation* had described a thousand-year reign of the Christ before the final new heaven and new earth.[8] In his monumental *City of God*, Augustine associated *revelatio* with the thousand-year reign of Christ's church following the death/resurrection of Jesus. *Revelatio* occurred in the past as described in the Gospels and Epistles, while *apocalypsis* still referred to the future as described in the Book of Revelation."[9]

In the centuries after Augustine, revelation was not a central topic of discussion, but the assumption was that God's revelation had been made complete in the life, death, and resurrection of Christ. The *Bible* was the written record of the *revelatio* what had been revealed and which had been transmitted from apostolic times to the church in the present.

The teaching of the bishops could be trusted because it was based on "God's word." There were differences in the way people understood "the word of God." If the phrase were taken in its most literal meaning, the *Bible* would be understood as dictation from God. But there was recognition by the time of Augustine that some passages of the Bible should be interpreted as allegory or as some other form of language that allowed for several meanings of a verse.

Thomas Aquinas was not a biblical scholar. Not knowing Greek, he accepted the Latin text of the *Bible* and the official teaching of the church. Like Augustine, Thomas insisted that teaching be based on the literal meaning of the *Bible* while allowing for more than one meaning within what is literal. When he used the term revelation it was often as object of a preposition: by, through, from, according to. Instead of writing that "revelation says …" or that something has been revealed, he refers to what we know "from revelation" which leaves the nature of revelation unclear.[10] Where Thomas does use "revelation" in the nominative case it is often a paradoxical meaning: "Revelation does not tell us what God is, and thus joins us to him as an unknown."[11] Sacred doctrine is based on "articles of faith" that involve articulation by the church of the revelation that occurred in the lives of believers.[12]

The middle ages were a time of closed rational systems that are often ridiculed. To the extent that church writers assumed that God had provided a revelation of the truth to interpret the world, there was less inclination to study the world of human experience. But historians in recent centuries acknowledge that there was more to the middle ages than deadening logical arguments. The beginnings of empirical science can be traced back to the twelfth century, as well as developments in mathematics.[13] To the extent that Thomas Aquinas was classified as a follower of Aristotle and understood to be intent on showing the compatibility of reason and "Christian revelation" (a phrase he never used), his work is dismissed as closed in on itself.

Modern studies of Thomas Aquinas bypassed the summaries of his work in seminary manuals and returned to his texts and to the influences on his work. What emerged was an understanding of Thomas's work as a complex joining of several philosophical traditions.[14] Thomas quotes, second only to Aristotle, the author known as Pseudo-Dionysius, who was mistakenly thought to be a disciple of St. Paul. This writer was a chief conduit to Thomas of the neo-Platonic tradition, which shaped the mystical strand of the middle ages.[15] This part of the story has usually been overlooked in any history of revelation but in fact mysticism is central to the story.

The mystical strand that runs throughout the middle ages emerged in the writing of Joachim of Fiore in the twelfth century. Joachim profoundly influenced not only the Christian Church but secular writing as well. The division of history into ancient, medieval, and modern is largely due to Joachim. In his complex system there was an age of the Father, an age of the Son and now has begun the age of the Holy Spirit. Joachim relied on the *Book of Revelation* for his understanding of this age of the spirit. He was not against institutions, but he thought that revelation could occur in the lives of individuals.[16]

It hardly needs to be said that the church officials have never looked kindly on mystical experience in which the individual claims to be "oned" with God. The category of "private revelation" was invented as a means to isolate whatever the mystic might claim to have experienced. In contrast, what the bishops claim has been transmitted from Jesus and his disciples is called "public revelation."

It must be admitted that people who claim to have mystical experiences can be unbalanced and dangerous. Listening to no institution or guidance from others, the mystic can be rebellious and violent. Nevertheless, religious mysticism can be a positive force for freeing society's underclass. The Marxist Ernest Bloch said of Meister Eckhart: "He who believes he is in union with the Lord of Lords does not, when it comes down to it, make a very good serf."[17]

A history of divine revelation would have to include the lives of people known as mystics, such as Eckhart, Hildegard, and Teresa of Avila.[18] It would also have to include mystical elements in many Christian writers. That category would include Thomas Aquinas who, although skeptical of Joachim and his followers, had his own mystical tendencies in the paradoxical language that he used of God, and in his prayer life that culminated in silence toward the end of his life.

The Protestant reformers showed the influence of medieval mysticism in their emphasis on the individual and the private reading of the scriptures. Martin Luther opposed the radical wing of the Reformation that threatened the political and religious order of the time, but Luther's reform let loose forces beyond his control. Luther was skeptical of the *Book of Revelation* but the brilliant artwork accompanying that book in Luther's Bible made the book more popular than ever.[19] The reform that traces its origin to John Calvin had less of an inclination to the mystical, but it also could not control every radical movement in Calvin's name.

The Catholic Church of the fourteenth and fifteenth centuries was torn by factions claiming to represent the one true church. The division between competing popes in Rome and Avignon was settled by the Council of Constance (1431–1449) that installed its own pope. On what authority a council claimed to decide on a papal leader raised new questions about the ultimate authority in the church.

The Council of Trent (1548–1563) was called to affirm the authority of the pope, and the bishops when they are in consort with the pope.

The Council did its work well insofar as it stabilized the Roman Catholic Church for centuries. On the question of divine revelation that it claimed for support, the Council of Trent fixed revelation as an object in the possession of legitimate authority. Revelation could be found "partly in scripture and partly in tradition."

The phrase "Christian revelation" had occasionally been used in the years just before the Council of Trent. After the Council, "Christian revelation" became a common way of referring to divine revelation. The phrase "Christian revelation" might seem to be an acknowledgment of the Christian Church's limitation; it leaves room for claims of Jewish revelation, Muslim revelation, and other parts of the complete revelation of God. But what the phrase "Christian revelation" did was to objectify revelation into a thing that can be divided and possessed.[20]

The Roman Catholic Church entered the modern age with its teachings well defined for those who were believers. The development of the empirical-mathematical sciences (or what quickly became "science") posed a new challenge for the church and its claim to possess a revelation. The sciences laid claim to a revelation of the workings of the universe. This "natural revelation" did not require any leap of faith; it demonstrated its truth by mathematical and logical conclusions. Science proved its value by inspiring the "practical arts" (which became known in the nineteenth century as "technology") to make improvements in human life.

The Roman Catholic Church countered the scientific claim to the revelation of the natural world by claiming that its revelation was "supernatural." The most important questions about the origin and destiny of human life could not be answered by natural revelations but only by a revelation from beyond nature. The church seemed to be saying to modern science: You can have this world; we have the world to come. The drawback was that a supernatural revelation could become increasingly removed from the daily lives of Christians and from the church's influence on public affairs.

In the nineteenth century, an increasing clash between the church and the political changes in the surrounding world led to the calling of a new council. The (First) Vatican Council (1869) intended to lay out and reaffirm the structure of church offices. It did not get far before it was interrupted. It dispersed having only covered the role of the pope. However, its pronouncement that the pope is infallible on certain matters was a startling claim that reverberated throughout church teachings. Popes would seldom claim to speak infallibly but the very idea seemed to seep into every papal pronouncement and filter down to much of what bishops said. Acceptance of the pope as the first among the bishops was nothing new, but the pope as infallible leader of the church made clear that the church was a pyramid with authority located in one man at the very top.

The (First) Vatican Council did have time to produce a document on the nature of faith.[21] A collection of statements on faith presupposed a corresponding understanding of divine revelation. The Council let stand what the Council of Trent had said about divine revelation. The idea of revelation was locked into a collection of truths that have come directly from God.

At the time of the (First) Vatican Council, modern biblical studies had already begun to undermine the claim that the *Bible* provides "proof texts" for every church teaching. The Council of Trent's assertion that revelation is contained in scripture became more problematic. As scholars went back to ancient documents they found many cases of error and mistranslation. Are these mistakes part of God's revelation? If not, what criteria distinguish between what is revelation and what is not? Most scriptural scholars preferred to avoid conflicts with church authorities. They asserted that all the scripture is "inspired" by God but is not necessarily revelation. They left the theological debates about what is divinely revealed to other church people.

The bishops confidently pronounced some things to be part of divine or Christian revelation. Any doubts could be removed by appealing to papal authority for a final judgment. Catholic scholars first concentrated on the Hebrew Bible where there was less danger of conflict with the bishops. But as Catholic exegetes in the twentieth century turned their attention to the New Testament, conflicts were inevitable. Catholic and Protestant scholars shared their findings and found agreement on the meaning of texts. The centuries-old battle between Protestant and Catholic versions of the Bible gradually disappeared.

As I noted in the Introduction, the papal proclamation in 1950 of the Assumption of the Virgin Mary was the event that opened a new discussion of the sources of revelation. Neither scripture nor tradition provided an adequate basis for this doctrine. Catholic scholars could not appeal to a higher authority because it was the pope himself who had brought about the crisis by proclaiming the doctrine to be an article of faith. The shaky basis for a "Christian revelation" needed to be examined but church officials did not show much interest.

The Second Vatican Council attempted to articulate a better understanding of divine revelation. But there was no effort to track the history of the idea and term revelation. The Council's *Constitution on Divine Revelation* is also known by its opening words *Verbum Dei* (word of God). The conflict between these two metaphors, hearing and seeing, was glossed over. Biblical scholars were more attuned to the Word of God, but they had been asked to write a document on the revelation of God. They tried to keep the two together.

The shocking thing about the document is that there is no reference to the *Book of Revelation*. How could authors write a document about revelation in the *Bible* and have nothing to say about the Book that is called Revelation? The answer is that the Roman Catholic Church has never known what to do with the Book of Revelation and still does not. Revelation was a threat in the early church before it was brought inside the canon. The *Book of Revelation* was isolated from a discussion of revelation by being called the Apocalypse. The divine revelation included only the organized set of beliefs that constituted orthodoxy. Prophecy, mysticism, and prophetic calls for action were outside the divinely revealed truths that were officially recognized as the church teachings.

Divine revelation and divine speaking were protected in the modern church by being located in a logical system. The modern sciences were rendered incapable of disproving these supernatural truths. The price of that protection was that the church teachings lost any influence on the political, economic, and ecological questions of today. The divine revelation that the church claims to possess was completed two thousand years ago. What relevance do these fixed truths have in exhortations to live peacefully and justly in today's world?

Pope Francis has been courageously outspoken in addressing major issues of the day. He has succeeded in changing the face of the Roman Catholic Church for millions of people both within and outside the church. Unfortunately, he is hobbled by an idea of revelation that gets in the way of vigorous dialogue with all people of good will. He has not been helped to rethink the idea of revelation as it still functions in seminary education.

For example, in his encyclical, *Laudato si,* Pope Francis writes: "Alongside revelation properly so called, contained in Scripture, there is a divine manifestation in the blaze of the sun and the fall of the night."[22] The statement reflects the Council of Trent's understanding of divine revelation. In this document, Pope Francis urges church involvement in discussions of environmental problems. But he treats the revelation of creation as an extra, alongside the real revelation in the *Bible.* I suspect that if a Francis of Assisi or Thomas Aquinas were alive today, he would start a discussion of divine revelation as coextensive with creation. The environment is not a problem to be addressed by revelation but the beginning place for everyone to understand the revealing of the divine, and the context for all other claims to divine revelation.

If there are no revealed truths possessed by the bishops, then what is the basis of the church teachings? The answer is: The tradition of the church understood not as truths accompanying the *Bible* but as the totality of church history, including the *Bible*. No individual knows that entire tradition. As a result, it is indispensable for the church to draw upon the scholars and saints who best know the history and practice of the church.

In its current form there is no organized way for the church to draw upon the contributions of all the people who represent the richness of its tradition. I suggest in the last chapter of this book that an authority based on a pyramidic structure is severely limited in its flow of information. The main flow is one of a demand for conformity coming from the top for obedience from below. Revelation understood as the truth already unveiled fits well within a pyramidic structure.

The alternative for the church is to become a community, which was the form of the original Christian movement. The church's failure to become a worldwide community of communities was not entirely its fault. Not until modern advances in education, travel, and communication has it become realistically possible to have an organization that is communal at every level. Given the limitations of human nature, the odds are still against creating and sustaining such an organization, but the effort should be made in that direction.

What would typify communication in such an organization would be speaking and listening that best embody the biblical metaphor of God's word. Plato used as the test of political community the limits of the human voice. Today a person's voice can be heard worldwide. Political organizations at the national level are threatened by authoritarian movements, which are sustained by violence. A religious organization can either offer more of that same authoritarianism or it can dare to follow the best lights of its tradition and listen for the truth in the hearts and minds of its members

CHAPTER FIVE:
The Morality Crisis

The intellectual crisis of the church, which was discussed in Chapter Four, is paralleled by a crisis at the foundation of its moral teaching. Like "revelation," the crisis is centered on one term, "natural law." Both terms were intrusions from outside the biblical tradition. Neither concept was a perfect fit for Christianity, and today both terms are inadequate and misleading in the way they are used. As the foundation of its moral teaching, "natural law" affects the church's stand on sexual morality, as well as on abortion, care of the dying, the state execution of prisoners, human rights, the environment, and more.

The following points trace "natural law" through history and they suggest some of the research and study that needs to be done. However, like "revelation," no one scholar could manage to do what is needed. A team of scholars would be necessary to address the many facets of the problem. During the last fifty years there has been a group of scholars who have advocated a "new natural law," and their scholarship should be helpful. So far, however, their approach seems far too narrow and arbitrary.

1. "Nature" (*phusis*) was coined by Greek philosophers for an inner principle of living beings. It quickly became a way to classify what kind of thing each being is. The ancient Jews, not being

philosophically inclined, had no need for a term such as nature. There was no equivalent word in the Hebrew Bible.

2. "Nature" had acquired many meanings by the time of the Christian era. The most important meaning was a collective use of natures for the whole world of things that humans encounter. This meaning of "nature" was found among the Stoic philosophers. Stoicism was the chief competitor to the early church.

3. "Nature," "natural," and "unnatural" entered the New Testament in Paul's letters, which were written in Greek. He was not writing a philosophical treatise and did not use the terms consistently.

4. Cicero, a prominent Stoic, coined the term "natural law." He described three kinds of law: natural law, civil law, and the law of nations. Natural law meant that humans must obey nature's laws. Although humans can resist nature, death is the evidence that nature always wins in the end. Christian writers for fifteen hundred years regularly cited Cicero's three kinds of law.

5. Christian morality was profoundly shaped by the philosophy of Stoicism. Christians admired the strict moral code of the Stoics.

6. The coining of "person" in the debates about how to speak of God and Christ's relation to his Father was a brilliant invention of Christian thinkers. The concept of person proved to be invaluable for describing each human being. A person is who I am; human nature is what I am.

7. Even in winning out against Stoicism, the church absorbed much of the language of Stoicism. There was a danger that Christian morality would be understood as a submission to the law of nature.

8. The church's moral teaching was shaped for more than a thousand years before Aristotle's influence through Thomas Aquinas reemphasized "nature" as a way to characterize beings rather than as a cosmic power.

9. Thomas Aquinas used the term "natural law" but in a distinctive way. He said that there were three applications of natural law, one for the world, one for nonhuman animals, and one for humans.

10. Natural law for humans might have been better called "personal law" because humans do not submit to nature. Natural law for humans can be changed or added to. Thomas uses the example that nature gives us a body, while "art" gives us clothes.

11. Sin is to act against the good of one's person. The contradiction or destruction of one's nature prevents the person from the realization of his or her good.

12. Beginning in the seventeenth century, moral theology manuals focused on classifying sins as failures to obey the law. The ten commandments of the Hebrew Bible were given prominence as divine and natural law.

13. In the 1950s, a shift began to occur that was inspired by New Testament study. The emphasis in morality was placed on the person, goodness, and virtue. The fundamental law in Christianity is not the "ten commandments" but "love thy neighbor as thyself."

14. Human life has always been a combination of what is "natural" or given by birth, and the artificial, including technological inventions. The artificial can be good if it enhances or completes the natural. The artificial is bad only if it is opposed to or does harm to the natural.

15. Law remains an important element for morality but there is always a gap between a principle that applies to many situations and knowing how to act in a particular situation. Thomas Aquinas says application of natural law for humans requires "determinations" from history, science, and experience.

16. Modern science reappropriated the Stoic meaning of "nature." The difference was that "man" now had the tools to penetrate

nature and control elements of nature. Nonetheless, there are laws of nature to which man must submit.

17. The church is right to condemn both the destruction of the natural in the nonhuman world and violence toward the natural in a person. Obvious examples are ecological destruction, torture, state execution of prisoners, sexual assault, and all violence done to persons.

The Story Line

The above points provide an outline for the story of natural law and its place in the Roman Catholic Church. The full story starts with the ambiguities of the term natural. "Nature" is perhaps the most ambiguous word in the English language. Aristotle had already identified six meanings of nature.[1] A study by two of the great scholars of the twentieth century found over six hundred meanings of "nature."[2] Obviously, some meanings proved to be much more important than others.

What creates such ambiguity in a term is that it does not refer to an object outside the mind. This fact does not invalidate the term. "Nature" has been an invaluable aid to thinking about human life, but it can also be used for ideological purposes and there is no way to refute such a meaning. For example, the term "human nature" is widely assumed to have a single fixed meaning. A person or a group of people can be persecuted for violating human nature because they conflict with what most people assume are the limits of "human nature."

The recognition that "nature" does not exist, that is, there is no thing or object outside the human mind that corresponds to nature, is especially difficult to recognize in today's world. Science makes constant references to nature and to what human beings are doing to nature. There is indeed a massive problem of survival for the human race but defending nature will probably not work. Breathable air and potable water are real in a way that "nature" is not.

In writing about the history of nature it is imperative to trace not an idea or ideas of nature but rather the meaning of the term nature. There is some control in speaking about what "nature" means, although it is still an extraordinarily complex undertaking. I have chosen to emphasize some of the major shifts in the meaning of "nature" for the purpose of clarifying the Roman Catholic Church's use of "natural law."

The origin of "nature" can be pinpointed with more accuracy than is true of most highly ambiguous terms. Aristotle is the main source of our knowledge of the invention of "nature" during the early period of Greek philosophy. Aristotle saw the great potential in "nature" as the inner principle of a living thing. "Nature" soon became a way to classify things, linked to what Aristotle called the "essence" of things.

The Israelites not being philosophically inclined had no need for the concept of nature. The *Bible* speaks concretely of men and women, plants and animals, rocks and rivers.

The terms nature and natural entered the biblical tradition through St. Paul who was writing in Greek. Like people then and now, he used "unnatural" for things that shocked him, such as men having sexual relations. (Rom. 1:26-27). But he also used "unnatural" for a range of things, even for something that is good as in his description of the relation between the church and the Jews. Paul says that God will act "contrary to nature" to save the Jews. (Rom. 11:24)[3]

Aristotle already listed six meanings of "nature," although he failed to include the meaning that already existed in his time and was to become most prominent by the time of the Common Era. In that meaning, "nature" was said to be an all-embracing principle or an ultimate context of everything. The two philosophical traditions that most influenced early Christianity – Stoicism and Neo-Platonism – gave nature a place superior to humanity.

Especially as interpreted by Plotinus in the philosophy of Neo-Platonism, Plato was seen as compatible with or even a supporter of the Christian idea of a creator. Plato referred to the One beyond being who is the source of all things.[4] Stoic philosophy, however, was more directly influential in shaping the lives of ordinary Christians insofar as it provided a language for moral life and a moral code. Christianity was understood to be a way of life similar to the philosophical traditions that it competed with.[5]

Where Christianity and Stoicism ultimately differed was in their idea of nature. For the Stoics, mother nature was the ruling principle of the universe and the origin of us all. For Christianity, nature was the creation of God the Father and it was only one principle in the universe. The Christological debates of the early church led to a key distinction between nature and person. God was said to be three persons and one nature; the Christ was one person and two natures.

The invention of person proved to be an invaluable tool for the description of human beings. In the secular world, it became standard to use "person" as a way to talk about the individual human being. Nature, in contrast, was taken to be common to the human race and constitutive of its difference from other living beings.

Christianity won the competition with Stoicism even while absorbing the moral language of Stoicism ("religion," "moral," "natural," "natural law," "pious," "sacrament"). However, the Christian victory might be seen as temporary insofar as the Stoic idea of nature returned with modern science. In the seventeenth century, nature re-ascended to an all-embracing position in the universe.

At first, nature was seen in modern science as the enemy to be conquered. Francis Bacon fixed the meaning of nature as all that opposed "man." Bacon warned, however, that nature had to be respected even as it was penetrated and controlled.[6] The human race has recently come to recognize that it has been destroying the environment, that is, the immediate sources of its own existence. Nature, it is now said, is not to be conquered but instead befriended.

Christians who now refer to "mother nature" may be unaware that they are speaking the language of Stoicism. Francis of Assisi who is said to be the patron saint of nature never used the word. Instead, he spoke of a wolf as his brother or a bird as his sister.[7]

Pairing the word "law" with nature has always been problematic. Neither Aristotle nor other Greek philosophers conceived of a "natural law." The Bible has no philosophical idea of nature and has no references to a natural law. The apostle Paul in the New Testament, while declaring some things unnatural, nowhere refers to a natural law. Paul is very much concerned with law, but his references are to the law of Moses and to the relation between law and grace.

The term "natural law" was coined by Cicero as one part of his juridical reflections.[8] For Cicero and the Stoics, there is ultimately only one natural law, namely, the submission of the human to cosmic nature. The Catholic Church would later refer to natural law as divine law, a usage more Stoic than biblical. Cicero also writes of civil laws and the law of nations. Civil laws were the products of human legislatures. Cicero's third kind of law was never entirely clear; it was replaced by the idea of international law, which begins in the seventeenth century.

It is surprising that the Christian adoption of "natural law" left the term in the singular. Thomas Aquinas speaks of three applications of natural law. The first of his natural laws that applies to the whole world is very close to Cicero's meaning. Thomas's second natural law is the law as applied to nonhuman animals. His third natural law, which governs human life could have opened a new discussion of whether "natural law" is an appropriate term for discussing human morality.[9]

Thomas says that "natural law" is a peculiar form of law that is not manifested outside the human mind. Further, he thought that to be useful this natural law for humans requires "determinations" from history and experience to be applied to particular situations.[10] It seems unfortunate that Thomas did not jettison "natural law" as a way to talk about human morality. Christian moralists might have concentrated on learning what is and what is not destructive of human nature.

The Roman Catholic Church's reliance on "natural law" was no match for the "laws of nature" that modern science articulated. The sciences adopted a meaning for nature's laws that could be discovered by careful experimentation. The church kept advocating a meaning of nature and a view of human nature that everyone supposedly knows. When conflicts arose between science's laws of nature and a religious morality based on natural law, science offered answers based on evidence. For much of the world, morality was included within the new sciences.

For many centuries, the church seemed to have a credible case that some moral principles were recognized everywhere. The nineteenth century explorations of cultures appeared to have demolished that claim. Anthropologists found a striking diversity among different peoples as to what constitutes a moral code. The term moral relativism indicated that judgments of good and bad were relative to place and time. While moral judgments about many practices indeed vary by culture, the conclusion that there are no universal principles was premature. The twentieth century had to engage in sorting out some moral judgments that are relative to a culture and some practices that the human race could not long endure.

The human race was confronted in the twentieth century by two experiences that threatened to wipe out human civilization: war and environmental destruction.

War has been part of human history as far back as history can be traced. Plato expressed concern that wars between Greeks be limited because after the war the vanquished would need to have the resources to rebuild.[11] The Christian Church led the way in trying to set limits to the destructiveness of war. Starting with Augustine of Hippo, the church distinguished just and unjust wars.[12] Augustine and Thomas Aquinas were not trying to justify war but rather to limit its destructiveness.

The rules for fighting wars were regularly breached but some limits were acknowledged, for example, avoiding the killing of non-combatants. Even at the beginning of the United States Civil War, war was imagined as a game in which each side fielded a team of soldiers who would fight until one side was exhausted. However, the savagery of that war proved to be a harbinger of wars that followed.

Technological developments, especially the airplane, made traditional rules of war unenforceable. The destruction in World War II finally convinced national leaders that a repeat of such a war could not be endured. Albert Einstein said: "I know not how World War III will be fought but I do know that World War IV will be fought with sticks and stones."

There were attempts after the war to create institutional protections against nations stumbling into war. War trials fixed some responsibility for the prosecution of crimes in World War II. The founding of the United Nations was a pledge that nations would talk to one another instead of fighting. The UN's *Universal Declaration of Human Rights* had little legal force, but it represented the acceptance of a moral principle in international dealings. The idea of human rights has slowly gained credibility in much of the world.[13]

The other looming disaster for the human race, environmental destruction, has not yet been brought into clear focus and remains a deadly threat. The steps that are now being taken may be already too little and too late. The empirical sciences have gathered the necessary information of the perilous journey that the human race is on.

Unfortunately, the sciences are not effective in generating activity based on moral convictions. The scientific picture of "man" as an inconspicuous element in nature's universe does not inspire moral convictions about a respect for the human environment. In contrast, the stories found in traditional religions have the potential to inspire activity for the good of one's family and that of future families.

The Roman Catholic Church's history of trying to persuade its members to act in accordance with God's creation could be an effective voice in addressing the grave problems that have come from greed, ignorance, and lack of discipline. The history of the church might have led it to be supportive of movements of nonviolence that respect all peoples and their environments. But talk of "natural law" is usually a non-starter.

A "new natural law" has been talked about since the 1960s, but it remains a cottage industry, most prominently among conservative Roman Catholic philosophers.[14] The most detailed theory of natural law from this group is by John Finnis.[15] His theory begins by claiming that there are seven goods or values that are found in human nature. From there, Finnis claims that one can work out a natural law. He makes an important connection between rights and natural law.

I would think his approach would be more helpful for the current discussion of human rights than for a theory of natural law. Unfortunately, he collapses any difference between human rights and natural rights. "Human rights," as I discuss later, arose in conflict with "natural rights" in the nineteenth century. It can be argued that the concept of natural rights had been distorted and that the idea of natural law and natural rights was a precursor to human rights. But it is "human rights" that is widely accepted today, and "natural rights" is used by a minority. The new natural law has had fifty years to make its case but has not succeeded beyond a small group of political and religious conservatives.

The bishops' invocation of natural law is usually limited to sexual morality, abortion, and euthanasia. I address these issues in later chapters. The fact that "natural law" is mainly brought up in the context of sexual morality undercuts the official church's attempt to apply the term more widely.

Church officials seem to imply a negative meaning for "artificial" when they refer to natural law. They condemn "artificial contraceptives" as a moral means of birth control. If one starts from "natural" instead of "natural law," it is obvious that the artificial – the making of art – is the indispensable companion to the natural. We humans are born with a nature that distinguishes us from the other animals. Humans are rather slow getting going but they surpass the other animals because of their artistic inventiveness. Human nature is art.

Starting at its beginning, the human race had to be creatures of artifice: gardens for growing food, protections against heat and cold. Some art – including technology – has been destructive even if the original intention was positive. Time is often needed for deciding whether technological developments are compatible with the good of human nature. If Roman Catholic Church officials wish to influence public policy or even just guide their members, they have to participate in the fallible human effort to learn about the conditions that improve human life.

PART THREE

CHAPTER SIX:

The Basic Principle of Morality

When I began teaching courses on ethics at New York University in the 1980s, I was forced to think hard about the basis of ethics. I had previously dealt with ethics within the context of the church's history and teaching. At NYU, I was confronted by students who held a wide variety of religious and nonreligious views of life. NYU at that point still had a large Roman Catholic population but that fact was not something I could directly draw upon.

The principle on which I based my moral conviction was not separate from my formation as a Roman Catholic. But I had to present morality to students in a different way. Instead of saying "Jesus teaches us to forgive our enemies" and assume that Catholics would agree when confronted by the New Testament, I had to present a diversity of voices on the issue that includes the great prophet Jesus of Nazareth.

From many sources, especially the teaching of the church, I decided that the principle that I have lived by is: "Do violence to no one." There are positive actions that can be drawn from that principle, but renouncing violence is the basis of ethics. That principle is firmly rooted in the New Testament as I show in a later section of this chapter.

A discussion of nonviolence is often assumed to be about national policy and the horrors of nations at war. Such a discussion is urgently needed. But a nation will never be characterized as nonviolent unless its citizens avoid violence in their personal lives. Each of us who are citizens of the United States find that we have been born into a strangely violent environment. Other nations may be as violent, but the United States pictures itself as peace-loving and marked only by occasional spasms of violence.

To live a nonviolent life in the United States requires two levels of resistance. First, a person has to puncture the myth that envelopes United States history and is indoctrinated into every child in the country. Second, a person has to develop self-understanding and a personal discipline.

In the Preface to my book, *America in the United States and the United States in America,* I wrote that during the United States war in Vietnam I began a fifty-year journey to try to understand why the United States is such a violent country, while at the same time most of its citizens think that the country is only seeking peace on earth.[1] Like almost everyone who grew up in the 1950s, I was indoctrinated with the vision of a country that has gone to war only as a last resort for the purpose of defending itself and other freedom-loving allies.

The distinction that I urge in the book between the actual nation of the United States and "America," the name of the promised land, allows one to understand the actual history of the country. "American history" (in contrast to United States history) is filled with myths about a country that does not exist. "America" can be a beautiful ideal, but it has also been a way to hide the faults of the country and to obstruct obviously needed reforms.

The United States has always been a violent country. The attitude to guns is a puzzle for many of its own citizens and for people around the world. No matter how many violent massacres occur in the country, defenders of the second amendment to the U.S. Constitution are unmoved. The rest of the world looks on with astonishment at the willingness of the

United States to live with an endless string of mass shootings and almost a hundred deaths by gunfire each day.

The violence of the country is also shown in its retention of the barbaric practice of the state executions of prisoners. Most of the civilized world has ended the practice. In this case, Catholic groups have been in the forefront of activists demanding an end to state executions. Pope Francis has gone further than his predecessors in asserting that the official teaching of the Roman Catholic Church rejects all state executions.[2]

When Roman Catholics arrived in the United States by the millions, they were viewed with suspicion and sometimes violence. They were accused of not being sufficiently "American." The result in the first half of the twentieth century was an exaggerated patriotism on the part of the church. Officials of the church were always ready to assure political leaders of Catholic allegiance to "America." That cozy relation reached a high point when the government and the church collaborated in anti-communism.

Roman Catholics were strongly supportive of the government's beginning of war in Vietnam, but the war seemed to bring about a changed attitude among a new generation of Catholics. The bishops even published a document indicating that church officials were willing to stand for peace in opposition to government policies.[3]

Unfortunately, in that same period of the 1970s and 1980s the country became badly split, a division that has only become deeper in time. There are many ways to describe what divides the country. The longest running basis for the disunited states of America is race, with a division of white and black that is enduring and profound. In such a split country, the Roman Catholic Church has not been well positioned. When Roman Catholic immigrants flooded the country in the middle of the nineteenth century, they were not accepted as white. They might have joined with blacks in a fight for freedom but that is not what usually happens among oppressed people.

The Roman Catholic Church of the twentieth and twenty-first centuries remained distinctly white in complexion. Racism has been a reason for Roman Catholics, especially the bishops, to support right-wing politicians whose views of racial justice, social welfare, and militarism conflict with the church's official teaching. Since the 1970s, the issue of abortion has been a driving force for the official church's involvement in politics. Abortion raises a legitimate question of violence, but it is not obvious that the bishops' support of the politicians they have backed has been on the side of reducing violence in the United States.

The second level of resistance to violence requires a journey of self-discovery. The human being is not born violent, but from the beginning of life he or she has an aggressive side that has to be directed to healthy expressions.[4] The fears that are unavoidable in a child live on and can prevent a person from living peacefully. Religion can be a help in this process; although, when religion is badly incorporated into personal life it can increase fears and a tendency to violent activity.[5] A person cannot serve the needs of the poor and suffering unless he or she has come to terms with the inclination to violence in his or her life.

This personal journey is a discipline for each individual. Nonetheless, the individual is influenced by the pronouncements coming from the institution and especially by the lives of public figures. When the Second Vatican Council decided to condemn "total war," despite the objection of several U.S. bishops, individual Catholics in the United States were given a boost in their personal opposition to violence. The example of a handful of bishops in the United States whose personal lives in the 1980s demonstrated a commitment to nonviolence was an invaluable support for Catholic groups such as Pax Christi.

The Teachings of Jesus

All Christian teaching of morality supposedly starts from the teachings of Jesus in the New Testament. That teaching is summarized by a collection of texts called the *Sermon on the Mount.* It is found in the *Gospel of Matthew,* chapters five to seven. An understanding of the teaching requires the context of the New Testament, including similar texts in *Luke's Gospel,* and the larger context which includes the *Hebrew Bible.* As a Jew, Jesus stands in a long tradition so that much of what he says echoes previous teaching in the tradition. He gives new meaning or new emphasis to previous teachings, but one cannot make sense of what he is saying without some knowledge of what he is modifying by imaginative reconstruction and syntheses.

In a series of well-known contrasts, Jesus describes "what you have heard said" as opposed to what he says. For interpreting these contrasts, it is indispensable to notice the passage in Matthew that just precedes the contrasts: "Think not that I have come to abolish the law and the prophets; I have not come to abolish them but to fulfill them." (5:17). The word fulfill can have several meanings but here it should be consistent with the next verse: "For truly, I say to you not an iota, not a dot, will pass from the law until all is accomplished." (5:18). These two verses and the following two that lead into the contrasts make it impossible to read Jesus' teaching as a rejection of "the law and the prophets" in favor of what would be their opposites.

The series of so-called antitheses ("You have heard that it was said to the men of old … but I say to you …) should be called super-theses, an intensifying of previous teaching. The meaning of the Greek word, which is translated as "but" in the middle of each contrast, is conveyed in English by "but also." For example, when Jesus contrasts committing adultery and looking lustfully on a woman (5:28), he is not replacing the first with the second; he is trying to deepen a law against adultery rather than abolish it. If a Christian were to assert that the second half of each statement excludes the first half, that would seriously distort both Jewish and Christian traditions.

Jesus as a Jewish prophet uses startling metaphors to heighten the contrasts he makes. Presumably, no one took literally his suggestion to pluck out your right eye if that is the only way to control your body (5:29). However, one of the most often quoted verses in the New Testament is Mt. 5:38: "You have heard that it was said 'An eye for an eye and a tooth for a tooth.'" The peculiar thing about this quotation from the book of *Exodus*, (21:24) is that the verb is omitted.

A common assumption by Christian readers is that the omitted verb is "take," which would be an approval of vengeance. The actual text in Exodus is, "If any harm follows, then you shall give life for life, eye for eye, tooth for tooth ... " The concern is not vengeance from the side of the person harmed but restitution by the offender.

True, there are parallel texts – Lev. 24:20, Dt. 19:21 – where the viewpoint is different. The one who has been offended is told "not to take more than an eye for an eye, tooth for a tooth." The law was a restraint upon, not an approval of violent retaliation. This advocacy of a rough equality between the suffering of wrongs and compensation for them represented an ethical advance. Jesus believed that the human race could do still better than restraint in seeking restitution for wrongs.

When the contrasts are set in their proper context, it makes sense to conclude: "In each case, Jesus is taking the Law, the Torah, so seriously that he extends prohibitions regarding action to prohibition regarding thought, Jesus does not oppose the law; he extends it. His attitude toward it is not liberal but highly conservative."[6] Many nineteenth- and early twentieth-century writers imagined a liberal Jesus in their own image. But like all genuine reformers, Jesus was deeply conservative as opposed to superficially conservative.

Jesus says, "You have heard that it was said, 'You shall love your neighbor, and hate your enemy.' But I say to you, 'Love your enemies and pray for those who persecute you'" (5: 43-44). Jesus cites here a verse from Leviticus 19:18: "You shall love your neighbor as yourself." Several things should be noted about the gospel text. First, the word neighbor is in the dative rather than the accusative case. That is, a more accurate translation would be "love to your neighbor."[7] The love Jesus urges is not a pious feeling but concrete actions. Second, there is nothing in Leviticus about hating your enemy. Jesus or the evangelist is quoting what may have been a popular inference from a restricted meaning of neighbor. Third, the verb is in the future not the imperative: "You will love your neighbor," rather than "Love your neighbor."

Critics often complain that telling people that they should love does not work. Jesus does not tell people to feel love instead of hatred. Jesus' teaching of love to your enemies is a practical, long-range program of reducing personal and institutional hatred. Faced with hostility, we can perform actions that show we are not doomed always to be enemies.

One's actions can "de-hostilize" the situation so that over time we may find a way to live on the same planet or even in the same neighborhood. If you act in kindness, it will lead to an affirming of both your neighbor and yourself. There is no restriction of "neighbor" to a friend or someone who lives next door. The neighbor is anyone who is close by and is in need. This principle is not restricted to personal encounters; nations can also practice the same activities of "de-hostilizing" an enemy nation.

The assumption that the *Sermon on the Mount* is a platform of spineless passivity is particularly based on 5:39: "But I say to you, do not resist one who is evil." From comparison to other similar passages in the New Testament, the meaning of the text can be clarified. Paul's teaching in Rom 12:21 expresses what most likely is Jesus' meaning: "Overcome evil with good." Jesus probably said something close to "Do not compete in doing injustice" or "Resist evil with kindness." Thus, the sense of the text might be not to use violence in resisting the action of an evildoer.[8]

There are other counsels in the text that are puzzling and paradoxical. The second half of 5:39 reads: "But if anyone strikes you on the right cheek, turn to him the other also." The detail of the right cheek is significant. An attack of an opponent would usually come from the left. Being struck on the right cheek would be a back of the hand slap, as in challenging a person to a duel. The strange gesture of turning to present the other cheek is a refusal to be drawn into violent conflict.

There were several events in Jewish history that used this tactic of "passive resistance." The most famous is a story recounted by Josephus in his history of the Jewish people.[9] A group of Jews who, when they were confronted by violent actions on the part of Roman soldiers, threw themselves on the ground and offered their necks rather than break the law. The Romans were taken aback by the gesture, which was not suicidal in intent but a challenge to the humanity of their oppressors. This gesture is commonly done by other animals that are smart enough to substitute a gesture of nonresistance for a fight to the death.

Similar acts of "nonresistance," or what is actually nonviolent resistance, are suggested by going two miles if forced to go one, or to give away one's cloak along with a stolen coat (5:40-41). An understandable reaction to such acts of nonviolent resistance is to call them foolish or crazy. Jesus' own family said: "He is out of his mind." (Mk 3:21). But these actions are not an absence of response to violence. Jesus calls for action that is at times paradoxical but always makes an appeal to the humanity of both parties.

When someone is violently attacked, there might be a variety of legitimate responses. What is excluded in Jesus's teaching is a symmetrical response of violence for violence. The situation itself has to supply the exact way to respond to corruption, evil, and violent oppression. In all cases, Jesus says, his followers must be gentle as doves and wise as serpents (Mt 10:16).

The *Sermon on the Mount* as a whole and as a summary of Jesus' teaching has been misunderstood in two ways: By damning it with faint praise or by just damning it. The first of these misunderstandings is the more common one. The *Sermon on the Mount* is praised as a beautiful poetic ideal that an individual might try to live by. Of course, the ideal is assumed to be highly impractical so that few people, except saints, try to conform their lives to this ideal. Nations, it is said, should not try to observe this individualistic ideal. It would be suicidal for a nation and its leaders to follow the *Sermon on the Mount*.

The second misunderstanding, which I call "just damning it," denounces the *Sermon on the Mount* as a slave morality. It is not only impractical, but it also glorifies poverty, suffering, and subservience. This reaction is actually more respectful of Jesus' teaching than the reduction of the words to a pious but individual and impractical ideal. A frontal attack on the teaching as dangerous admits or at least implies that the Sermon has important social, economic, and political implications. Jesus's life and teaching challenged the powers of religious and secular empires at the risk of his own life. The *Sermon on the Mount* is not a series of nice thoughts about love.

Many nineteenth- and twentieth-century scholars and politicians expressed admiration for the *Sermon on the Mount* – before dismissing its relevance to politics. Herbert Marcuse took the *Sermon on the Mount* more seriously in a 1968 speech to students in Berlin: "With *the Sermon on the Mount* one cannot revolt. Nothing is more abominable than the preaching of love: 'Do not hate your enemy' – this in a world in which hate is everywhere institutionalized."[10]

Marcuse was right that hate is everywhere institutionalized. But does not hating one's opponent only add to the problem? Marcuse was contemptuous of the preaching of love. Certainly, preaching love is worse than useless unless it is an advocacy of action in a community that already professes belief in these actions. Preaching love in general is likely to be a sentimental cover up of situations that require intelligence, dedication, and risky action. The *Sermon on the Mount* is far from being sentimental preaching.

Force and Violence

One of the most important distinction for an ethic of nonviolent activity is the difference between "violence" and "force." If those two terms are conflated in meaning, then there is no hope for an ethic of nonviolent action. In most situations we easily recognize a difference between force and violence but in international discussions "force" is very often a euphemism for violence and war.

The U.S. Senate in 2002 approved legislation that George W. Bush should use all needed "force" in Iraq. Bush subsequently said that he hoped he could avoid force; shortly afterward, he unleashed the full violence of war. Some Senators later complained that they had not voted for war but, if so, they should have distinguished between force and violence, force, and war. The United States had been using force against Iraq for the previous decade in policies such as a no-fly zone.[11]

"Force" is commonly used in everyday life. We use force whenever we exert physical pressure against something that resists our will. It is always questionable to use force against a person. Sometimes we use force where another option might be better. But at times force is indispensable. If a child is running into traffic, then a forceful restraint is the effective and appropriate reaction. An ethic of nonviolent action cannot work without the person acting forcefully for what he or she believes in.

It is often claimed that not even Jesus could live up to the ideal of nonviolence. The scene of Jesus driving the money changers from the temple is the one passage that is inevitably cited (Mt. 21:12-17). Jesus's actions as reported in the gospel were undoubtedly forceful but there is no suggestion that they were violent. There were no broken bones or bloodshed. A nonviolent life is one that is supported by using force when it is appropriate.

Human Rights

It is tragic that the church's strong commitment to "natural law" did not lead it to be involved in some of the main movements in modern times. For the most part, the church invokes "natural law" to condemn sexual practices that are supposedly against such a law. Two areas that might have followed from the discussion of "natural law" could have been opposition to violence, including ecological destruction, and support of the development of human rights.

What might have been central to the church's mission is the movement for human rights. Instead, the church is seen either on the sideline of human rights discussions or an opponent of human rights. The idea of human rights has a long but somewhat shaky history and could use all the help it can get. The term "human rights" was not coined until the nineteenth century but church discussions of natural law and natural rights in the later middle ages is an important part of the story of rights, including the eventual emergence of human rights.

Even the supporters of human rights find the basis of such rights difficult to establish. The policy adopted by most politicians is not to bring up that topic. At the time of the United Nations' *Universal Declaration of Human Rights* there was a philosophers' group that sought to provide grounding for human rights. When the head of that group, Jacques Maritain, was asked about their findings, he responded: "Yes, we agree about the rights but on condition no one asks us why."[12]

This pragmatic attitude may be the best approach. Compliance to the observance of human rights is more important than philosophical and historical discussions of where human rights come from. Nonetheless, there remains an uneasiness about the basis of human rights.

The literature on human rights tends to be preachy. There is nothing wrong with (well prepared) sermons in church but they are of limited value in the political arena and for international dealings. An effective sermon requires that the congregation and the preacher share basic beliefs. The sermon is intended to rouse people to go forth and act on the beliefs that they profess. The international scene does not provide fertile ground for sermons.

There may be some value in tracing how the church participated in the historical process that led to the idea of human rights. The same study might suggest to church leaders how and why they should be strong supporters of human rights today. The Roman Catholic Church lacks credibility today to be a major voice in the human rights movement, but in combination with other religious bodies, including Islam, the church could be a supporter rather than a perceived opponent of human rights.

In reading about the origin of human rights I have seldom seen any reference to medieval discussions by moralists and canonists about the idea of "natural rights." Authors usually go back no further than the seventeenth century. Or they go all the way back to the Stoics. But as Tom Holland points out: "Natural rights derived, not from ancient Greece or Rome, but from the period of history condemned by all right-thinking revolutionaries as a lost millennium, in which any hint of enlightenment had at once been snuffed out by monkish book-burning fanatics. It was an inheritance from the canon lawyers of the Middle Ages."[13]

"Natural law" was a common term in the late middle ages. The term, as I have noted earlier, was coined by Cicero and was central to Stoic philosophy. Christian moralists took over the term, but they tried to give it their own twist. Brian Tierney who has thoroughly researched the origin of natural rights in the middle ages, writes: "Stoic authors when they wrote of *jus naturale*, were thinking mainly in terms of cosmic determinism; the canonists were thinking more in terms of human free choice."[14]

The term *jus naturale*, which Tierney refers to, could be translated not only as "natural law" but also as "natural right." Natural law implied duties that are based on such laws. The correlate of duties was rights. If I have a right to something which I have loaned to someone, the person has a duty to return it. If I have a right to life, others have a duty not to kill me. This reciprocity of duty and right has generally been forgotten or obscured in modern times. Rights are celebrated but duties or obligation do not get the same embrace.

Before the radical split in modern times between the objective world and subjective experience, "objective" and "subjective" were taken to be poles within a unity. Thus, "right" (*jus*) started by having an objective meaning before it moved to the subjective pole of a person's experience and could be claimed as a possession. There is still a trace of this reciprocity in the English language in which "right" can mean what is correct, as well as meaning a personal claim to a good.

The eighteenth-century philosophers who spoke about rights called them "natural rights" but did not acknowledge the source of the idea. An important conduit for the idea and language of rights was John Locke, a British philosopher and political theorist who directly influenced Thomas Jefferson's Declaration of Independence.[15] Locke forwarded the claim of medieval canonists that every man has inalienable rights to life, liberty, and property.

Moralists and church canonists had distinguished between some rights that could be given up and other rights, such as the right to life, that could not be "alienated" because such rights pertain to the nature of the human. A person has a duty to preserve his life; he does not have a right to renounce his life and "as by nature, no man may abuse, torture or afflict himself, so by nature no man can give that power to another, seeing that he may not do it himself."[16]

The case for life and liberty as being inalienable – belonging to human nature – seemed obvious. An inalienable right to property was a more contentious issue. In Latin, "property" referred to what is proper to a person's existence. But even in medieval times the term "property" could be extended to luxuries beyond life's necessities. Opponents of property as an inalienable right argued that "property," in the meaning of private possessions, was not inherent to human nature but was instead a result of sin. They thought that humans were designed by nature to share all things in common.[17]

John Locke was aware of the ambiguity of "property." He defined the word as meaning that "every man has a property in his own person. This nobody has a right to but himself."[18] Locke is criticized for saying that men put themselves under government for the preservation of their property.[19] He is seldom given credit for retaining the more ancient meaning of property. The medieval writers who opposed property as an inalienable right correctly foresaw that the right could be used as a defense of greed. I doubt that they could have imagined a world in which a few billionaires have more wealth than billions of poor people..

Thomas Jefferson in the *Declaration of Independence* substituted a right to the "pursuit of happiness" for Locke's right to property. It was perhaps an effort to avoid a dangerous split between the rich and the poor. One might argue that until recently the United States managed to prevent severe economic inequality. But the claim of property as necessary to someone's pursuit of happiness became a central feature of the country's laws.

Many writers on human rights assume that "natural rights" and "human rights" are equivalent in meaning. That is not the case. In the nineteenth century, "human rights" arose in opposition to the way "natural rights" were being employed. Natural rights had arisen in church discussions as one element in a configuration of natural law, natural duties, and natural rights. The natural rights celebrated in the eighteenth century were called by Jefferson "self-evident," which is hardly the case.

Unmoored from historical context, property or pursuit of happiness were subject to unlimited greed. Rich people seem to think that more money gives them power, which of course it does in political terms. But they soon find, as the gospel warns, that it gives them no protection against sickness, aging and death, which come to rich and poor alike.

The most scandalous idea of "property rights" was its application to slavery. It was regularly asserted that a "slave owner" could not have his property taken from him. The infamous Dred Scott decision (1857) by the U.S. Supreme Court backed the idea that a slave was property and had no standing before the court. Chief Justice Roger Taney invalidated government attempts to limit slavery. The slavers claimed a natural right to own a human being. They assumed that the African slave was not fully human. He or she therefore had none of the rights proper to a person.

Writers who trace human rights back to ancient philosophy or to the eighteenth centuries miss something obvious. None of those philosophies were ready to admit all human beings as sharing an equal humanity. Even when they tried to speak about humanity, they were hampered by a lack of knowledge of how diverse humanity is.

The term human rights could only come from an audacious group who were demanding recognition of their full humanity. I searched for what I could identify as the first use of the term human rights. I came upon a use by Frederick Douglass in his autobiography in the 1840s.[20] I later discovered that Douglass had used the term earlier than that. I would not be surprised if somewhere in the abolitionist literature of the early nineteenth century the term human rights had been used. The term arose from people actively engaged in trying to establish their place in the human family.

The term human rights was used at the women's conference at Seneca Falls in 1848. Frederick Douglass spoke at that conference and urged the women to demand suffrage. He might have been the reason why the term human rights was used by the women. However, the claim by women makes sense on its own without the contribution of the great abolitionist. Men were running the world (or at least thought they were) and women were not acknowledged as equals in political and social rights. A spokesperson for the woman's cause, Sarah Grimké wrote: "I know nothing of men's rights or women's rights; I know only of human rights."

Neither the movement for black freedom nor the woman's movement of the nineteenth century succeeded in making the term human rights widely known. Part of the problem was a tragic split and opposition that developed between the two groups. Instead of working together for their human rights, blacks and (white) women went their separate ways in appealing for justice regarding their respective causes.

One can find the term human rights occasionally used in literature of the early twentieth century. The adjective human shows up as a modifier of rights but with no apparent intention to assert a distinct kind of right. In 1933, two "Human Rights Leagues" were formed but they did not use the term with the intention of asserting a new kind of right. The Supreme Court used the term six times in the 1940s. It would double its usage in each of the three decades that followed. World War II, the Holocaust, and the Nuremberg Trials convinced governments and advocacy groups that international controls were needed.

The UN's *Universal Declaration of Human Rights* has provided the framework for the twentieth and twenty-first century discussion of human rights.[21] There was intense disagreement in the UN committee about the nature and origin of human rights. One of the main contributors René Cassin proposed that the document begin: "As human beings cannot live and achieve their object without the help and support of society, each man owes to society fundamental duties which are obedience to law, exercise of a useful activity, acceptance of the burdens and sacrifices demanded for the common good."[22]

Cassin's passionate advocacy of this principle as the context of human rights, which was essentially the same as the basis of rights did not get much support. The idea that rights are correlated with duties did get into the final document; the idea was watered down and was buried in article twenty-nine: "Everyone has duties to the community in which alone the free and full development of his personality is possible." No one is likely to interpret that statement as the context in which the idea of human rights developed and as the necessary context for the success of a human rights movement.

Liberty is a favorite word in this country. For the right-wing it usually means the absence of governmental regulations and the existence of low taxes. But the primary meaning of liberty for human rights is the ability to move without coercion or imprisonment. Freedom of movement for an individual is needed to lead a full human life with other people.

Society may sometimes need to temporarily restrain some people who are an imminent risk to themselves or others. But the incarceration of millions of people in sub-human conditions is a gross violation of human rights. The Israeli writer Avishai Margalit, in searching for the most fundamental principle of what he calls a decent society, concludes: "A decent society is one that does not humiliate its prisoners." That is a test for whether the human rights of all people are respected.

It is tragic that the Roman Catholic Church is widely believed today to be an opponent of human rights. It is obviously a tragedy for the church, but it is also a great loss for the human rights movement. The church's stand on abortion is all the evidence that many commentators need for concluding that the church is opposed to human rights. The generalization is unfair, but church officials have not persuaded critics that their concern with abortion is part of a larger concern with the rights of human beings who are vulnerable to injustice. Most writers on human rights are oblivious of the church's central role in the development of rights. It is difficult to argue for the relevance of that history amid skepticism about the church's concentration on abortion.

An important conversation that does not get much attention in human rights literature is the possible contribution of religions. I think a Roman Catholic has to be restrained in a claim that the church is a supporter of human rights. It is more effective to argue for the place of a coalition of religions. I would argue that unless human rights are acceptable to Christians and Muslims there cannot be peace in the world.[23] Beyond that, a conversation across religious lines would be a helpful contribution to the human rights movement. Jews, Christians, and Muslims provide a more solid basis for human rights than an abstract concept of nature.

In the 1980s, I was given the opportunity to teach a course in NYU's program of international education (despite my thin credentials to do so). The director of the program trusted me from knowing about my courses on ethics. He always referred to the course as the "human rights course," but I called the course "international ethics." It was a challenge to teach the course but a joy to work with the intelligent and interested students who were often doing international work already.

I taught the course for about twenty years and gradually filled in my large areas of ignorance. I slowly came to understand the strengths and the weaknesses of the idea of human rights. I am still suspicious of university courses on human rights. I think that such a title encourages a preaching of human rights rather than an academic examination of the basis of such rights and the ethical dimensions of dealings between nations.

When I was asked in recent years what course I was teaching, I would answer "International Ethics." The most common response I would get was: "Isn't that an oxymoron?" I would smile as if I had never heard that gem of wisdom before, and answer: "It might be. But it might also be one of the most urgent problems that the world is now facing." There has always been an ethical dimension in the dealings between nations but today the ethical issue is front and center. Environmental problems, immigration questions, and the prevention of war are issues that cannot be addressed without confronting the question of ethics.

Peace

The history of the Roman Catholic Church's attitude to war has been decidedly mixed. The Christian gospel condemns violence, which would include war. The early Christian Church took a stand against war, and its members refused to fight in the empire's wars. By the fourth century, however, when the church became part of the empire its official attitude shifted.

Augustine of Hippo composed a doctrine that is usually referred to as "just war theory."[24] Augustine laid down principles for whether a nation could morally go to war and further principles to be followed when fighting a war. He assumed that war will always be with us and his principles were less a justification of war and more an attempt to restrain the violence of wars.

Thomas Aquinas did not make any major changes in Augustine's doctrine. This "just war" teaching became a central part of the Roman Catholic Church's approach to peace. The idea that a nation was going to war for a just reason was easily manipulated but the principles did manage to put some restraint on wars. When the church was no longer a leading voice, similar principles were adopted by secular governments, such as in the nineteenth-century agreements known as the Geneva Conventions.

Pope John XXIII's encyclical *Pacem in Terris* represented a shift in the official church's attitude to war.[25] The existence of nuclear weapons had changed calculations from previous discussions in the past. Wars became out of control at least since World War I when the whole population was involved in the war rather than only the soldiers. One of the tenets of just war doctrine was that "non-combatants" would be protected. In modern wars, more civilians than soldiers are killed.

Pope John's condemnation of war carried into the Second Vatican Council where a lively debate ensued. Several U.S. bishops were vocal in defending the United States' military machine including its nuclear weaponry. The Council was hardly daring in its condemnation of what it called "total war," but the conclusion was nonetheless a clear signal of a shift in direction. The phrase anathema sit meaning "let it be condemned," which had been liberally used by previous councils to condemn heretics, was used by the Second Vatican Council only once for the purpose of condemning "total war."

The 1960s anti-war movement in the United States was led by some unlikely people, including a woman on a lonely journey of resistance to all violence, a Jesuit poet, and a Trappist monk. Dorothy Day and her colleagues at the Catholic Worker remained steadfast in their opposition to all wars. Daniel Berrigan, along with his brother Philip, led an aggressive protest against the war and against violence. Thomas Merton, a Trappist monk, inspired many young people with his writings on nonviolence.

Both Merton and Berrigan acted in tension with the superiors in their religious orders but did not break with the church. They brought out the sacramental and mystical nature of Catholicism at its best. Young Catholics today are still inspired by Thomas Merton's writings; he was accidentally killed when on an ecumenical journey to the East. Daniel Berrigan, who served time in prison for his protests, continued until his death in 2016 to oppose the militarization of the United States.

The U.S. bishops achieved some success with their document in 1976, *The Challenge of Peace*. While the bishops were composing their document, word of what they might say leaked out. Political conservatives were worried about the influence that the document might have. Government officials had always counted on the support of church officials for militant opposition to communism. When the bishops published their document, it seemed clear that they were catching up to most of their members.

I was hardly an activist opposing war, but I tried to do my small part during the United States war in Vietnam. That war seemed particularly unintelligible at its beginning and it just kept getting worse. The government after a while had no rationale for sending 500,000 soldiers into a civil war in a small country that the United States did not understand. The violence done to the people of Vietnam and surrounding countries was horrendous. Daniel Berrigan was considered extreme in his tactics, but a look back at the insanity of the war might lead to the conclusion that millions of Roman Catholics should have been out on the street with him.

CHAPTER SEVEN:
Morality at the Beginning of Life

The Roman Catholic Church's reliance on "natural law" has implications for the sexual process that leads to pregnancy and birth. In its insistence that nothing "artificial" interfere in the process, the church has condemned artificial birth control and the interruption of pregnancy. The human race until recently had a limited understanding of this process. One important reason for this ignorance was the absence of a public voice for women on these matters. That has been rapidly changing worldwide. Women now speak about their own experiences and their right not to be violated. Catholic officials have lacked a knowledge of women's experience; the official teachers are all men. They even are supposed to lack sexual experience.

It does not follow that church officials should have no voice on sexual matters. They are legitimately concerned that ancient principles might be swept away in the tidal wave of new information and a variety of social movements. But new information and the new assertiveness of women place a special burden on Roman Catholic officials to listen carefully. Sexual practices ranging from self-pleasuring to early abortions need to be placed in an adequate context. I have recounted in an earlier chapter the official attempt to ban artificial birth control. The effort largely failed to convince Catholics. The ban is still an official doctrine but generally priests and bishops seem to accept that the ban has been rejected.

The bishops have left themselves with only one doctrine in this area: the condemnation of all abortions. Their overall position is self-defeating because the most effective way to reduce abortion is by ready access to the means of birth control. Despite their insistence that abortion is about a right to life, it is also about sex and about the assertiveness of women to have their own experiences taken seriously.

The bishops did have grounds for skepticism about the widespread practice of abortion. The principle of nonviolence needs to be considered in abortion practice. On that basis, later abortions are a more serious moral question than early abortions. Church officials may argue that all abortions involve violence, but they ought to make some distinctions about the way abortions are performed, including how far into the pregnancy the abortion occurs.[1] The move to recriminalize abortion or the attempt to eliminate the facilities for legal abortions can have the unintended effect of increasing violence in the abortions that would continue to be performed.

When I taught ethics in undergraduate and graduate classes there was only one ethical question that I refused to discuss in class: abortion. I said that I would be glad to discuss abortion but only when the conditions would make possible a useful discussion. A classroom with several dozen students and within a time limit of less than an hour was not a place for a civil discussion on this emotion-laden topic. Unfortunately, the classroom, which should be a place for thoughtful discussion and debate, is on this issue too much like the rest of society. The first sentence about abortion that someone utters classifies him or her on one side or the other, and the discussion goes downhill from there.

Even in writing, it is difficult to get a reader to suspend temporarily his or her convictions about abortion and consider the possibility of a different perspective on the morality of abortion and what public policy should be. When on rare occasions I have spoken or written on abortion, almost the only response that I receive is the question: Are you pro-life or pro-choice? My response to the question that I am neither (or both) is taken to be a refusal to answer the only real question about abortion.

I would argue that the pre-condition for any useful discussion of abortion is a refusal to admit into the discussion the slogans of "pro-life" and "pro-choice." Both phrases are obstacles to thinking about the history, philosophy, religion, social science, biology, and anything else that might aid in an understanding of the subject. The two groups that use these slogans for political purposes do not represent most of the country.

Sometimes the public is said to be inconsistent because they hold views that cross the lines of the opposing parties. But the inconsistency more likely indicates that the two slogans are inaccurate and useless. Everybody who is not dead is in favor of life, but everybody draws distinctions about life. Everybody is in favor of choice, but everybody draws distinctions about choice. The two slogans make a discussion of abortion impossible, let alone progress in what to do about abortion.

The people who support the legality of abortion often use absolutist language. A common phrase in public discussions is "abortion rights" that makes no sense and is inflammatory. Why the term is always in the plural is a puzzle. More important, abortion is not a good which people have a right to. No young girl thinks, "When I grow up, I really want to have an abortion; it is my right."

A phrase that is used interchangeably with "abortion rights" but has a different meaning is "reproductive rights." For its own good, society should guarantee that women have support in exercising their power to have a child or not have a child. Although the support of men is indispensable, it is women who have a right to decide what happens to their bodies. The plural form "reproductive rights" makes sense here because there are several possibilities, the choice of an abortion being only one of them.

The phrase "pro-choice" is not helpful because the issue of abortion cannot be reduced to that of choice. Human choice exists in situations that lead up to the choice and produce consequences that follow from the choice. Abortion is a social issue involving the government, the medical profession, and the women and men who decide what happens during a woman's pregnancy. People who talk almost exclusively about choice undermine their own cause. There is a need for abortion facilities and for physicians and midwives who perform abortions.

There is no possibility of a genuine conversation between people who talk about "abortion rights" and people who accuse their opponents of murder. At present, the suspicion on both sides of the public rift means that something desirable to most of the population cannot even be discussed. For example, there would likely be widespread agreement that reducing the number of abortions would be a good thing. And the conditions for that to occur are well-known, especially the ready availability of birth control devices.[2]

The Catholic bishops have broken with their long tradition of acknowledging a major difference between early abortions before a person exists and later abortions. By claiming that an "unborn child" exists from the moment of fertilization, they weaken their argument against late abortions. Even if the bishops continue to teach that all abortions are wrong, it still makes sense for them and for Catholic politicians to discuss improving public policy on matters of abortion.

I have never had to deal directly with abortion in my own life, something that has advantages and disadvantages in achieving an accurate view. The simple fact of being a man almost excludes one from taking part in a public discussion of abortion. I can understand why many women think this way, but men do have views and men wield power in the policies on abortion. I have very slowly come to a conviction about abortion and about public policy regarding it. I remain open to changes in my convictions, but I admit that my main conviction is not likely to undergo a big change.

The Moment when Hilary Clinton lost the Election of 2016.

Because abortion was surprisingly played down in the presidential election of 2016, it might seem to have been of minor importance in how the election was decided. But 81 percent of Evangelical Christians and 52 percent of Roman Catholics voted for Donald Trump, and those two groups made up 49 percent of the electorate. Add the fact that when these voters were asked why they would vote for someone whose views conflicted in innumerable ways with what Evangelicals and Roman Catholics each profess to believe, their most frequent answer was abortion. Donald Trump's own view on abortion could at best be described as inconsistent. But these voters were referring to who Trump would nominate for Supreme Court vacancies and the hope that a decisive vote would be added for overturning *Roe v. Wade*.

The question of abortion emerged in the presidential campaign at the final debate on October 19, 2016. Chris Wallace, the questioner, first asked Trump whether he was in favor of overturning *Roe v. Wade*. As was his custom, Trump did not answer the question directly. He did say that his nominee for the current opening on the Supreme Court would be someone who would vote to change the law and that the issue of abortion would be returned to the states. Wallace then turned to Hilary Clinton and asked, "You voted against a ban on late-term partial-birth abortions. Why?" While Trump had spoken to his supporters who think that abortion should be illegal, Clinton had the opportunity to speak to the whole country or at least to the almost two-thirds of the population who support *Roe v. Wade*.

Clinton missed her opportunity. She gained applause from her ardent supporters, but she did not win over those voters, especially Roman Catholic voters, whom she needed. She probably lost thousands not millions of votes but in our weird electoral system the election was determined by a few thousand votes in crucial places.

The strange thing about Clinton's failure is that what she said was true enough. The transcript shows a reasonable and measured statement based on a thorough knowledge of what she was talking about. Trump used inflammatory rhetoric about something he was obviously ignorant of. But most people judged Trump to have been the winner in that exchange.

Clinton's failure was in her tone of voice and in what she did not say. By any reasonable standard, that judgment of failure was unfair, but political debates are not scored on reason alone. Abortion is a terribly divisive issue in the country and has been for decades. Without giving an inch on the rights of women, Clinton could have acknowledged the ambivalent feelings that millions of people have about abortion – even if they support the law allowing abortion. Instead, Clinton immediately provided an explanation for why she voted against the proposed ban that Chris Wallace had referred to.

Her main failure was her willingness to answer the question as it had been asked. Wallace had introduced the misleading, and biased phrase "partial-birth abortion," which led into Trump's inflammatory rhetoric of "ripping babies from the womb a few days before birth." By not rejecting the phrase "partial-birth abortion," Clinton gave the impression that she was approving what Trump was condemning.

Clinton needed to provide a bigger picture (admittedly difficult in two minutes) of when and why abortions, especially late abortions, are performed. The idea that many women are waiting until the seventh or eighth month of pregnancy for deciding that they would like to have an abortion is wildly inaccurate, but many people know only the wild rhetoric that is in much of the news media. Clinton could have indicated how rare are late-term abortions and that they are performed only for dire reasons. Instead, people heard from her only the standard rhetoric delivered in a militant tone of voice.

Many Roman Catholics who could have been won over by Clinton were put off by her tone and her one-dimensional response. They didn't necessarily vote for Trump, but they also did not vote for Clinton. Nearly all Roman Catholics, whatever their politics, have a sacramental sense of the human life cycle. A sense of the sacredness of life means that life in all forms should be respected.

This "respect for life" can be appealed to in a defense of human rights, the protection of the environment, a condemnation of war, and opposition to the state execution of prisoners. That sensibility puts most Catholics in the liberal column, according to today's political categories. On abortion, most Catholics support the legality of abortion, but they are concerned with respecting the life-process. Interrupting that process is understood to be serious business for which serious reasons are needed.

Many Roman Catholics stand with the bishops in condemning every abortion as murder. But there are many other church members who make some distinctions about the gravity of abortion according to the situation. Those are the people who Hillary Clinton could have won over with just a change of tone and some attention to the ambivalence that millions of people, including most Catholics, feel about abortion.

Historical Perspective

Throughout human history there presumably have always been abortions. In the distant past there was not much conversation about the practice but also not much public disagreement either. Abortion would have been frowned upon for a variety of reasons, but it was nonetheless practiced. The disagreements would have been within families or in hidden places in the society. Abortion was legal in the early part of United States history. Abortion was thought to be a problem only after "quickening" occurred, that is, when the woman was able to feel the movement of the fetus. The criterion was obviously not precise, but the judgment did depend on the pregnant woman's experience.

In the second half of the nineteenth century, a change occurred with the rise of the medical profession. The professionals, who cornered for themselves the word "doctor," thought it was their province to control all medical procedures. They favored laws that would stop privately performed abortions.[3]

The physicians were joined by evangelical Protestants who were concerned that abortions by Protestant women were reducing the birth rate for Protestants while Roman Catholics were producing very large families. Protestants feared that they would be overrun by Catholics. Anti-abortion laws were therefore anti-Catholic. Roman Catholic Church officials were not very vocal on the subject.[4]

Despite the passage of these laws outlawing abortion, it was evident that many women were having abortions. The main means was toxic medicines, which were sold under the pretense that these medicines had other purposes. In addition, for performing abortions women used home remedies, many of which were dangerous to their health.

Physicians would grant permissions for "therapeutic abortions" that were judged to be necessary to the health of the mother. The system was arbitrary but rich women could usually find a physician to provide a permission for abortion; poor women continued with their home remedies. Kristin Luker, in one of the best books on the subject, notes that "neither the public nor individual physicians appear to have been very troubled by the discrepancies."[5]

There are no reliable statistics on how widespread the practice of abortion was in the late nineteenth and early twentieth centuries. By the middle of the twentieth century some physicians had become uneasy about the arrangement, which could put them in legal and professional jeopardy. Some states began to legalize abortions under certain conditions.[6]

Many people seem to think that the Supreme Court's *Roe v. Wade* decision in 1973 just suddenly decided to make legal what everyone had previously thought was immoral. Instead, the Court was trying to regularize a confusing situation, but it did not entirely succeed. It is not clear what people today who are opposed to the court decision think would be the result of overturning it. Do they think abortions would stop? Are they sure abortions would decrease?

Roman Catholic Official Teaching

It is well known that the Roman Catholic Church is an unyielding opponent of abortion. At least the official doctrine of the church admits of no qualifications or grounds for compromise. The exact number of Roman Catholic women in the United States who have had abortions is impossible to determine. However, responsible surveys by the Guttmacher Institute and the Pew Research Center estimate that almost a fourth of Catholic women have had abortions and the numbers have remained consistent.[7] The majority of Roman Catholics support the legality of abortion. The attitude of Catholics toward abortion differs from the general public but not so much as the bishops would like.

In 1974, the Vatican published a document, *Declaration on Procured Abortions*, which traced the history of the church's teaching on abortion. It claimed to find a consistent condemnation of abortion from the time of the *Didache* and the writings of Athenagoras and Tertullian.[8] But the document is misleading if not disingenuous. It mentions, "Excellent authors [none is named] allowed for this first period more lenient case solutions than they rejected for following periods."

What is vaguely referred to here is a tradition at least as old as Jerome and Augustine, which acknowledged a difference between early pregnancy and the time after *animatus*, the moment when the soul (*anima*) is infused by God.[9] The *Declaration* insists, "it was never denied that procured abortion even during the first days was objectively a grave fault." That is true but it is also true that this grave fault was distinguished from homicide.

The term *animatus* was a philosophical-theological term, not a biological or empirical term. An English translation as "animation" or "quickening" misleadingly suggests that *animatus* referred to physical movement, which can be tested empirically.[10] Instead, the term assumed that there must be some development of the living organism before a soul could be infused. Thus, abortion, said Jerome, "is not reputed homicide until the scattered elements received their appearance and members." Augustine agreed that for early abortions, "the law does not provide that the act pertains to homicide for there cannot yet be said to be a live soul in a body that lacks sensation when it is not formed in flesh and as yet endowed with sense."[11] In other words, homicide requires the existence of a person.

The *Declaration* fails to point out that this distinction made by Jerome and Augustine was the main tradition throughout the Middle Ages. Gratian, whose collection of laws became the basis of the Code of Canon Law, said that abortion is not homicide until the fetus is formed. Pope Innocent III agreed.[12] Perhaps most important, Thomas Aquinas had no doubt that the soul could not be infused until there was some development of embryonic life. Roman Catholic Church officials are usually quick to invoke the authority of Thomas Aquinas but on the question of abortion they are usually silent about Thomas' opinion, or say only what the *Declaration* does: "St. Thomas, the Common Doctor, of the church teaches that abortion is a grave sin against the natural law."[13]

That statement is simply a refusal to acknowledge Thomas Aquinas's position.[14] Thomas was clear in saying, "ensoulment did not take place at conception. Abortion was a sin but not the sin of destroying a man."[15] Thomas did not profess to be a biologist. His reflections on the human soul and the nature of the person are metaphysical in nature. His philosophical principle is not dependent on embryology. It is based on a common sense understanding that a speck of matter is not a baby.

Catholic tradition remained committed to this view of early abortion until at least the seventeenth century. When moral theology took a turn to "casuistry" and a focus on individual acts of morality, there was no room for allowing any ambiguity about the moment of "ensoulment." Since there is no clear marker during the process of pregnancy for when the person is "formed," it was thought necessary to protect ensoulment by assuming that it could happen at any time after fertilization.

In the nineteenth and twentieth centuries there continued to be an admission that we do not know when "ensoulment" occurs. In the *Declaration on Procured Abortions*, a footnote says, "This declaration leaves aside the question of the moment when the spiritual soul is infused. There is not a unanimous tradition on this point and authors are as yet in disagreement."[16] How can this central question be dismissed in a footnote? It is true that "authors are as yet in disagreement" about the "moment when the spiritual soul is infused." There will probably never be an agreement. But that did not stop teachers in the past from being clear that this moment is not fertilization or the weeks immediately following.

In the anti-abortion movement since the 1970s there has been no change of opinion about ensoulment. Instead, what happened was a change of language so that the bishops speak about the beginning of life instead of the beginning of the person.

As a Roman Catholic who has been formed in my thinking by the church, I am profoundly affected by church tradition. But from the study of the past, I have concluded that the Roman Catholic bishops have radically changed church teachings. I am the traditionalist on abortion, agreeing with leading thinkers of the past who held that early abortions are not homicides. The bishops today are the radicals who have abandoned that position, ceding their authority to what they take to be scientific truth.

Catholic Bishops and the Soul

When did Roman Catholic bishops stop believing in the soul? When I was a child it was drummed into me that nothing was more important than my immortal soul. That drumbeat continued until the 1960s. The idea of a soul never generated much enthusiasm in me. The belief that my soul would survive my body at death and continue without a body was not an attractive proposition. Thomas Aquinas acknowledged that a soul without a body is not a person. There was the consoling fact that the soul would re-unite with the body at the general resurrection but there did not seem to be much emphasis on that belief.

The concept of a soul was one of early Christianity's many imports from Greek philosophy. Because the *Bible* was short on philosophical concepts, Christianity was bound to assimilate some philosophical ideas from Aristotelian, Platonic, Neo-platonic, Stoic, and other philosophies. The *Bible* knew nothing of a soul, but the idea did seem to support the belief that there is more to a human being than what can be seen and touched. The biblical image was one of God breathing life or spirit into each human form. The spiritual and sacred dimension of each individual human seemed captured by the concept of a soul.

The belief that every individual is composed of body and soul was always in danger of leading to a dualistic philosophy in which the soul was what was important. The body was at best an amiable companion and at worst it was a constant source of temptation to sin. Body and soul had to be integrated as dimensions of something greater. Here is where Christianity created a philosophical concept unknown to the Greeks. The concept of person was a brilliant invention that originated in\the Trinitarian and Christological controversies.

Thomas Aquinas's philosophy showed the importance of person not only for theological expositions but for metaphysics and morality. Body and soul remained as dimensions of the personal but the emphasis in Thomas's philosophy is the union of body and soul rather than their conflict. According to Thomas, "Person signifies what is noblest in the whole of nature."[17]

Thomas's person-centered morality is not what dominated Catholic moral thinking after the Council of Trent. Confessors were trained with manuals that catalogued sins and the seriousness of each sin. Morality became a question of how to avoid "occasions of sin."

In the middle of the twentieth century, emphasis began shifting to a more positive approach about morality. One of the important contributions to this change was Bernard Häring's three volume work, *The Law of Christ*, which turned moral theology upside down.[18] The Law of Christ that Häring refers to is the command to love God and to love one's neighbor. Häring and other theologians made use of the work of New Testament exegetes who provided an abundance of material on the moral implications of Jesus' teachings.

New Testament scholarship also directed attention to the resurrection as central to the life of Jesus and the lives of his followers. Works such as F.X. Durwell's *Resurrection*, provided a new emphasis that the "resurrection of the body," rather than the immortality of the soul was the New Testament belief. Catholics expressed belief in the resurrection of the body each time they said the apostles' creed. The translation of the biblical doctrine as resurrection of the body could be misunderstood as referring to body as opposed to soul. In the biblical framework, the belief might be better translated as resurrection of the bodily self.

The result of these historical, biblical, and philosophical studies in the 1960s was a healthy emphasis on the person as the moral agent who is called to a life of justice and love, and eventually resurrection. Sin is a failure to live up to that calling but sin can be overcome by going beyond sin to a healthy unity of the whole person.

For the application of moral principles there is need for an enlightened conscience and an understanding of the total situation of any moral activity. There was less talk about the soul undergoing judgment at the moment of death and more talk about the resurrection and the final judgment. This shift of emphasis from talk about saving souls to emphasis on personal-communal existence in a material world is a big improvement.

Pope Paul VI's *Humani vitae* that forbids contraceptives was met with loud protest because it reduced the meaning of human sexuality to a biological process similar to the sexual practices of nonhuman animals.

Catholics who had become aware of theological and scriptural emphasis on the person opposed the encyclical precisely because it clashed with the best of Catholic moral thinking and with their knowledge of the situations in which they lived. Millions of Roman Catholics left the church; others decided to remain in the church while following their consciences on sexual matters.

The bishops decided to make an absolute stand on abortion, especially after the 1973 Supreme Court decision that made abortion legal in the United States. Roman Catholic groups immediately began mobilizing to express opposition to the Court decision.

The bishops since the 1970s seem reluctant to talk about the soul. That reluctance could have been a positive step for bringing in the scriptural studies and moral theology that emphasized the integrity of the person. Unfortunately, when the bishops gave up on soul talk, they switched to talking about "life." The key question of when a new person comes into existence was left aside. The only question entertained was when does life begin.

The concept of life taken alone is one of those philosophical abstractions that the ancient Greeks were good at. Living beings exist but life itself doesn't exist. Simply saying that one is in favor of life does not offer any needed distinctions. If Roman Catholic Church leaders are not prepared to talk about the soul, then they need to find other categories which retain the idea that it is the human being or the person or a bodily-spiritual individual who is being defended and not only a life process.

While people who are not Roman Catholic may have expected Pope Francis to modify the official church teaching on abortion, he has not suggested any change of doctrine in his comments on the issue. At a speech before an Italian anti-abortion group, Pope Francis quoted the Second Vatican Council's words, "abortion and infanticide are unspeakable crimes." [19]

When the Pope warned church officials about having too narrow a range of moral concerns, he was not playing down abortion. He wanted only to situate abortion in the context of what Cardinal Joseph Bernadine called a "consistent ethic of life." Many Catholic groups are admirable in their opposition to all forms of violence. A group such as "Consistent Life" describes itself as part of the "anti-violence community." Its supporters include Sister Helen Prejean who has written: "I stand morally opposed to killing, war, executions, killing of the old and demented, the killing of children, unborn and born."[20] What the killing of unborn children means is part of the question.

The church officials might have expressed an opposition to abortion by saying: "We are against abortion as a violent way to control birth; other nonviolent ways of regulating birth should be encouraged as the main way to reduce abortions." That is not the way the ideological battle developed. Instead of saying we are against violence to living beings, especially to human beings, they announced that they were in favor of life. The question then became, "When does (human) life begin?" which is not a question that needed debate.

The Beginning of New Life

For many centuries, there was an assumption that women had nothing to contribute to the process of generating a baby, except to provide a place for the man's seed (semen), a view that some feminists call the "flowerpot" theory of pregnancy. Some sects considered a man's "spilling his seed," the seed of life, to be equivalent to murder.

It has long been realized, however, that the woman contributes to the process of giving a new life. The clearest marker for when a new life begins is the fertilization of the egg. There is little room for debate here; the embryo is not dead, and it is not nonhuman. However, fertilization is a biological term that refers to something visible. When a human being comes into existence is a different question.

Robert George, a leading Catholic voice in opposition to abortion, writes: "The facts of human embryogenesis and early development make the conclusion inescapable: from a purely biological perspective scientists can identify the point at which a human life begins. The relevant studies are legion. The biological facts are uncontested. The method of analysis applied to the data is universally accepted." Those of us who have a problem with this statement are not disputing biology, but the question of when a person comes into existence cannot be determined "from a purely biological perspective."

George concludes: "Your life began, as did the life of every other human being when the fusion of egg and sperm produced a new, complex, living organism – an embryonic human being."[21] Calling the embryo an embryonic human being does not change the fact that a speck of matter is not a baby, a child, a person.

Peter Steinfels begins a thoughtful essay on abortion with two "simple statements." His first simple statement is: "Fertilization, a remarkable process involving the union of twenty-three chromosomes from each parent, creates a new, unique, individual member of the human species, a physically dependent but genetically distinct and self-directing organism. This is a scientific fact, not one dependent on faith or religious teaching."

Steinfels's second "simple statement" is: "The conviction taught by the Catholic Church and shared by many people, religious and nonreligious, is nowhere near as obvious as many of us who hold it suppose." That is a remarkably low-key way of admitting that not only is the conviction not obvious to most citizens but that it strikes them as wrong.

Steinfels proposes: "Catholics and others opposed to abortion should strive for the legal protection of unborn life not from conception but from that point where not one but a whole constellation of converging arguments and intuitions can be brought to bear." That point, he says is eight weeks of development when there is "an accumulation of evidence that should compel a majority even in a pluralist society."

The proposal sounds reasonable. But Steinfels is surely aware that there is nowhere near a majority who would agree to anything remotely similar. His opening statement that a unique human individual exists at fertilization kills any chance of anti-abortionists endorsing a legal approval of murder.

Steinfels, like many opponents of abortion, invokes an analogy to slavery. The comparison to slavery might be helpful to the cause of restricting late abortions. But for asserting that a fertilized ovum should have the rights of a human being the case of slavery is contrary to that position.

Aristotle thought that some men were born to be slaves; he did not think that slaves were not human beings. When Columbus encountered the Arawak or when Africans were brought to the United States to work the tobacco and cotton fields, any sane person could see that they were human beings. They were thought to be inferior to the white Europeans who were prejudiced in ways that are obvious today.

Slave holders were acutely aware that they were dealing with human beings, which is why it was important to humiliate the slaves and it was illegal to teach a slave to read. Only because of a powerful ideology could anyone deny what was apparent to the senses and reason, that a slave was a human being. Those who say that in the future a fertilized egg will be recognized as a human being are on the ideological side of rejecting what the senses and reason recognize as a human being.

Church officials have ceded their authority to biology for determining when a human being comes into existence. It is strange that in this case Roman Catholic Church officials choose to rely on the data of modern science rather than draw upon their own tradition. "Life" is a category in biology ("the science of life"). Many biologists have gladly accepted the role of declaring what life, including human life, means.[22]

Two questions that must be faced by Roman Catholics who think that a new human being exists at fertilization are:

1. Are they ready to call tens of millions of their fellow citizens murderers?

2. Do they believe that the billions of abortions that happen, most of them without external intervention, result in one-celled human beings that go to heaven and enjoy a vision of God – while awaiting the resurrection of the body?

After the bishops had decided on the strategy of condemning all abortions, they had nothing more to say. No negotiations on public policy were possible. For them abortion is an unspeakable evil and anyone who participates in it takes part in a murder. Roman Catholic politicians who face complex questions of public policy are ordered to have no strategy other than to be against abortion and to oppose any legislation that tries to work out helpful compromises on abortion policy.[23]

A Strange Alliance

In a strange coalition that has continued to the present, evangelicals have joined with the Roman Catholic Church in making abortion a top moral concern. When *Roe v. Wade* was decided, most evangelicals believed that abortion was a deeply personal issue in which government should not play a role. In 1971, the Southern Baptist Convention had adopted a resolution supporting legislation to "allow the possibility of abortion under such conditions as rape, incest, clear evidence of severe fetal deformity; and carefully ascertained evidence of the likelihood of damage to the emotional, mental and physical health of the mother." A resolution in 1974 affirmed that stance as "a middle ground between the extreme of abortion on demand and the opposite extreme of all abortion as murder."

Shortly after the court decision was handed down, W. Barry Garrett in the *Baptist Press*, a wire service run by the Southern Baptist Convention, praised the ruling: "Religious liberty, human equality and justice are advanced by the Supreme Court's abortion decision." The essay said that religious bodies can continue to teach their own particular views to their constituents with all the vigor they desire. "People whose consciences forbid abortion are free to practice their religion according to the tenets of their personal or corporate faith."[24]

By the 1980s, however, resolutions from the Baptist Convention expressed concern about "abortion on demand" and the use of taxpayer money for any abortions except to save the life of the mother. Some Evangelicals were hesitant to oppose abortion because they saw it as a "Catholic issue," and worried about the influence of Roman Catholic teachings on American religious observance. But Evangelicals had emerged as a political force in the country, and they had decided to make opposition to abortion a top priority.[25] They did find it politically necessary to make exceptions for victims of rape and incest. Ronald Reagan and the National Right to Life Committee supported this distinction.

Any such exceptions, however, were illogical. If there is a baby from the moment of fertilization, then all abortions are murder. It was not until 2019 that states began passing abortion bans that had no exceptions. That change shocked many people as lacking in compassion, but groups that are opposed to abortion were finally being logical. The killing of an "unborn child" for any reason could not be justified.

In 2019 David French in the *National Review* declared that it was time "to throw down the gauntlet, declare to the world [that] the era of incrementalism is over and show that the people are ready to embrace life."[26] What does "embrace life" mean? Is French ready to defend the life of every flea and cockroach? The human beings are killers, but some killings are more serious than others.

We recognize intuitively that killing a mosquito and killing an elephant cannot be judged within the same framework. In a few generations it is possible that our contemporary treatment of chickens, pigs and cows will be looked back upon with horror. How could human beings have slaughtered millions of their closest animal kin? However, it is not likely that humans will stop the killing of insects or viruses that spread disease and death among the human population.

Killing human life exists in a special moral universe. Cancer surgery is a justified killing of exuberant human life because the success of cancer cells is at the expense of the person. The direct killing of a person is almost never justified, although the Roman Catholic Church in the past did allow for exceptions. The killings in "just wars," was accepted for centuries until it was finally challenged at the Second Vatican Council. The state execution of prisoners was not directly opposed until Pope Francis proposed to change church teaching.

The killing of a human embryo is a special case because of its potential. Under the right conditions it will become a person. There must be a serious reason for interrupting the process by which a new human being comes into existence. Opponents of abortion in the past realized that rape or incest was a serious enough reason for abortion. They might have recognized that there were other reasons why women thought that an abortion was necessary. The current law is simply an acknowledgment of that fact.

Roman Catholics admirably profess belief in the equality of human beings. The church professes to be especially concerned with the most vulnerable human being whose right to exist is frequently threatened. An old person, a sick person, or a severely handicapped person still deserves the respect that is due to every person. There is no reason for the church to cease being a voice in the defense of all human beings.

The U.S. Supreme Court drew a line at the end of the second trimester of pregnancy for the legal acceptance of abortion. Some groups that are concerned with the moral side of abortion think that the line should be much earlier, and that late abortion should only be performed for very exceptional reasons. And in fact, an estimated 98 percent of abortions occur before twenty weeks; nine out of ten occur in the first twelve weeks.[27]

It should be possible to get agreement that an individual human being does exist when the organism is able to live outside the womb. Many state laws stipulate that abortions in the last trimester can only be performed to save the life of the mother. There are a small number of other cases when abortion should be allowed. Such is the case when the fetus will be stillborn or will exist only briefly and in pain. The operative principle here is that it is ethical to do something to lessen pain for a dying person even though the means will hasten death. Many parents face the difficult choice of abortion as the least bad decision when birth will only bring on a brief and pain-filled life for a baby. Their grief should not be met with accusations of murder.

The Roman Catholic Church is surely right in insisting that the entire process of pregnancy should be respected. Abortion at any stage of pregnancy is a moral concern. There should be a good reason for an intrusion into the life cycle. The destruction of the human embryo for trivial reasons is surely wrong.

The category of person is regularly used today by lawyers and psychologists for their own purposes. "Person" was and still is a philosophical category to identify a member of the human family. In Christian history, persons are created by God who placed the man and woman in a garden and told them "to dress and keep it." A person is a responsible agent, that is, one who responds to its environment and eventually becomes morally responsible for his or her actions.

A recent political strategy has been to get "personhood" amendments on state ballots, assigning the rights of a person to the fertilized egg. The legal fiction of "personhood" was created a long time ago for corporations, such as universities. They have been considered legally as persons because they are responsible public actors with rights and duties, but no one mistakes General Motors for a person.[28] Even if a fertilized egg were assigned personhood, it would still not be a person.

CHAPTER EIGHT:
Morality of Sexual Diversity

When Roman Catholic officials invoke "natural law," it is most often in referring to sexuality. And the most direct application is to the area of homosexuality. There is seldom any explanation of that judgment because they assume that homosexuality is obviously against "natural law." What could be more obvious than the fact that God created man and woman, telling them to multiply and fill the earth. It is true that most people do fit that image; they are sexually attracted by the other sex. That does not mean that everyone is constituted that way. Nor it is obvious that homosexuality contradicts human nature or is destructive of nature. If a man's orientation is to same sex love, then marriage to a woman would be "unnatural."

This chapter is mainly about the gay/lesbian revolution, but that revolution is now in the context of questions about a wider diversity of sexuality. The acronym LGBTQ opened the discussion beyond homosexuality. There is a question whether LGBTQ is the name of a community or instead whether there are several interest groups who sometimes agree and sometimes are in conflict. The full range of implications in the discussion of the relation between sex and gender is not entirely clear yet.

If most of us older people are candid, we have to admit that we have been largely ignorant of the struggles of people who are sexual minorities.

What has stunned many of us is to discover that we are not talking about an isolated case here and there but a large enough group to be significant for public policies. It would be rash for anyone to pronounce a final judgment of what has been emerging in the last fifty years.

Fifty years ago, one might have been skeptical about the claims and the demands of gays and lesbians. Most people, now known as "straight," were only beginning to grasp how large this minority is and what they were asking for. The officials of the Roman Catholic Church shared in this ignorance. But these church officials have not seemed very interested in at least learning how to talk about gays and lesbians. Pope Francis surprised people by dropping the English word "gay" into the conversation. But most church officials seem content to keep referring to "the homosexuals" as if they were talking about a different species. In fact, the official church has never fully affirmed the existence of gay and lesbian people, that is, the existence of people who are oriented to same-sex love and whose expression of that love is integral to their human nature.

The Roman Catholic Church does not get as passionate in denouncing homosexuality as do Evangelical groups. The word "unnatural" was practically invented for Paul's condemnation of sex between men. A word in the Hebrew Bible for sex between men was translated as "abomination," The connotations of this word accumulated its meaning by referring to sex between men. The *Bible* has few passages that can be interpreted as references to sex between men or between women.

Despite what is regularly asserted, the *Bible* does not condemn homosexuality. The authors could not condemn it because they did not have either the idea or the word. The Bible literally says nothing about homosexuality. To moralists who say that it is obvious what the Bible is referring to, my response is that sexual relations between men may or may not be a case of homosexuality.

An interesting psychological question, which will not be pursued here, is why many men become apoplectic in their reaction to homosexuality. That sometimes leads to violence against gay men. In some parts of the world, it can lead to a death sentence. For men who are not comfortable with their own sexuality, the reality of homosexuality seems to threaten their self-conception.

Even before Pope Francis, the official church seemed to wish to avoid a direct condemnation of "the homosexuals." Church officials encouraged a reaching out "pastorally" to such people and encourage them not to give in to their "deep-seated inclinations." Many gay and lesbian people find this attitude hypocritical, and I suspect many church officials know it is an untenable position.

A further twist in the church history is that the leadership of the institution probably had (and has) a high percentage of gay men. While no one has the full picture, it seems safe to assume that the percentage of gays in the clergy is at least as high as it is in the population as a whole, and there is good reason to guess that it is higher. In any case, the presence of gay men among the people who formulate church statements about homosexuality would seem to have some influence on what the official church teaches. Logic might suggest that church teaching would reflect favorably on homosexuality, but personal struggles to keep one's sexuality hidden can reverse that tendency.

The term homosexual is a clumsy half-Greek and half-Latin word which was invented in the 1870s. Before that time there were no heterosexuals or homosexuals. There were just "normal people" (like us) and perverts, sickos or queers.

A helpful invention of language a half-century ago was the phrase "sexual orientation." The term's significance is not immediately obvious, but the term is indispensable for describing how a person's sexual desires and attractions are stimulated. The term was introduced to establish the fact of homosexual identity. Unfortunately, people seem to assume that only gays and lesbians have a "sexual orientation." Like the problem that "gender studies" tends to be bracketed as referring only to women, "sexual orientation" does not apply only to gay and lesbian people.

It seems amazing now that until the middle of the twentieth century "homosexual" meant both sexual acts between people of the same sex and people whose main orientation is gay or lesbian. Alfred Kinsey, an early student of human sexuality, claimed that 40 percent of men have engaged in sexual acts with other men. Whether that number is too high, it is nonetheless clear that many heterosexual men have engaged in same-sex activities and that their behavior should not be described as "homosexual."[1] Some of it is experimentation. Much of the behavior in our outrageous prison system is often described as homosexual and some of it is, but it should often be described as heterosexual rape.

The historical relation between the Roman Catholic Church and homosexuality would probably be a fascinating story but it is mostly unknown and will remain that way. The last generation of people from before the gay and lesbian revolution are dying out and their experience is likely to remain unrecorded. Historians can piece together some of the story, but first-hand testimony becomes scarcer each passing day. The same is true, of course, about the whole human history of homosexuality. What Roman Catholic history adds is a suppression of sexuality that would have been especially pronounced in the lives of gay people.

Reflections on 1945–1969

Any surveys about homosexuality during the period from the end of the World War II to the 1960s would be suspect. The one study that certainly got attention was Alfred Kinsey's study of the sexual life of the human male in 1948. I was thirteen years old at the time. All that I knew then of the Kinsey study was that it was crazy and untrue. I never heard about the Kinsey report's numbers on sexual activity between men.[2]

I admit to having been sexually innocent growing up, but I was not alone. From conversations with men who grew up in the same era as I did, I think my experience was typical. It may seem incredible to people today but during my entire childhood I did not know of the existence of homosexuality. That was in part because the word was hardly ever used, and I also did not know any substitute word because I never imagined what the word homosexuality meant. When the term was coined in the 1870s, it was to name a crime and/or a sickness. That meaning remained true in the larger society up to the 1960s.

The Roman Catholic Church was totally opposed to homosexuality, but the strange thing is that it was very seldom referred to. There were no sermons denouncing it; religion classes did not deal with it. Every parish mission and retreat featured a fiery condemnation of "self-abuse." But if sexual relations between boys was discussed, I missed it. The priest in confession did ask discreetly whether a sexual sin was committed "alone or with others." I assumed he was referring to a girl not another boy.

Gatherings of boys in the neighborhood talked about almost everything and it might be expected that homosexuality would have been an obvious topic, but it was not. I remember rumors about one boy who did strange things with other boys. His activities seemed to be beyond the pale. My own reaction was disbelief or repulsion. I spent many hours with one friend in a loft of his family's home. I don't think anyone was suspicious of what we were doing. It certainly never crossed my mind that sex might be suspected.

The all-male high school I attended might be thought to be a place where sex between boys would be common. There may have been some of it occurring, but it was not spoken about. Even in the locker room and showers of the gym where I spent endless hours trying to be an athlete, homosexual talk or behavior were absent in my experience. In the standard sexual banter among the athletes there might have been coded references to gay sex, but all the surface talk was about girls or "your mother."

A novitiate full of young men might seem a likely place of gay sex. At the time in the 1950s that thought never occurred to me. I think a brotherhood was less likely than the seminary to attract boys who were homosexually oriented. A pairing of gays in the novitiate or in the scholasticate was almost impossible to manage. Boys who were thought to be gay were not accepted or they were weeded out early. On a few occasions a boy disappeared from the ranks with no explanation. The fact that it might have been because of homosexual activities never crossed my mind.

In the novitiate, athletics was second in importance only to prayer. Manliness was quietly impressed in the life of the brother. Every minute was programmed between rising at 5:00 a.m. and lights out at 9:30 p.m. There was not even a stimulus to think about sex. In the mandatory walks on the grounds, there was a warning against "particular friendships." I did not understand that phrase until many years later. (Were there non-particular friendships?). The people in charge were always watching out for signs of the sin that could not be named.

Even when I was teaching in an all-boys high school there was no discussion of homosexuality and no homosexual behavior acknowledged. Later when I began graduate school, homosexuality was not on my radar. I cannot remember when I first heard the word "homosexual", but I think it was not until I was a young adult.

One incident in the early 1960s crystallizes the era for me. I was in graduate school in Washington, D.C. My younger sister, who was a brilliant mathematician, was applying for a job which she got at the National Security Agency. In those days, the NSA was an obscure building with no name on it in Ft. Meade, Maryland. After her day-long interview, my sister came down to visit me. She was somewhat shaken by the experience because they had repeatedly asked her about her sexual life with women. They did not care what she did with men, but they were fearful of her being lesbian. The agency had recently been rocked by the blackmailing of two gay men who gave up government secrets. My sister was about as innocent of such matters as I was. In later life, she told me that in sixteen years of all-girl Catholic schools she had never heard lesbian sex discussed and had not encountered it among the girls.

Changes From 1969 to the Present

The gay revolution is usually dated from 1969 when at the Stonewall Inn, a popular bar in Greenwich Village, there was a clash between gay men and the police. The police had regularly harassed the patrons of the bar but usually early in the evening. On June 28, the police arrived at the peak hour, demanding ID's and arresting men who were wearing clothes that were "not appropriate to their gender." A riot ensued and lasted for six days. The "Village" had been a place where gay men had lived for decades in relative peace and had developed a culture of their own. The police thought that it was necessary to intervene in the lives of people who were not doing harm to anyone.

I was living in a community of six men not far up Broadway from where the uprising occurred. It was impossible not to be aware of it and to have an opinion about gay men. I thought at first that it was a small group who were causing a lot of noise. Then, I started discovering that many of the men I knew, some of them close friends, were gay. What I knew or imagined as homosexual behavior was still something that repelled me. But I could not condemn "homosexuals" because the category included men I knew who were morally outstanding.

One person, Kevin, whom I had been friendly with since the time of the novitiate came out as gay when he left the Christian Brothers. He told me that he was unaware of being gay throughout his childhood and adolescence. I think he began trying to reinvent himself after leaving the brothers; he was a bundle of energy, sexual and otherwise. He moved to San Francisco living on Castro Street, which was then the center of gay activity in the city. When I visited him there, I found the activity exhausting. He became a chief spokesperson for the Catholic gay community, much to the chagrin of the local bishop with whom he regularly tangled.

Kevin became my chief link to what was happening among gay men, especially gay Catholics. He enlisted me for a committee that he assembled to speak out on gay rights. I was accused by a Christian Brother on the west coast of being a scandal because I was living an openly gay life. I found the accusation humorous because it was so far from the truth. At the time I was having a difficult time trying to manage my relationship with Maria.

Maria, like myself, found herself identified with the gay and lesbian movement. She had become a supporter of gay and lesbian students in the Protestant seminary where she taught. She had not adopted homosexuality as a cause; she was simply a person who was sensitive to outsiders. The young women in the seminary trusted her. She was also a friend of Kevin's. When the three of us were together, as often happened, it would strike me that the two of them were more emotionally compatible with each other than I was with either of them. I was the introvert to which each of them related.

A typical incident occurred when Kevin called me one morning and told me he needed me to come down to the steps of City Hall. He was holding a press conference to express support for a gay rights bill that was opposed by the Cardinal of New York and the Catholic clergy. I said I would be there, but I was not a spokesman for the gay community. He knew that but he said he needed bodies. I supplied a body and joined other bodies that he had rounded up. He also had every television channel in New York City there to get his statement and to answer questions. I was impressed by his ready answer to every question that reporters asked. Afterward, I told him that he was born to hold press conferences. He said the secret was to have the answer ready whatever was the question.

I vividly remember the afternoon when Kevin came to see Maria and me after he was diagnosed with AIDS. In the early 1980s, AIDS was a death warrant. We discussed how he was going to manage and how we could help. We also planned for how he might die and exactly how his funeral was to be conducted. He fought valiantly and continued working as a professor at Brooklyn College. When I found that he was going to AA meetings, I asked him why he did so because he did not drink. He said he found that group to be the best support he had.

He finally collapsed one morning in the subway on the way to work. He lasted only a short time in the hospital before he died. He was grateful that he had lived to the age of fifty. Most of his friends had died at a younger age.

During the AIDS epidemic, it was difficult to find an undertaker who would accept gay men; a professor at Union Seminary helped me with that. Kevin was buried in a lonely plot in New Jersey in zero-degree weather. Few people were able to get there. The big sendoff that he wanted was what I prepared for in the months that followed. When the memorial was finally held, people came from near and far. The participants in that memorable event at Union Theological Seminary, the place he had insisted it be held, gave him the production he would have loved.

From the early 1970s until his death in the late 1980s Kevin had struggled with the official position of the Roman Catholic bishops. He and many thousands of gay Catholics insisted that they had a place in the church. At the least, the official church could have been supportive of the rights of a minority in society.

The claim was commonly made that gay people were by their existence a danger to marriage and the family. I can understand that it would take time for many people to reorient their thinking to accept the fact that a significant percentage of people are oriented to homosexual love. It is surprising how fast things did change once homosexuality was finally brought out for public consideration. Straight people who had imagined homosexuals as a different species suddenly discovered that they had friends or family members who were gay or lesbian. People fighting for their rights may think the change has not been rapid but considering how big the change has been and how long it took in comparison to other movements (such as our glacially slow change in race relations), the pace of the gay/ lesbian revolution is astounding. I doubt that anyone at Stonewall in June 1969 could have imagined June 2019 when lower Manhattan became one grand celebration of "pride."

What puzzles me are philosophers who construct "natural law" theories and draw the conclusion that this entire revolution has been misguided. Millions of people who claim to be oriented homosexually are just sick or give in to their "homosexual inclinations." Famous scholars, such as John Finnis, can issue that judgment without any seeming doubt about the adequacy of his theory because he is kind to those people.[3]

The church did not have much history of public condemnations of homosexuality but at the beginning of the 1970s that was generally the case with society's institutions. In 1975, the Vatican's Congregation for the Doctrine of the Faith laid out its view of homosexuality. The document was blandly titled *A Declaration on Certain Questions concerning Sexual Ethics*. The document's opening words, "According to contemporary scientific research …," were encouraging. But by the end of that paragraph, the document is concerned with condemning "licentious hedonism."

The fourth paragraph of the *Declaration* confidently asserts that the church "ceaselessly preserves and transmits without error the truths of the moral order and she authentically interprets not only the revealed positive law but also … those principles of the moral order which have their origin in human nature itself." The important word in that quotation is "principles." The claim to transmit moral principles is one that might be defensible, but what to say about homosexuality has certainly not been passed down from antiquity.

That quotation from the *Declaration* manifests an attitude of not admitting that the church has much to learn and that it has made obvious mistakes. What the document calls "revealed positive law" makes no sense. There is no such thing. Moral principles may have their origin in human nature but the church's application of principles to human practice has involved many mistakes. The Roman Catholic Church could not be immune from error when the knowledge necessary for interpreting those principles was not available.

The most surprising thing about the document is that it tried to make a helpful distinction that seemed to reflect the findings of the Kinsey study of men. (I doubt that the authors of the document were including women when they referred to "homosexuals"). The document distinguished two kinds of homosexuals. In the first category were men who have sometimes engaged in same-sex practices; the second category was, in the words of the document, "homosexuals, as such."[4]

The writers of the document deserve some credit for trying but their distinction is illogical. Their first category of men is not accurately called "homosexuals." They are heterosexual men engaging in sexual practices with other men. The Declaration says that these actions are the result of a false education or a lack of normal development. That could be true, although the activities might be just ordinary experimentation by boys or an outlet in repressive all-male institutions.

The *Declaration's* second kind of homosexual is, "homosexuals who are definitively such because of some kind of innate instinct." If the sentence had ended there it would have seemed to endorse what was central to the gay revolution, namely, that homosexuality is innate. There are not two kinds of homosexuals; rather, there are two orientations of people: heterosexual and homosexual.[5]

Unfortunately, the sentence did not end there. It continued, "or a pathological condition judged to be incurable." The whole sentence does not make sense. The phrase "innate instinct" is redundant. Instincts by definition are innate. While instincts clearly belong to nonhuman animals, humans are not usually said to have instincts. However, the *Declaration's* use of "instinct" seemed intended to root homosexuality in human nature itself. But then to equate this "innate instinct" with a "pathological condition that is incurable" creates a strange picture of a human being with sexual desires that are at once natural and unnatural.

Many church people saw an opening here. They could accept the phrase "some kind of innate instinct" while disagreeing with the description of a pathological and incurable condition. Those people probably included some U.S. bishops who were acutely aware of the revolution happening around them. And what is seldom admitted is that some of the bishops were probably gay. The Vatican felt the need to issue a corrective to an "overly benign interpretation given to the homosexual condition itself."[6]

If one reads through the discussions at the U.S. bishops' meetings in the 1980s, it seems that many of the bishops were looking for a positive perspective on gay and lesbian people. They could not openly disagree with the Vatican, but they did repeatedly use the term "sexual orientation" even after the Vatican had condemned the phrase.

The official line was that we respect the dignity of homosexuals who should receive the pastoral care of the Catholic Church. But at the same time, we reject the existence of homosexuals. By 2006 the U.S. bishops were with the program. The title of their document says it all: *Ministry to Persons with a Homosexual Inclination: Guidelines for Pastoral Care.*[7] Instead of the existence of people whose homosexuality is "natural," there are people who have an (unnatural) "inclination" to homosexual practices. The inclination is not a sin, but the practice is. Therefore, the pastoral care must help people resist the inclination. One recommendation was that people with such an inclination should not associate all the time with people who have a similar inclination.[8]

I find ironic their choice of "inclination" to indicate that homosexuality is a violation of "natural law." In Thomas Aquinas's exposition of natural law, the law and behavior are connected by inclinations. Pamela Hall writes: "Thomas's own emphasis on the natural law is first in terms of inclinations, ways of being directed to our end and not in terms of any set of rules."[9] Even the Vatican's own International Theological Commission refers to "the moral principles that derive from reason's consideration of the fundamental inclinations of the human person."[10] Thomas Aquinas did not have today's access to the testimony of millions of people as to their fundamental inclination. Contemporary bishops do not have that excuse.

Pope Francis became famous for answering a question about gays by saying: "Who am I to judge?" That was a good initial response, but it demanded a follow up analysis which never happened. The pope's answering a question with a question received praise in nearly all quarters. Late night comedians in the United States would have none of that. They pointed out that the pope's job is to judge. Every time he asserts a church teaching, he judges.

As far as gay and lesbian people are concerned the pope must assert something different from what the Vatican has been saying, otherwise he is endorsing that teaching. The Pope has subsequently cited the *Catholic Catechism's* use of "ingrained inclination" as the official Roman Catholic language to describe a gay person. The phrase "ingrained inclination" might have been used to indicate that homosexuality is compatible with the law of human nature but instead it was used to condemn gay sex.

In 2014–15 there was a Synod to consider the family. It is surprising that a discussion of homosexuality was included in the synod's discussion. But what was genuinely surprising was that an interim report after the first week of the Synod gave a very positive report on homosexuality. Apparently, many bishops in the Synod were also surprised. It seems that a small group of bishops had managed to get their opinion into this interim report even though the matter had not been thoroughly discussed.[11]

The final report of the Synod dealt with homosexuality in the illogical way that Vatican documents have spoken since the 1970s. Gay organizations were disappointed and felt that they had been duped. Nevertheless, two things should be noted: First, the fact that homosexuality was discussed at all in this setting gave legitimacy to a question which the Vatican would prefer not to discuss at all.

Second, the phrase "sexual orientation" found its way into the final document. I suspect that many bishops did not even notice the inclusion of that phrase, but it is one that had always been avoided or condemned. If "sexual orientation" exists, then the existence of homosexual people is admitted. That is the primary thing that the gay community wants from the pope and bishops: not pastoral care but the recognition that they exist.

Gay and Lesbian Marriages

Roman Catholic official teaching is in a bind because if it admits that people are by nature oriented to same-sex love, then it follows that there should be an outlet for expressing that love. The sacramental principle in Catholicism would dictate that conclusion. Official teaching insists that the sexual drive finds sacramental expression in marriage. The official church acknowledges and praises people who are virgins and celibates for the kingdom of God. But it recognizes that this way of life is a special vocation, not something to be imposed on a major part of the population.

Same-sex marriage is now a worldwide phenomenon, which the church might recognize as a conservative movement that shores up a troubled institution. I was somewhat puzzled that gay and lesbian people were so anxious to join an institution that fails more often than it succeeds. The upper classes in this country still consider marriage to be a mark of respectability but a sizable part of the straight population has disconnected marriage and babies. And a great many people also have doubts that sexual companionship is helped by the stereotypes that the idea of marriage still carries. I thought that perhaps heterosexual couples would increasingly join gay couples in establishing unions with desirable economic protections and social approval but outside marriage.

The argument for same-sex marriage before the U.S. Supreme Court was disingenuous on both sides. On one side, opponents of same-sex marriage argued that marriage has had the same meaning for millennia.

Advocates replied that marriage is always changing. Neither side was entirely forthcoming.

Marriage today has a different meaning than in the past. Justice Kennedy in the majority opinion said that marriage makes "two people greater than they once were." That was hardly the case in most of history.[12] In the distant past, marriage was about a man's property, which included a woman or women who could bear the children that he would father.

Even in the nineteenth century the common-law rule of "coverture" collapsed the woman's legal identity into that of her husband's. A wife was legally invisible. It was a long journey for women to get to the place where marriage could realistically be called a partnership. Not much progress toward that arrangement had been made until the human race began producing more babies than the earth or two parents could manage. Marriage understood as a contract to have as many babies as God or nature sends needed adjustment.

In the 1920s, there was discussion of two kinds of marriage, traditional and companionate. Even the Roman Catholic Church in the 1930s accepted companionship as a secondary purpose of marriage. The primary purpose, according to the church, was the birth and education of children. The church altered its position in the 1960s by saying that there is no hierarchy of ends. Within such a framework, the Roman Catholic Church could be a supporter of same-sex marriage, which is suited to the companionate function of marriage and presents no problem of interference in the process of pregnancy and conception.

Marriage that includes parenthood does involve more complicated questions than only a stable sexual partnership. Some of marriage tradition makes sense for the upbringing of children. The problem with all the attention given to who can marry is that the related question of who takes care of the children can get underemphasized.

The term marriage could have been rerouted to its historic role of a contract to start a family. Gay couples raising a family could have strengthened or reconnected the bond between marriage and family. The government could then have concentrated on the quality of childcare in this country where one out of five children is born into poverty. Stable sexual unions other than marriage could be blessed by the church. The government should stay out of the sex lives of both straight and gay couples who wish to contribute to society in ways other than by parenting.

The moment has passed when that linguistic direction could have been taken. The legal recognition of same-sex marriage is progress insofar as it provides gay people with the respect that they deserve. But a confusion about the nature of marriage remains. Same-sex marriage will more likely strengthen than weaken the institution of marriage, but the institution needs more help than the addition of a new population. The country needs an honest discussion of how to improve family life and to have government policies that help rather than undermine families.

After the court decision, the U.S. Catholic bishops said, "marriage remains unchanged and unchangeable." That statement is simply a denial of reality. Marriage has obviously undergone changes over the centuries; there is no eternal essence of marriage.

Opponents of same sex marriage, however, had a strong point in that marriage had always been a man-woman relation. While proponents of change were right about constant change in marriage, it was not honest to imply that the man-woman relation was only an incidental fact about marriage. Perhaps it was time to change that tradition, but in proposing to do so one must respect the history of an institution as to whether a proposed change does or does not make sense.

A second problem in the arguments for same-sex marriage was the phrase "marriage equality." It is an effective slogan because if "equality" is the issue, opponents are in a corner. Do they really want to be on the side of inequality? But like most slogans "marriage equality" clouds rather than clarifies the issue. People who argued against same-sex marriage logically raised the question of the limits of that equality.

In an essay in the *New York Times,* William Baude argued for polyg-amy as the next extension of marriage equality.[13] He concludes the essay: "Once we abandon the rigid constraints of history, we cannot be sure that we know where the future will take us." Indeed, once we abandon those rigid constraints of history, we can call anything by any name but there is nothing left to argue about.

A plural marriage could conceivably fit within some logic of mar-riage, but the case would have to be made within the perception of an historical evolution. The marriage of one man and several women would be nothing new and it could even be construed as regression. These days we are presumably including one woman and several men, as well as all numerical combinations of men and women. But what is the limit?

Can five people have a marriage? How about fifty or five hundred? Is there any advantage in calling a union of fifty people a marriage rather than, say, a community? It is true that "we cannot be sure that we know where the future will take us" but wherever it takes us we will not be free of our history and the imperfect institutions that have helped to shape us.

The Roman Catholic Church has begun a massive change in its atti-tude toward gay couples adopting children. In 2003, the Vatican denounced gay marriage claiming that "allowing children to be adopted by parents liv-ing in such unions would actually mean doing violence to these children."[14] (No evidence was offered for that claim). In a welcome change of tone, the Synod in 2014 said, "the Church pays special attention to children who live with same-sex couples and stresses that the needs and rights of the little ones must always be given priority."[15]

The Roman Catholic Church could make a great contribution to society by continuing to say that there are two ends of marriage that are not hierarchically ordered. These two kinds of marriage could be sacramen-tally distinguished. They might be called family marriage and partnership marriage. Both straight and gay couples who intend to raise children need the support of family-friendly policies by the government and the support by the church.

Other married couples need legal recognition of their economic partnership and they also need social support for their union. If the Roman Catholic Church were to come on board, a new way of looking at marriage might emerge that respects tradition but acknowledges the irreversible trends of the last seventy-five years. Women's equality and help for family life could be given the attention they deserve.

PART FOUR

CHAPTER NINE:

Morality at the End of Life

One of the things that the Roman Catholic Church was historically good at was managing dying and death. It still provides more help than most institutions do when a person comes to the end of life, but in recent decades its leadership has been seriously undermined. Many people simply assume that the church is as obstinate about humane treatment at the end of life as it seems to be about the beginning of life.[1]

Pope Benedict XVI asserted, "there may be a legitimate diversity of opinion about waging war and applying the death penalty, but not however with regard to abortion and euthanasia."[2] What he seemed unaware of is that the term euthanasia has changed its meaning in recent decades to include medical practices that the church has long approved. I do not like what has happened to "euthanasia" but if someone is going to make an absolute ethical condemnation of euthanasia, he or she should know that the term is ambiguous.

This chapter examines aspects of death and the period preceding death. First, I examine the new phenomenon of a large age group that is really old. Second, I look at how the living deal with death in the rituals of burial and mourning. Third, I examine what it means to care for the dying and what "aid" to the dying might include.

A New Time for Old Living

Old age has been the subject of philosophers since Plato and Aristotle, and it continued through Cicero, Montaigne, Bacon, and Beauvoir. Plato has generally positive things to say about old age as a time for philosophy when the passions of youth have quieted.[3] Aristotle was harsh in assessing the same condition: "Men at this time of life are often supposed to have a self-controlled character; the fact is that their passions have slackened and they are slaves to the love of gain."[4] In recent times, Simone de Beauvoir presents a depressing picture of society's attitude toward the old. She does not have much use for the Stoic image of life ripening into old age: "We harden in some places and rot in others. We never ripen."[5]

There have always been a few really old people. But suddenly there is a new population of old folks, and the rest of society has not yet come to terms with that reality. When I was young, the age of sixty-five was the assumed time for retirement. And when men retired from their job they quickly retired from living. It seems just a short time ago when the average life expectancy for men in the U.S was sixty-six. Women (the stronger sex) usually did better because they knew how to take care of themselves.

When I passed the age of sixty-five, I did not sense an experience of being old; actually, I felt that I was just settling into my job. Even when I passed seventy, I did not feel old. I did retire from full-time teaching at age seventy-five, mainly to give a younger person a chance to be appointed as a professor. There is no retirement age for professors, which is not a good arrangement. The age of seventy-five seems about right though exceptions could be allowed. I assumed that I could get part-time work for ten years or until I could not do the job (or a friend told me that my time was up).

When I hit eighty, I could not deny that I was now old. Not many people in the human race get that far. Like many men my age, I had survived several health problems including cancer and heart failure. At this age, one cannot avoid an awareness of death, not as a monster hiding in the shadows but as a daily companion. I tell people that I am living in sudden death overtime. Younger people think that description is morbid. I think it is simply realistic. Death can take any of us on any day but in your eighties the odds get high.

We have more old people now and they are living longer and longer. This fact is a cause for rejoicing among those who only recently would not have been alive. It does create a crisis in health care services. In 1950, children under the age of five were 11 percent of the U.S. population, those over eighty were one percent. In thirty years, there will be as many people over eighty as there are under five. The same pattern is emerging throughout the industrialized world.

One of most neglected pools of teachers in the country are grandparents. Everyone who becomes a grandparent seems to get transformed. Leslie Stahl writes, "In various surveys, nearly three-quarters of grandparents say that being a grandparent is the single most important and satisfying thing in their life. Most say that being with their grandkids is more important to them than traveling or having financial security."[6] The enthusiasm of grandparents is healthy for both the old and the young and it also makes life easier for the generation in between.

More than half of the very old now live without a spouse and have fewer children than ever before, yet we give little thought to how they will live out their later years alone. The obvious problem of old age is a decline in physical strength. There are people who live into their nineties with no major health problems, but the general story of old age is one of vulnerabilities that include illnesses, injuries, and medications.

The old who live alone are asserting their ability to take care of themselves and to cope with the ordinary frailties of age. Their determination may be admirable but there can be self-deception in this outlook. It is a responsibility of family and friends to check in on the old who either by choice or necessity are living alone. That concern especially applies to driving an automobile. In a culture built on the car, relinquishing one's driver's license can seem like a death sentence. Nevertheless, most people over eighty should have their driving skills regularly examined.

Living alone at any age requires a structure to one's daily existence. The problem of many old people is that their lives have had a firm structure, and then it suddenly disappeared. The death of a spouse is the most dramatic instance of a person needing to reinvent a world of order. People may assume that they know the problem of being a widow or widower, but it is difficult to know what that is like before it is experienced. "People say: 'I know the problems of age.' They don't. Nobody's been old but the old."[7]

Many widows have written about the change of attitude among their friends; either the widow is treated as an exotic specimen or else she becomes invisible. Order is a "social construct;" a seventy- or eighty-year-old widow should not have to build a new world alone. But millions of people must do the best they can without strong social support.

When a structured life has suddenly disappeared, a new order has to be built ritual by ritual. The United States has from its beginning been an anti-ritual nation. We take pride in our informality, which at times cuts through all kinds of traditional forms that hide reality. But it is unwise to think that human beings do not need habits, rituals, ceremonies, and daily practices. The small rituals that I refer to below may seem trivial but in both manners and morals the rule is to take care of the small things and the big things will generally take care of themselves.

Widows and widowers share the same basic problem but the differences between men and women can be pronounced in this situation. Women seem to cope much better with the problems of old age, in part because women have carried the burden of life's necessities all through their lives. As Margaret Mead said, "Men are more likely to die when they retire, while women just keep on cooking."[8] Things may change in future generations but for now there remains a big difference in how most men care for themselves and their surroundings.

Old people who live alone often do not eat well. The problem is not that they do not know how to cook a meal; even men can easily learn the minimum skill needed. The real problem is that they do not see the need for a ritual of cooking a meal when the meal is only for themselves. After my father died, my mother, who was an excellent cook, was not eating well. When she was asked about that, her reply was: "It is not worth the bother to cook for one."

Eating as well as other basic human practices need rituals that are performed every day. Rituals do not exist if their practice is regularly skipped or routinely violated. No ritual is more important than going to bed and rising at approximately the same time every day. There is a well-known connection between insomnia and depression; it is not always clear which is cause and which is effect. Being able to get up when the body is rested and to take naps during the day are benefits of old age, but the pattern needs consistency.

Personal grooming is often neglected, especially by men. Why shave, shower, or dress with clean clothes? It seems an unnecessary bother. Men need to be convinced that such rituals are good for health, happiness, and whatever social interactions the day may bring. Dishes left in the sink and a bed unmade are signs that life is not under control.

It is often said that breakfast is the most important meal of the day. Millions of people deny this principle by their actions. Some people skip breakfast on the mistaken notion that it is a good way to lose weight. Other people claim to be too busy. Young people who skip breakfast may use the excuse that they need to rush off to work or to school. Retired old people have no such excuse. For the old person living alone there is no excuse for not starting the day with a big, healthy, leisurely breakfast. For people who tend to be slow-moving in the morning, it helps to prepare everything that will be needed for breakfast the night before.

In developing a basic routine for the day there are radical differences according to one's economic situation. Having a membership in a gym or exercise clinic is helpful but it is beyond the means of many people. That makes it even more important to have a regular pattern of physical exercises, starting with daily walks.

For people who are not forced to hold a low-paying job for their economic survival, volunteer work is usually helpful. "Work" as distinct from a job is the contribution that an individual makes to society. Everyone needs work especially after they retire from their job.

Everyone also needs beauty in their surroundings. The rich can easily afford beautiful things, although they are often too dull to appreciate simple things of beauty. Whatever the limitations of one's budget, it is important that one's immediate surroundings have aesthetic touches for the walls, shelves, and entrance to one's home.

Whatever one's ear for music, everyone's life is helped by music that he or she can appreciate. Music is the natural companion to silence. An old person living alone has long stretches where there is no conversation with others. The absence of sound does not automatically create a calm, meditative silence. One must learn how to appreciate silence as the gift of a life separated from the noise and hyperactivity of today's world. C.S. Lewis describes heaven as the place "where all that is not music will be silence." [9]

An old man living alone may forget to smile and to have a pleasant expression when confronting others. Preoccupied with minor aches and pains, he might seem to be a grumpy old guy when in fact he has simply become unaccustomed to smiling. A positive outlook on life is good for one's health in addition to having a smoothing effect in social contacts. Laughter is good medicine as Norman Cousins documented in his *Anatomy of an Illness*.[10] Good humor does not cost anything; it just requires an attention to the face that one turns toward the world.

Aristotle said in his Ethics that no one would wish to live without friends.[11] The older one gets, the more cherished are long-standing friendships. Family members, who have been occupied with their own family and work, often rediscover family bonds late in life. All friendships require cultivation. Women seem better at maintaining a few close friends across decades and distances, something that men need to work at.

The cell phone, e-mail, and more exotic technology are a great boon to old people who live alone. Many of the old are struggling to become familiar with today's devices. There is no reason why, with just a little help, they cannot use these means of communication to their benefit. Some grandparents have their lives enriched by now being able to see as well as to talk to their grandchildren who live far away. One of the few good things about the Covid-19 pandemic is that old people became familiar with programs such as Zoom or Facetime.

If it is possible for the old person, going out to dinner or a movie, especially with a companion, but even alone, is a healthy element to include in a weekly routine. Old people who are shut-ins and have meals delivered to them need someone to talk to. If the person bringing the meals cannot do that, neighbors or friends have to regularly provide conversation.

Some people remain healthy into their eighties and nineties, but everyone eventually needs help in doing some ordinary activities. Old people often complain that they have become invisible, and that younger people do not offer help. Some of the feeling of being left behind is inevitable. I never realized how fast people walk in Manhattan until I found that it was impossible for me to keep up. Generally, however, I find most younger people to be kind and solicitous.

I was shocked when I was first offered a seat in the subway. Did I really look feeble? Now I just gratefully accept the offer, which is usually made by a woman or a black man. I have fallen four times on Manhattan streets and each time eight or ten people have rushed to my aid. Most people are kind and helpful if the problem is clear to them.

The city has 500,000 home health care aids. Most of them are immigrants who do this difficult work for a minimum wage. They are certainly underappreciated. There are also tens of thousands of people who volunteer their services to help the poor and aged.

When Maria became sick and needed constant supervision, I thought I might have to quit my job. The professional agencies were not flexible enough for what I needed. I finally hit upon putting up a notice in a local church. The woman who responded was a perfect companion and just what we needed. While I was at work, Maria and she would sit quietly or listen to music. I forget what I paid her, but that kind of help was something money cannot buy.

Some people in their seventies or eighties are not content to settle into living alone. They may be looking for a new partner. Why not? Their behavior can be upsetting to their children; the old are often liberated in a way that scandalizes the middle-aged. The closest ally for an old person is often a teenage grandchild. Teenagers know the experience of rebelling against the people in charge.[12]

The children of the old should, of course, be listened to. They may have legitimate concerns. Some people are shocked to discover that there is a lot of unprotected sex these days in nursing homes. Young people may suspect that their dad is just looking for someone to take care of him. Or it may seem that an older woman is too quick to jump at the chance of financial security. Ultimately, the old need to find their own way with the help of family and friends. The middle-aged son or daughter is not the parent.

In today's world the old have greater possibilities than at any time in the past. Except for people in poverty, there is easy access to food and drink; there is a world of entertainment at one's fingertips. There are medicines that can ease the pains of old age. Without some rituals of order, however, benefits can become dangers. Television, which now spills beyond the television set, is a great pacifier of children and the old but too much of it saps one's vitality.

A glass of wine at dinner is a delight, although alcohol is one of the silent dangers of old age. A person living alone does not have a built-in ritual for the use of alcohol; the result is that there is no place to stop when one drink follows another. The rate of alcoholism among old people is a serious but mostly hidden problem. For the person who eats and drinks alone, it is imperative to have a ritual that makes sense for that person.

The old person living alone is someone who may feel that he or she no longer has an identity. The old person needs to re-create not an entirely new identity but a new way of being the person that he or she has been. It is not a mechanical or robotic process. There can be a wonderful sense of liberation in old age when one can drop most of life's pretensions and simply be a self that respects the wisdom of the past and is open to learning from every possible source in the present. Especially after a serious illness, the old person knows that every day is a bonus.

The Roman Catholic Church should be one of the main institutions that can be a help for old people. The church today is (unfortunately) skewed toward the old. But that fact provides a special mission that is widely neglected in the larger society. Many orders of nuns and brothers have been doing an excellent job of caring for their old even though they realize that there is no future for the order. Their care of the old can be a model for other groups.

Many Roman Catholic parishes have organizations for people who are recently widowed. These groups can benefit from someone who has training in group dynamics or psychology. But I have seen many groups that did not need professional guidance. Old people have extensive experience to draw upon. What is most needed to provide support for a new widow or widower is companionship and conversation. Experts are welcome but are not indispensable.

Catholic social agencies continue to do excellent work sometimes under very difficult conditions. Volunteers for local needs and missionaries who go overseas give a witness to Christian belief. Religious congregations of men and women used to be the backbone of work with the poor, the aged, and the sick. There are still young Catholics who would be willing to work with other dedicated people in such efforts, but they need institutional support.

Death and Mourning

The Roman Catholic Church still provides an ancient ritual for death that many mourners find comforting. Perhaps only Judaism has a more elaborate ritual surrounding death. The Second Vatican Council made a drastic change in the central funeral ritual of the Mass. In this case the transition was smoother than with other liturgical changes.

Until the Second Vatican Council, the funeral liturgy emphasized fear and the frightful judgment of God. I can still remember from my childhood the booming sounds of the medieval "Dies irae, dias illa ..." (Day of wrath, day of mourning/David's word with Sibyl' s blending/Heaven and earth in ashes ending). Even without knowing Latin, the sentiments of fear and dread came through in the music and all the trappings of the Mass.

In the years after the Council, the funeral Mass became positive in tone. There is more talk of Jesus' resurrection than his death on the cross. There is talk of the joys of eternity. The music is bright and joyful and the deceased person's life is celebrated. I thought at the time of the changes that the shift might be too abrupt as did happen with much of the liturgy. Those who are mourning need a place and a time for sorrow and grief. Happy talk can be a denial of the reality of death, a denial that is common in society today.

As usual the church can find elements in the past tradition to create a more balanced ritual. At the funerals I attend – when one is old going to funerals is a main part of life – the joining of sorrow and hope seems reasonably well done.

One development that occurred despite resistance by church officials is a family member or friend speaking about the person's life. Unfortunately, the comments by someone who knew the deceased person well are not allowed where they should be given after the reading of the Gospel. The priest continues to think that his words about the person are needed.

Usually all I can think about while the priest drones on about someone he probably did not know is: *Why can't he just shut up?*

When my father died, my sister and I went to see the local pastor. We knew what we wanted and what we did not want in the funeral liturgy. He did not object. My sister, who is a member of the Sisters of Mercy, was much better than I at this procedure. She specified readings and other elements of the liturgy. She also supplied a choir of nuns.

My sister is the kind of person who is a natural as a priest. When my brother recently died, she arranged for a group of family member to come to the burial at the cemetery. I usually dislike the performance at the cemetery when the mourners are subjected to more stilted prayers and pious comments from the priest or the funeral director. In my brother's case, my sister made a brief ritual the appropriate conclusion with family members speaking and a prayer that my sister had composed.

A part of the church ritual that does not seem to have survived so well was that the priest used to be called in when death was imminent to administer what sounded to a child's hearing like "extrimunction." Calling in the priest was a signal that death was about to occur. There was often resistance to bringing in someone who was the angel of death. The Council tried to give a more positive twist to the priest's role as that of administering a sacrament of the sick.

A main reason why the priest was thought necessary was to hear the last confession and get rid of any mortal sins before the person faced the stern judge. The Catholics whose deaths I have witnessed in recent years seem to have died peacefully and have not felt the need for a confessor or a last confession.

It is too bad if the Roman Catholic Church loses a role here. Chaplains in large institutions, such as prisons, hospitals, and nursing homes, usually have access to the clients or inmates. The religious representative can be an ally on the side of good care and be a witness against the institution's failures. In the past, and sometimes still in the present, the chaplain could be a support to the family of a dying patient. The church represented by parish members can be an important help, especially to widows and widowers.

One other distinctive part of the Roman Catholic Church's ritual of death is the wake. The wake was undergoing some changes even before the Council, but its essential function has remained among most Catholics. The busy lives of the friends and family of the dead person have cut into the amount of time, which was once reserved for the wake, but there is still the feeling that some time is needed for expressions of condolences.

The Irish American wake was the most famous sendoff, but other ethnic groups had their own ritual. In the nineteenth century, the Irish immigrants made the wake a substitute for the funeral Mass. It took a while for the clergy to convince their parishioners to combine the wake with the official liturgy in the church.

The old-time wake was still common in the1950s. I can vividly remember my grandmother's wake in 1958. The wake was held in the family home and went on for three days and three nights. I can picture the women gathered in the living room where the embalmed corpse was enthroned. The men paid their respects with a quick prayer at the coffin, and then retreated to the kitchen. The kitchen I can recall was smoke-filled and alcohol fueled. As I was neither a smoker nor a drinker, I was at a disadvantage. I probably did not know most of these people who were friends or acquaintances of grandma, Margaret McDermott Moran from Galway.

This old-time wake had an important purpose of supporting the mourning family as the first step of the church's detailed practices of bereavement. The need for time was realistically faced. Food and drink were deliberate symbols opposing death. Unfortunately, a long wake in the family home could create a burden on the mourners. And the home was often too small a physical space for the many mourners.

When the funeral home began to take over the arrangements after death, some people protested. The funeral business since the nineteenth century has often been an operation of shady and exploitative practices.

People are at their most vulnerable when a death in the family occurs. They can be persuaded to spend money foolishly if the funeral professional gives them a hard sell. Nevertheless, enlisting professional help was in most ways a good and necessary development.[13]

I know of idealistic Catholics who have gone into the funeral business to try to change the role of funeral director to a religious vocation. Their main intention is not to become rich but to respond to the needs of the mourners. The schools that train funeral directors have been pressured to emphasize the humane aspects of death and mourning.

Funerals used to be a family business; the children would follow the parents in serving their neighbors. Each ethnic group had its favorite parlor. Large corporations started taking over the local family operations. One funeral director whose family had been in the business since the nineteenth century told me he had to sell the operation to a big company because none of his children was interested in continuing the family tradition.

The companies were out to make a big profit by using "economies of scale" by making funeral homes identical. Funerals seemed a sure way to have a steady income. But some of the big companies went bankrupt because they were oblivious of the importance of the local ties that funeral directors previously had.[14]

I taught a course on death for twenty-five years. It was by far the most popular course I taught; the topic was obviously more of a draw than I was. I used to set the computer at fifty students lest a hundred or more students register for the course. I think universities cheat students by having courses in auditoriums with several hundred students. Particularly on the subject of death I wanted to make sure that I could get to know all the students and that personal interactions were a main part of the course.

The course was entitled "The Meaning of Death," which seemed to me to promise too much. At the first class, I would say that I could not tell them the meaning of death nor could I teach them how to die. A grandparent, a friend or a public figure would need to show them the way. My job, as I saw it, was to introduce them to a conversation about death that the human race has been having for thousands of years.

During one of the first times that I taught the course, an NYU student committed suicide in a dramatic manner that reached the front page of the *New York Times*. I was afraid to look at the name of the student. I was concerned that an unstable student might have gone over the edge because of something said in class. That particular student was not in the course on death. I eventually decided that someone considering suicide would not be inclined to take a course on death.

It is not widely known that there are a considerable number of suicides among college students each year. One year there was a spotlight on NYU when the suicides of several students were noted in the *Times*. People around the country were asking what is wrong with NYU, but every large university had similar rates of suicide that year. NYU, for better and for worse, is more likely than most universities to be noticed by the powerful newspaper up the street. The suicides of young people are nevertheless shocking and raise questions about society.[15]

It puzzled me why so many students were interested in taking a course on death. It was not a required course for students in any field. The students were usually serious and thoughtful. I decided after a few years that most students seemed to be taking the course for highly personal reasons. Often a parent or grandparent had recently died. Sometimes the student was concerned with AIDS. To a large extent, what the students most wanted was to hear adults speak truthfully and with genuine emotion about the reality of death.

I remember a parent who called me to ask whether it was a good idea that their son, whose brother had recently died, was going to take the course. All I could tell them, not knowing the student, was that a person might have different reactions to talking about death so shortly after a death in the family. The assurance that I could give the parents was that I would never exploit raw emotions, which a student might be experiencing after a death in the family. Anyone teaching a course on death must remember that the classroom is for understanding not for therapy. Understanding can have its own therapeutic effect but going directly at fear, sorrow, or sadness in a classroom is an abuse of power.

At first, I co-taught the course with two women who were the experts. Their full-time work was with the dying. One of them had done her dissertation on the lives of three-year old children who were dying or whose parents had died. I told one of the women that she could be doing stand-up comedy. Humor might seem out of place but if your work is only with the dying you need some humor to keep things in perspective. For the first few years I handled the history and philosophy parts of the course. The classes of the two women were much more to the students' liking.

One book we used in the course was *Death and Dying*, a famous book by Elizabeth Kübler-Ross. I had not intended to do more than mention it. The book was published in 1969. I naively believed everyone would already be familiar with it. But the book was a complete revelation to most students. I also had thought that the book was not appropriate because of its many faults, which had long been known. Kübler-Ross almost accidentally found herself in hospital work and constructed a scheme of emotions that a dying patient experiences. There was nothing scientific about the "stages" that she put forth. It was based on a very unscientific sample and her own idiosyncratic interviews and observations. Despite the limitations of the book, which I would point out, most students were enthusiastic about it.

I had to accept the fact that students liked the book because it gave them a definite pattern to sort out their own feelings about death. It is interesting that Kübler-Ross's "five stages" have become cultural lore but they are almost always referred to as the five stages of grief. What she claimed to find was five stages of dying. Grief and dying do have some parallel development, but the obvious difference is that one of them ends in death, the other leads away from death. The culture is much more comfortable with what leads away from death.

The two women with whom I taught eventually moved on to other things. I wondered if I should continue the course because I lacked the credentials and the experience for dealing with some elements of the course. I decided to invite in speakers who could help me in areas where I was weak. A funeral director, a grief counselor, a rabbi, and others agreed to help me out. One woman who proved to be invaluable was a hospice nurse. She was nervous the first time she came to the course because she had no previous experience in classroom teaching. I encouraged her simply to describe what she does. The students were enthralled by the stories she told them. I made sure to bring her back each year.

During the twenty-five years of the course, I did gain some first-hand experience of death. Both of my parents died, my closest friend died, several other friends died, and finally my wife, Maria, died. Maria's death profoundly affected the course one year. I could not hide the fact that her dementia and finally her death forced on me a special perspective on the subject under discussion. The students turned out to be an important support to me after her death. I was present for every class during the semester when she died, not from any heroic effort but because I found teaching, including teaching on death, to be a way of working through personal grief.

Aid in Dying

The Roman Catholic Church's teaching in this area – perhaps to some people's surprise – is quite nuanced. The church helped to develop the language for talking about what should and should not be done in caring for those whose dying seems imminent. The most basic distinction was between ordinary and extraordinary means for keeping a person alive. A person has a right to ordinary means to stay alive. A person, or a patient's proxy, has a right to decide whether or not extraordinary means should be employed to keep the person alive. The practical difference, therefore, was between killing a person and allowing a person to die.

This principle or some further development of it remains important. One of the things that distinguishes today's society is that questions of who dies and under what conditions they die have become extremely complex. It is often unclear even what it means for a person's life to end, that is, to sort out the contributions of various people and many impersonal factors in someone's death. Laws can be passed that exclude some actions as untenable for a society; but laws cannot provide the details needed for decisions today that involve modern medicines and technology.

The heading of this section, "aid in dying," is intended to introduce ambiguity or flexibility in thinking about the way a person who is close to death should be cared for. In my book, *Missed Opportunities: Rethinking Catholic Tradition*, I tried to make a careful change in what I had previously thought about what is ethical in the treatment of the dying. I think that the aid that people need when they are close to death may include helping the person to complete the act of dying. There is a danger in moving in this direction; the intention of the person providing the aid and the kind of aid that is provided need to be carefully considered. I think such a shift in the context of contemporary medicine is compatible with Catholic tradition.

The moment of a shift in my thinking was one day in the hospital when I looked at Maria who had four or five lines running into her body to keep her alive. I had approved each of these procedures, but I wondered if this was just a form of torture. There was no hope that she was going to get better, so what was the point? There was a part of me that just wanted to keep her alive, but we had passed the point where letting go was called for. What does this question mean for millions of people who are in similar circumstances?

Faced with the bewildering complexity of today's situations, there is a strong tendency to rely on slogans that set up two camps. Instead of a serious discussion of morality and mortality, we have a conflict of political lobbies. Physicians and families who are doing their best do not need the added burden of outsiders protesting the decisions. It can happen that parents, while leaving the hospital after their child has been disconnected from a "life support" machine, are met by shouts of murderer. When two lobbies have taken shape, I think that a thoughtful person might have to refuse membership in both camps.

Two things are needed for an ethical discussion of these situations: a firm grasp of first principles and an admission of uncertainty on some points.

Finding anything that can qualify as a first principle here is difficult. When people make judgments on morality/ethics they usually imply a universality to their statements. People do not say that murder or torturing people is sometimes wrong or that it is wrong in my part of the world. Instead, people make moral pronouncements that murder or torture is wrong always and everywhere. And yet, there is an obvious limitation to any moral/ethical statement, starting with the fact that every language is particular, not universal. Perhaps there are statements that can approach universality ("it seems to be true almost everywhere" or "surveys have found this is always the case"). The range of uncertainty can be narrowed but it cannot be eliminated.

The term "principle" is the best choice for the role of ultimate guidance in these matters. The word suggests what comes first and can be relevant to almost any situation. However, there is a built-in ambiguity in the use of "principle"; it is comprehensive because it leaves out the details of a situation. There can be strong disagreements about how a moral principle is implied or embodied in a particular situation.

We have an understandable desire to want rules or precepts that can be applied with no ambiguity. There is a tendency to slide from principles to rules. Laws exist in the form of rules. Laws are useful for excluding some practices that a society cannot abide. Laws are not very helpful in telling us how we should act.

In the 1960s there was a movement that was misleadingly called "situation ethics." It dismissed moral principles and rules in favor of doing whatever the moment seemed to call for. All ethics is situational, but the situation must be open to guidance from the wisdom of the past and from present knowledge that goes beyond an individual's "value choices." A morally good action is based upon a moral principle, a good intention, and an understanding of the circumstances of the action. All three of those elements are needed for morally good activity.

Perhaps the most obvious moral principle in this situation is that human beings are deserving of respect. At a minimum, respect for someone means not violently intruding on a person's bodily life. The twentieth century enshrined the term human rights as the way to express acknowledgement of a person's legitimate demands upon the human community.

The principle of respect for human beings is accepted everywhere, that is, the principle is accepted but not necessarily its consistent application. In the past, some human beings, for a variety of reasons, were excluded. On this point we like to think that we have made great progress in the inclusion of people and no doubt we have made gains. But the human race is still a long way from respecting every human being whatever his or her condition.

Roman Catholic officials prefer to say we should respect "all life." But saying that we should respect life has the danger of being an abstraction. Life does not exist; living beings, human and nonhuman, exist. My focus is human lives; in addition, a respect for human beings implies respect for the human environment of living beings.

I wish to use this principle of respect for each person in drawing a parallel between the beginning of life and the end of life. It would seem likely that there would be connections about how a person begins and how he or she finishes life as a human being. There would likely be one or a few moral concerns that would be relevant to both the beginning and the end of a human individual.

It can now happen in hospitals that we are uncertain whether a human being exists. Here is where a similarity arises between the beginning and the end of a person's life. If in doubt, we should surely proceed with caution. But respect for a person differs from protection of the life process.

We can say with certainty that life begins when the contributions of a man and a woman join in human fertilization. But the coming into existence of a new person can only be judged by external signs of development during the weeks after the beginning of pregnancy. Science can provide help to interpret those signs, but the human judgment of whether a person exists remains fallible.

At the end of life, a person should be respected whatever his or her condition. But it may not be certain that an organism is a person, that is, an organism can be kept alive for many years when it is unknown if it is still a living human being. As is true of the beginning of life, we can only fallibly judge from external signs whether the living organism has ceased to be a person.

Just as the fetus in the early stage of pregnancy may or may not be a person, so also an organism that has been a person does not necessarily continue to be a person when there is heart or brain activity. The big difference in the two situations is that the question at the beginning of life is resolved in the course of a few months while at the end of life the process can go on almost indefinitely.

The end of life poses legal and moral complications that are as great as the beginning of life, but the end has been less discussed than the beginning. Most of us do not like to talk about dying; it inevitably reminds us that we are soon going to die. Whether "soon" means two years or fifty years, we are reminded that the one sure fact of our life is that it will end.

Occasionally, the general public becomes aware of an organism being kept alive for years when there appears to be no reason for continuing the medical procedures, other than a physician's resistance to admitting defeat or a relative's refusal to accept the inevitable. It is praiseworthy that physicians are dedicated to keeping people alive; the law would best not tinker with that role. But the medical profession needs to cope with the unnerving fact that its eventual failure rate is one hundred percent. Everyone dies.

The occasional case that attracts the news media hides the fact of what regularly occurs in hospitals, hospices, and nursing homes. I do not refer to terrible scandals but to what medical professionals and ordinary people need to do in coping with everyday challenges. They must deal with the process that leads to death when death is in the near future but the path to that death is over a darkening plain. It is sometimes said that today a patient in a hospital dies when a physician decides it is time for the patient to die. That is an exaggeration in most cases; what more often happens is that there is a negotiation about the time and manner of death.

One of the strongest movements today that concerns sickness and death is called "physician-assisted suicide." There is controversy about this idea and the controversy is likely to intensify. Similar to what happened with abortion, we are in danger of having two lobbies, each with moralistic slogans, when what we need are open discussions that admit of uncertainty and compromise.

The movement for legalizing "physician-assisted suicide" uses as its slogan "dying with dignity." Who is going to oppose that? There are no proponents of dying with indignity. However, there are people who are horrified at a movement that can casually talk of suicide as a good thing. They say that God forbids suicide; no one has a right to take a human life that is sacred.

Everyone is in favor of dying with dignity and everyone recognizes human life to be of inestimable value ("sacred," however, is a conversation stopper). The phrase "physician-assisted suicide" is not a help. One reason that it is unhelpful is that it puts the physician in the spotlight instead of the person who is dying. Society has a danger of giving over the power of life and death to physicians.

I would acknowledge, however, that physicians do have an import-ant role in informing patients or their proxies about whether a proposed treatment makes sense within the context of a particular patient's condition. For exercising the right of the patients or their proxies to have their decisions based on accurate knowledge, the physician has a place. Here as in so many difficult situations the question is not who has the right to decide but how can there be cooperation between people with different contributions to make. Sometimes patients and their families demand a treatment that is futile. It can fall to the physician to state the hard truth.[16]

The term suicide is misleading in many situations today. The word was coined in the seventeenth century as a morally neutral term to replace self-murder or self-homicide. The first citation on suicide in The Oxford English Dictionary is a 1651 work in which Walter Charleston argues that "to vindicate oneself from inevitable calamity ... by suicide is not a crime." But in time "suicide" acquired all the negative connotations that self-murder previously had. I doubt very much that the term suicide can be rehabilitated for actions that are morally acceptable.

Susan Jacoby writes: "According to a Gallup Poll conducted last year, 72 percent of Americans agree that doctors should be allowed to help end a patient's life painlessly if there is no hope of a cure and the medical assistance is requested by patients and their families. The support drops to 65 percent if the phrase "doctor- assisted suicide" is used instead of "end a patient's life" – yet another case of the American preference for euphemism."[17] But perhaps some of the public recognize a significant difference between those two descriptions. There can be consistency in someone saying patients might be aided in completing their lives, but they are opposed to giving physicians the power to help a person kill him- or herself.

We need different terms to distinguish between the following cases: In the first instance, a ninety-year-old man, who is suffering from multiple diseases and believes that his life is complete, wants a peaceful sleep that brings an end to his life. Contrast that with a forty-year- old man who loses his job and is clinically depressed; he puts a gun to his head and shoots himself. The second case is a textbook illustration of the meaning of suicide. The first case is not about a man "taking his own life" but a man accepting that his body is saying that it is time to die.

The Vatican published an important document in 1980 which proposed that, instead of the language of ordinary and extraordinary means, a better distinction is between proportionate and disproportionate means. It said that a person has "a right to die peacefully with human and Christian dignity." It allowed a refusal of advanced medical treatment for a dying patient to avoid suffering or "burdensome prolongation of life." And stopping life support is not ethically different from not beginning such treatment.[18]

As early as 1958 Pope Pius XII wrote, "It is unnatural to prevent death in instances where there is no hope of a recovery. When nature is calling for death, there is no question one can remove the life support system."[19] It is interesting that Pope Pius XII here makes good use of the church's insistence on not violating nature. The nature that calls here is not a cosmic mother of life but the human-nature of a body that is dying. Whatever is disproportionate to the situation justifies stopping further treatment that may keep the person alive.

It has sometimes been protested that to remove a nutrition tube is starving a person. Certainly, a person has a right to food as an ordinary means of life. But when a person is no longer able to eat and has no desire for food it can be a sign that the body is preparing for death.[20] So long as a person can enjoy a meal, that fact is a good sign that the body still wants to live. But when that desire for food has permanently disappeared, forcing nutrition into the organism can be a violent intrusion. We ought to respect what the person's organism is telling us.

A principle that is often invoked in the care of the dying is that life should not be extended artificially. The principle is presumably meant to exclude technological means to keep an organism alive when there is no hope that the person will ever again function in the human community.

However, merely saying that life should not be extended artificially is misleading; it assumes a simple dichotomy of natural and artificial.

In 2019, the bishops of the Freiburg Conference published a thirty-page instruction saying that euthanasia is "radically against the Gospel message." They used a slogan that is popular in the anti-abortion movement that "a person's life must be protected from conception to natural death."[21] That saying is ambiguous about conception and wrong about "natural death," as an ideal. All of us could agree that dying from "unnatural causes" is not desirable. But a "natural death" is not the alternative. Everyone's life is a combination of the natural – what is given by birth, and human artifice, including technology. All of us live with artificial aids (clothing, houses, heating, water systems). This dependence on artifice inside and outside the body becomes more obvious as one gets old.

If I had wanted to die a natural death, I would have died a long time ago. I started having metal inserted into my body (to save my right arm) when I was fifteen years old; it is still there. In recent years, my heart has been hooked up to a machine in my body; three of my arteries are kept open by pieces of metal inserted by skilled surgeons. Those instruments are not natural to my body; I was not born with them nor did my body naturally produce them.

My case is not unusual; almost anyone my age and older is alive because of the marvelous advances in the use of materials that are not natural to the human organism. I do not wish to die naturally. I prefer that the path to death is eased by liberal uses of morphine or other helps. The ideal is not a natural death but a personal death, one that can include the wonderful creativity of human artifice.

The officials of the church are in danger of simply repeating slogans about euthanasia instead of making some helpful distinctions about natural and artificial. The world is rushing by them. They are right to resist much of what is being done in the name of progress, but general truths are not an answer to decisions at the level of practice.

The Catechism of the Catholic Church says, "the use of pain killers to alleviate the suffering of the dying, even at the risk of shortening their days, can be morally in conformity with human dignity if death is not willed either as an end or a means, but only foreseen and tolerated as inevitable."[22] That is a striking admission: Actions can be morally good even if the death is foreseen and tolerated as inevitable. Millions of people have been confronted with this situation; those people who have not been in this situation will likely find themselves faced by it in the future.

The situations can be endlessly varied, but the principle is the same: humans should be respected, including during the time when they approach death. Aid to dying patients can include actions or lack of actions that have a good intention of alleviating suffering while also hastening the end of life. No rule or law can remove the burden of deciding that a parent, a spouse, or one's child is soon to die and that the best that can be done is something that will hasten their death.

My mother lived for a few years after my father died but her bond was more to the dead than to the living. Her main interest in life was her grandchildren. She was happy taking care of some of her visiting grandchildren up to the day she had a massive stroke. The hospital immediately put her on a respirator to keep her breathing. Brain activity was completely absent. During the night as all her children sat in waiting, I thought I finally understood that night something about the origin of a "wake." It was a quiet time of staying awake to await the arrival of death.

After the all-night vigil by the family, we were asked by the physician what we wished to do. There was no doubt among us that the respirator should be removed. In those days removing a respirator was much debated. I remember asking the physician what the law was in that state; I did not want him to get into legal trouble. He said, "I don't know, and it does not matter; your family should do what makes the most sense." We stepped outside the room and within a few minutes she stopped breathing. If there had been a glimmer of brain activity the decision might have been more agonizing, but the same decision would have made sense. She would not have wished to be kept from completing the act of dying.

When my wife, Maria, died it was after several years of suffering from advanced dementia. People do not die of dementia. Some dementia patients live for a decade or more. My wife had surgery for a bed sore because as the surgeon told me, "if it were untreated, it would mean her demise." The surgery, however, was not successful. There was a recommendation for more surgery.

Her primary care physician spoke to me on the phone about what to do. I asked him if she were untreated would she die of infection? He said that she would. I asked him what it is like to die of infection or sepsis. He assured me that pain could be controlled. We agreed that more surgery made no sense in the situation.

With that phone call we decided that she would die within a few weeks. Was this a case of playing God? I viewed the decision as providing the best aid possible, which now included her dying as an unintended effect. Hundreds of thousands of people are faced with similar decisions in this country. Not to decide anything becomes a decision.

. When I later reflected on my decision, I wondered if I should have made the decision weeks or months earlier. Several times she was rushed to a hospital, a journey that was uncomfortable for her. There was no discernible benefit for her, but the nursing home and the rehab center were doing all they could to keep her alive. She was never going to get better and there was only a glimmer of mental activity in someone who had been a brilliant teacher and writer.

Like most caregivers, I could only think about getting through each day without some calamity occurring. One can easily lose sight of any long-term planning. During the early stages of the dementia we were able to discuss what to do. She accepted her terrible illness with astounding equanimity. She was the one who decided when a nursing home was necessary. However, in the later stages of the dementia she seemed to be living in some other universe. There were no conversations with the living on earth. Were the treatments she received, which were largely the result of my decisions, disproportionate to the situation?

When the physician arrived on the morning of the day that Maria died, I asked him what he thought. He surprised me by responding: "You have been the closest one on the scene, what do you think?" I said I thought the end was near. He agreed but he wanted to check her vital functions. After finding that her kidneys were no longer functioning, he said that there was nothing more to do. I tried to keep her comfortable by helping her to breathe. When she suddenly seemed free of the struggle, I thought I had made her more comfortable. Experienced nuns on the scene realized that she had stopped breathing. They took over from there.

Human decisions are fallible. Medical science has come a long way in a short time. It can provide valuable information about what is going on in the human body. This information can enable moral decisions to be based on a better understanding of what are the options for our own living and dying. It also provides invaluable help when we face life and death decisions for someone else.

Medical science will never be able to replace human decisions that are likely to be more complicated and ambiguous than ever before. Disagreements are inevitable and may increase. One can hope that ambiguous situations will not lead to accusations of murder against people who have tearfully accepted the death of a loved one. Whether one has religious beliefs or not, the decisions are in the hands of human beings who have to do the best they can in situations that outsiders should be hesitant to judge

CHAPTER TEN:

Presence

A threat to the existence of the Roman Catholic Church is revealed in a 2019 Pew Research poll, which found that only one-third of Roman Catholics believe in the "real presence" of Christ in the Eucharist. The Eucharist is at the very center of the church's existence. Attendance at Sunday Mass dropped precipitously after Roman Catholics decided that they would not go to hell for missing Mass. Attendance now depends on church members finding that it is a worthwhile experience for them to attend. The attraction must be at a deep level, if it is to be sustained.

The reaction of most bishops to the poll was predictable. According to Bishop Robert Barron, "It represents a massive failure on the part of Catholic educators and catechists, evangelists and teachers."[1] It is unfair to lay the problem on that group of people. The question of Christ's real presence is not a matter for better catechizing so that people would know the church's teaching. Most of the church's members are aware of the teaching, but it simply doesn't make sense to them. Taken in isolation, the idea of bread and wine becoming the body and blood of Christ is unintelligible. Earlier generations of Roman Catholics were able to believe in the real presence from within a sacred context and in a texture of other beliefs.

The Pew Research poll found that 22 percent of Roman Catholics believe in "transubstantiation." I was surprised that that number was as high. The term "transubstantiation" was introduced by the Fourth Lateran Council (1215) and it was affirmed by the Council of Trent. A detailed study of the history of the term is available in Brett Salkeld's book, *Transubstantiation.*[2] The book shows that a common belief that Thomas Aquinas forced the Eucharist into Aristotle's philosophical language is not accurate. As is true of all Thomas's philosophy, Aristotelian elements are incorporated into a philosophy of participation or a sacramental way of looking at the universe.

A clarification of the original meaning of transubstantiation is important for ecumenical dialogue, but it is doubtful that the term can be made intelligible for most Catholics today. Insisting on the word transubstantiation is not the way to have Catholics understand the presence of Christ in the Eucharist.

The phrase "real presence" can be misleading. What other kind of presence is there? Sometimes people contrast real with symbolic, which is not entirely accurate. The symbolic is real, although it can be real in several ways. A symbol can be an arbitrary sign that is used to stand for something else. That is a symbol without much depth. Symbols can also be the outward expression of something that has spiritual depth; the symbol shares in the richness of what it expresses. That is the sacramental principle that is central to Catholic life. The sacraments, including the Eucharist, are based on this meaning of symbol. Flannery O'Connor wrote of the Eucharist: "Well, if it is just a symbol, to hell with it!"[3] The crucial word in that statement is "just." Is Christ's presence just or merely symbolic so that bread and wine are a stand-in to remind us of something else? No. Is Christ's presence symbolic and real? Yes.

The Roman Catholic Church urgently needs some profound thinking about real presence. There are probably some great thinkers in the church who would be up to the task, but they do not seem to be prominent.

We need a philosopher of the caliber of Gabriel Marcel, Martin Buber, or Karl Rahner to reflect on the meaning of presence.

Presence

Belief in the real presence of Christ depends on people experiencing real presence in their lives. One writer who tries to get at what that presence means is Richard Rohr in *The Universal Christ*: "Only presence can know presence and our real presence can know Real Presence. When Jesus spoke the words 'This is my body,' I believe he was speaking not just about the bread in front of him, but about the whole universe, about everything that is physical, material and yet also spirit-filled."[4]

Robert Orsi's book, *History and Presence*, is related to the topic of this chapter.[5] However, the presence that Orsi is interested in is supernatural beings that confront the human. He reports on an impressive collection of material about the past and present Catholic experiences of the supernatural. The presence of Christ in the Eucharist falls within this experience. However, the presence that he writes about is only obliquely related to the topic of this chapter. Orsi says very little about the meaning of presence in human experience that I argue is the necessary basis for the experience of the Eucharistic presence.

Presence refers to the present or, more precisely, to being present. Human beings are often encouraged to live in the present. But in our common image of time as a line in which the past is behind us and the future is in front of us, the present is not a part of time. It is simply the dividing line between the past and the future. How can human beings live in the present if it disappears at the rate of sixty seconds a minute?

If the past is no longer here, the future has not arrived, and the present is a disappearing point, where is a human being to live? The answer of great philosophers and religious mystics is that one should live in the depths of the present. For them, presence is not a point but a relation. It is a relation not first to time but to other human beings, and through them to the whole world. To be able to live in the present is to have discovered that the present has a dimension of depth.

In this meaning of time, a person stands upon the past, as in the image of standing on the shoulders of our ancestors. Some writers who talk about living in the present mean that we should forget the past because it no longer exists. But the attempt to escape from the past is a bad idea that does not work. As William Faulkner wrote: "The past has never died; it is not even past."⁶ Whatever is in the past must be accepted as the underpinning of the present.

The present has depth because of the millions of people who have gone before us. The Buddhist monk, Thich Nhat Hanh writes: "Our presence here means the presence of all our ancestors. They are still alive in us. Every time we smile, all the generations of our ancestors, our children, and the generations to come – all of whom are within us – smile too. We practice not just for ourselves but for everyone, and the stream of life continues. If you have made mistakes and caused your beloved to suffer, and if he or she is no longer alive, don't be frustrated. You can still heal the wound within you. You can make him or her smile."⁷

The future is a different kind of reality than the past. The future exists only in the possibilities of the present. The future is the source of possible good things and of possible horrors that will never happen. Anxiety about the future can prevent a person from ever living in the present. Humans can influence the future, but they cannot control it. They must act on what to them seems to be the best available choice for the future and not agonize over what might have been.

For anyone who lives a busy life of going and coming, who never stops long enough to wonder at existence, "presence" may be a meaningless term. But while philosophers and mystics may be the writers on presence, millions of people experience what those writers try to convey.

The experience of deep presence is usually in a silence beyond words although that is not to disparage language that is needed to draw near to a wise silence.

For some people, a deep presence is found when they are alone with mountains, oceans, or starry skies but before it is possible to experience presence in solitude there needs to be the presence of one or many human beings. People who lead busy lives, such as mothers of small children, may be mystics among us. People who do boring and tedious work may survive because of the presence of an interior life.

For someone to be genuinely present, there had to have been at least one other human being. Every human baby has at least one person who cared for it; otherwise, it could not have survived. Most people have several family members and friends who bring out their personal qualities and provide experiences of caring, friendship, and love. Anyone who is seriously lacking in such experiences is likely to be distracted by failures in the past and fear for the future. Living calmly and contentedly in the present is unknown to a person who is overwhelmed with regret for what happened in the past or anxiety about what may happen in the future.

Eating and Drinking with Friends

A central activity of sharing life with others is eating and drinking. A "companion" is someone you break bread with. Food and drink are a necessity for existence, but the human act of eating and drinking also has a meaning that goes far beyond mere survival. Other animals eat and seem to find it a pleasing experience, but humans can invest their meals with solemnity or joy. If a family does not at least sometimes sit at the table and eat a meal together, its future as a family is precarious. When friends meet for talk about what is happening in their lives, they very often share a meal and help along the conversation with a glass or two of wine.

Food like other good things in life can be misused. One of the cardinal sins is gluttony, which is usually assumed to mean eating too much. But undereating, for various reasons, can be a problem too. People who have an abundance of food should accept that gift with gratitude while also doing whatever they can to help people who lack food. Sometimes the poor who do not have enough nourishing food are our neighbors. Sharing food with a neighbor can be the beginning of a bond of friendship.

Philosophers who give serious attention to the importance of food, such as the Epicureans, unfairly get a bad name. The human act of eating is not a bad place to begin philosophical reflection on human life. Unfortunately, René Descartes began modern philosophy by sitting alone in a room until he decided that the basis of all knowledge is, "I think, therefore I am." If he had waited a few hours more, he would have said, "I am hungry, and I know how to solve that." Philosophy and ethics might have been based on the relation between the body and its necessities rather than on ideas in a guy's head. The newborn infant instinctively and immediately goes for the source of food. As a person approaches the end of life there is no better indicator of whether the body is ready to die than whether the person can still enjoy a meal.

Drink is a bigger danger than food for being abused. Humans early discovered the pleasure of some beverages that provide a heightened sense of life, at least for a while. Drinking too much of a beverage like alcohol has repercussions in the body and mind. The context is crucial. Drinking alcohol by oneself can lead to deadly addiction. Sharing a bottle of wine at dinner has a built-in control for the amount of drink consumed.

Many religions have rituals of fasting and abstinence. The practices do not imply hatred of food or the body. On the contrary, the temporary restraint is to remind us that food is a gift and that we need to be aware of those who are not as fortunate as we are. Catholics, like other groups, were encouraged to give thanks before every meal (Bless us Oh Lord and these thy gifts...). Lent is still observed by many Catholics as a time to observe some restraint. The best-known Catholic practice of meatless Friday was abandoned in the 1960s. Although that practice probably no longer made sense, the almost total absence of a comparable discipline does not bode well for the Roman Catholic Church's future. Orthodox Jews, Muslims, Buddhists, and Hindus still have dietary laws as a means of strengthening community bonds.

Food and drink play an important role in the accounts of the life of Jesus. Part of the reason for that prominence was simply because Jesus was a Jew of his time. He did, however, seem to give a special emphasis to the importance of food and drink; many of his parables and sayings concern food. Several of his best-known miracles were about food and one of them concerned wine at a wedding feast.

In the miracle of loaves and fishes, as recounted in Mk 8, it seemed to suddenly occur to Jesus and his disciples that there was a hungry crowd that had followed Jesus into the desert for three days. The disciples said that there were only a few loaves of bread and a few fishes. They brought these few loaves and fishes to Jesus who broke the bread and blessed the fishes. There was enough food for four thousand people and for seven baskets of leftovers. It seems unlikely that Jesus did a kind of magic act. It is also unlikely that the people had gone into the desert without any provisions. The miracle perhaps consisted of the disciples going through the crowd and persuading those who had an abundance of food to share what they had with their neighbor.

The many times that Jesus shared food with his disciples led up to a last supper the night before he died (Mk 13: 22). The disciples seemed to sense that there was something special about this meal. Jesus clearly wanted them to remember that evening. So he took bread and pronounced the strange words "this is my body." And stranger still were his words over the cup of wine, "this is my blood, which shall be shed for you." Then presuming that the disciples would meet for many meals like this one, he said, "do this in remembrance of me." The ritual received a first test with the disciples on the way to Emmaus after the resurrection (Lk 24:30). The disciples were impressed by their conversation with this stranger. But it was only at the breaking of bread that they recognized who this person was.

Body and Blood

A human being is a bodily being. The body hides much of what makes up a person. Nonetheless, the body is what a person presents to the world as a visible and acting self. We share bodily delights. And when something terrible happens to a friend we may not know what to say, but bodily presence is a crucial support. In *Waiting for Godot*, Didi says to Gogo: "Don't touch me, don't question me, don't talk to me, stay with me." Technology can be a big help today in providing an oral and a visual connection between friends and family members. But nothing can substitute for the bodily presence of a loved one.

A person begins as a tiny body some months before birth. A baby does not look like much at birth, but the potential is almost limitless. Among the animals, humans are the most helpless at birth, dependent on the care of a mother and the kindness of strangers. The men who produced the *Declaration of the Rights of Man and of the Citizen* wrote that "men are born free." I doubt that any mother would have written that line, having seen the condition of the newborn infant. What the infant does have is an awareness of the universe. The entire unfiltered world rushes in. All being is present and nothing else will be added, although the individual will spend a lifetime sorting out differences within unity.

From the moment of birth, the human baby is bodily present to anyone in its vicinity while the baby itself lacks awareness of its own presence. Self-awareness will bring all the joys and sorrows of human existence but that will require years of development. The human will must consult the bodily senses before deciding on a path for the self. To live in the depths of the present the body cannot be either dismissed as irrelevant or forced into submission. The body must be won over as a quiet ally in the journey to the center of the self.

One ability of the body that is neglected in philosophy is laughter. Meister Eckhart warned against a supposedly spiritual person for whom laughter does not lie at the center of spirituality.[8] Mary Midgley says that some cultures try to restrain laughter, "but far from showing they do not naturally have it, this indicates quite the contrary. They want to subordinate it to some other good. And however solemn the adults, laughter is found among healthy children everywhere."[9] A person who lives in the present can laugh heartily, especially at him- or herself. When we are chuckling in the present, it is impossible to regret the past or worry about the future. A person who never laughs does not know what it means to live in the depths of the present. A person who does not laugh cannot be trusted in political office.

Blood is the indispensable life force that flows throughout the body. The heart cannot take a timeout in pumping blood to the brain. Any injury that results in a great loss of blood is life-threatening. The anthropologist Loren Eiseley recounts how after an injury, which left him bleeding, his immediate instinct was to apologize to his blood. It is our precious friend that we must protect.

The donation of blood, especially to a stranger, is an extraordinary symbol of the unity of the human race. It is amazing that after any disaster there is a rush of volunteers who wait in a long line to give their blood. I am intensely aware when I have received blood that I have been given life by someone whose name I do not know. One of those occasions is indelibly printed in my memory. I was so anemic from cancer that I could barely reach the hospital. The transfusion lasted many hours during which I was fully awake. The nurse stayed with me the whole time. I marveled that everyone in the room was receiving a gift of life from a stranger.

Sexual Life

Sexual intimacy can be a deepening of the presence of a loved person. In other animals, sex is simply a drive to reproduce the species. Sex is not a constant preoccupation of nonhuman animals. In humans, sex is for reproduction, but it is much more. At its best, sex is the way into one of the most intense and genuine experiences of presence in someone's life. The joining of two as one can give a glimpse into the deepest mystery of human existence.

Because sex is so powerful, it requires discipline and restraint. A person may become entirely taken up with the pleasurable aspects of sexual activity and never get to its more profound meaning. Self-pleasuring is a harmless activity, but for men it can become addictive and create unrealistic fantasies of sexual relations. An undisciplined person can be preoccupied with pleasure and not be attentive to his or her partner. Sexual fantasies and sexual desires completely dominate many men's lives. Without healthy human relations, the expression of these desires can take a twisted or a violent form that further isolates the person.

Until the middle of the twentieth century the Roman Catholic Church's official teaching on sexual matters exercised a rigid control of Catholic lives and even beyond to the rest of the society. When change came it was in the form of a collapse of any agreed upon rules other than what counts as consent. There are still laws to protect children from sexual predators, but given the lack of restraints on sexual activity the line that stops at children is, not surprisingly, regularly violated.

The Roman Catholic Church in its effort to stem the tide of this sexual upheaval has made church teachings a target of ridicule. What is tragic is that the church may be right in resisting a revolution of mores that had been in place for centuries. Changes were overdue but on a matter which is as profound as human sexuality revolutionary speed could be dangerous. The human race may still be ignorant of the mysteries connected to sex so that as a result contemporary wisdom about sex may still have its blind spots.

What is also tragic is that church officials failed to listen to what was genuinely new learning about sexuality. The church was still insisting in the twentieth century that the only purpose of sex is reproduction and that the only moral use of human intercourse was between married people who do not prevent the act from bringing about pregnancy. Human sexuality was thus reduced to the level of sex in every other animal, that is, the meaning of sex is for reproduction.

In 1968, Pope Paul VI dithered over whether to change the church's teaching on contraceptives. His encyclical was dead on arrival. Whichever side he had come down on, the decision would have split the church. The church had a problem that it was incapable of talking about; church officials still cannot discuss sex. There was an almost total rejection of the pope's continued ban on "artificial contraception." There were and still are people who demand that every Catholic assent to the ban. But poll takers do not find many Roman Catholics whose practice reflects such a belief.

The most obvious case in which church officials failed to learn what most of society was suddenly confronting is homosexuality. Gay and lesbian people are one of the most persecuted minorities in history. In some parts of the world homosexuality can still get you killed. In the gospels Jesus does not indicate any fear about two of his apostles possibly engaging in sexual activity. *The Book of Leviticus* (18:22) (20:13) has the clearest condemnation of two men having sex but there was neither the idea nor a word for homosexuality. The men were to be put to death.

The church had a wonderful chance to rethink its attitude on homosexuality as part of rethinking its sexual code. Homosexuality could have been an entrance into seeing the wonderful diversity that is human sexuality. That would have aided understanding of what has now emerged in the discussion of transgender individuals.

Sex should be one of the greatest helps to the experience of presence. Most people may not reach the depth of union, which two people who love one another ideally attain. But any depth is helpful. In contrast, a stunted sexual life, which for many men seems frozen at about age twelve, is a definite obstacle to experiencing the presence of any person. The reality of love can be judged by whether the love shared by two people opens them to respect and care for every human being. Their presence to each other can create a sense of presence to humanity and to being itself.

The sense that we have at certain moments of life that we are related to the whole world is impossible to put into a verbal description. The sense that we carry the universe within us is beyond all rational calculation. We are regularly told these days that human beings are an infinitesimal and unimportant part of the universe. But the humans are not a speck in nature; nature was invented in the human mind and exists because there is a human mind. Unless and until other intelligent beings appear, the humans are the center of all intelligibility. If there is a reality greater in importance than the humans, it is not millions of miles of space. A greater reality would have to possess the qualities of a "who" not a "what" and be smarter and more skillful than the best of the humans.

The Presence of God

What do Christians mean when they say, "we are in the presence of God"? If one tries to imagine what that prayer means, we are likely to produce only a childish picture of a big being in the sky who has extraordinary eyesight to watch over each of us. That image is what eighteenth-century deism/theism gave us and it is still with us. We know that the image is a false one but people who loudly proclaim their atheism seem to be imagining that picture for the God they don't believe in. Noam Chomsky has remarked that he would be an atheist if someone could tell him what God he is not to believe in.

The presence of God is the experience of the depths of presence in which we realize that we have barely begun to grasp the mystery of existence. We inevitably live most of the time on the surface of reality as we move through our mundane existence. But there are moments, if one is attentive to them, when there is an opening to a level of being that we are usually oblivious of. It can be a moment that is profoundly shaking such as the death of a close friend. But it might also be the scent of flowers or the sound of a voice that throws open the mind to a usually hidden universe.

My own experience of a deep presence occurs when I regularly visit a community of Christian Brothers in Rhode Island. The experience can be called private because it is only mine, but it is an experience like that of numerous people past and present. The building that I visit was constructed as a novitiate and is now put to good use as a school for young men who would otherwise be put in prison.

I have been associated with the place since it was built in 1959. There is a plaque with my parents' names at the front of the building; there is a room on the second floor that has my wife's name. The office on the first floor is where the provincial council met when I was provincial. When I walk down that corridor, I always half expect a brother named Andy to appear. Brother Andrew was my novice director in 1954. In his last years, he was technically my secretary, but he was in fact my greatest supporter and my secret weapon in any argument.

I left the brothers thirty-five years ago, but all the retired brothers there treat me as if I never left. They have forgotten or have forgiven me for some irresponsible years. I am deeply indebted to the brothers for the education I received and for the friendships that have endured for a lifetime with current and former brothers. In the chapel prayers I am present to myself because I am present with others whose lives I deeply respect. Morning prayer begins with, "Let us remember that we are in the presence of God," which signifies to me the community of brothers.

I regularly visit the cemetery on the property. On one occasion while I was sitting there, a couple drove up; the woman had brought flowers to put on a grave. While she was doing that, the man walked over to me and said, "Do you know someone who is buried here?" With only slight exaggeration, I replied, "I know everyone here." I suspect he thought I was someone who had wandered into the place or maybe someone with dementia. But to me the names on the headstones are a main part of the communion of saints that brings together the past and the depths of the present.

Religious people seldom talk about God; they certainly are not foolish enough to try to describe God. Even to use the word God is close to blasphemy. The "presence of God" is most accurately referred to as the experiencing of the limits of one's awareness together with the acceptance that there is reality beyond what can be imagined, thought, or spoken.

Christ and Eucharist

Some religions, including Christianity, have a more intimate name for this greater reality but it is a name to be spoken only in the setting of prayer. That is where the Christian language of the presence of Christ or the Spirit of Christ comes into play. In the context of prayer, the "presence of God" in a Christian form is expressed concretely in a community acting in the name of Jesus the Christ.

Richard Rohr writes: "Christ's sacramental presence in the Eucharist was, we might say, an intensification of his sacramental presence in the world."[10] It is the experience of presence at its most profound. The real presence of Christ in the Eucharist depends upon the experience of the believers who are the Christian community. If there were no believers, there would not be a Eucharist. Christ or the Spirit of Christ is present in the church community not in the sense of what William James called the "will-to-believe," but as the deepening of the presence that is always there. The meal of bread and wine is the symbolic expression of that (real) presence.

The locating of the real presence in the community may sound at variance with the church's teaching. However, in the first centuries of the church the real presence of Christ was said to be in the church. Jesus said, "where two or three are gathered together in my name, there am I in the midst of them." He also said that he had to leave but that he would send the Spirit to be with his followers. The Eucharist is the presence of Christ not the presence of Jesus.

In the early church era, the Eucharist was called the "mystical body" of Christ. Mystical does not mean unreal; instead, it refers to a mysterious depth. In recent centuries, the "mystical body" was used as a metaphor for the church. Pope Pius XII wrote an encyclical on the mystical body (1943). I remember laboring through its prose in high school religion class. I think the "mystical body of Christ" is a rich image for the church, based on Paul's *Epistles*. Each organ of the body has an important part to play. The body has a head, but it depends on the cooperation of every other part.

The church as "the mystical body of Christ" seems to have fallen out of use. That is a shame. The fact that it has almost disappeared has a significant relation to the lack of belief in the (real) presence of the Christ in the Eucharist. The Eucharist is the real and mystical presence of Christ because the church is the mystical body of Christ. In Thomas Aquinas's philosophy of sacramental presence, "the true Body of Christ is also the sign of his mystical body, which is the church."[11]

The bishops at the Second Vatican Council in the document on the church surprised everyone by looking first at the church as a whole or what they called the "mystery" of the church. They referred to the members of the church as "the people of God," a phrase which was an immediate hit. I thought "people of God" was a terrible choice of terms that did not bring out the organic character of the church. The phrase "people of Christ" would have made some sense, referring to the people whose faith is in the Christ.

The "real presence of Christ," that is, the presence with the greatest depth, is found in the Eucharistic meal which is integrally linked to the scriptural readings. The scriptures are the symbolic "word of God." The homily is intended to be a few words of commentary on the readings by someone in the community who has reflected deeply on the words of scripture. Priests are not necessarily good preachers. Many congregations have church members who could occasionally deliver a good homily.

The meal of bread and wine is the central religious act of Christians because the most basic affirmation of life is eating and drinking. The church, following the example of Jesus, uses bread and wine that are staples of life. Wine is an intoxicant, which can be abused, but wine can also rouse the spirit and inspire the community. Richard Rohr writes: "In the act of drinking the blood of Christ at the Holy Meal, you are consciously uniting yourself with all unjust suffering in the world, from the beginning of time until its end. Wherever there was and is suffering, there is the empathy and sympathy of God."[12]

If the "real presence" of Christ is found in the Eucharistic meal, what does that mean for the many rituals and "sacramentals" that grew up as extensions of the central act? The answer depends on whether they have an integral relation to the Eucharistic meal. In the middle ages and the early modern era, devotion to the "blessed sacrament" sometimes overshadowed the Eucharistic meal.

Many people who call themselves conservative resisted the changes in the liturgy made by the Second Vatican Council. But the Council's emphasis on the Eucharist as a meal was a conservative move, a restoration of the original meaning of the Mass that had been obscured by some devotional practices. A traditionalist should welcome the emphasis of the presence of Christ in the community by the sharing of the Eucharistic meal.

The Mass had been looked upon by many Catholics as a ritual to produce the hosts for communion and for veneration. In the middle ages some people would come into church for the solemn moment of consecration.

The saying of the words of consecration became an isolated and magical moment. Enemies of the church coined the term "hocus pocus" from the words of consecration. (Hoc est …).

A devotion such as "Benediction of the Blessed Sacrament" was a gathering of church members who at least sometimes were aware that they were extending the Eucharistic meal. But as the practice of venerating the host moved to such things as the Corpus Christi procession, the devotion to the host bordered on the superstitious. However, the practice of bringing the host to a sick or an aged person is an appropriate way to connect an individual to the community's experience of the real presence in the Eucharist.

The corona virus crisis has forced the church to radically change its practice. What will emerge as a result during the next decade will either be an improvement of liturgy or a further decline in many people's meaningful engagement in liturgical prayer. Unless there is imaginative thinking and bold experiments by the church leaders, decline is more likely than improvement.

A true leader will enlist the best minds and most creative artists of the church to try out new forms of liturgy that put community and presence at the center. The Second Vatican Council taught that the Eucharist is a meal. To be sure, it is a sacred meal but nonetheless a real meal in which a community sit around a table and pass the food and drink to each other. There is a place for a person to preside over such meals. That is the role of priest, which needs to be carefully rethought in the Roman Catholic Church.

During the pandemic, Catholics were actually forbidden to go to church. For some people, this experience was one of separation from church and prayer. Modern technology became the imperfect means for keeping some connection to others and to the Eucharistic ritual. Perhaps this experience will make people reflect on what the point is for gathering with others in a building called a church and physically participating in a ritual of eating and drinking.

Television has long played a part in bringing the Mass to millions of people. My mother had been a daily communicant until she was physically unable to go to church. The daily Mass on television was a great comfort to her. I remember arguing with a prominent theologian who ridiculed the television Mass as not liturgy at all. For many old and sick people, their sense of community through televised liturgy is genuine.

Most Roman Catholics still think of the church building as filled with the presence of Christ. The presence of Christ and the Spirit is attenuated in the church building but the believer still experiences a presence there. The place where the Eucharist occurs retains a sacredness for many people. That attitude deserves respect

CHAPTER ELEVEN:

Community

This chapter addresses what is a central question about the nature and condition of the Roman Catholic Church. Is the church communal in its structure? The question and answer refer to whether the people who make up the church come first, and that any office of authority is at the service of the people. Or is the church a typical pyramidic organization intent on selling its "brand" and its product? For an organization of over one billion people the challenge of having and maintaining a communal structure may seem impossible to meet.

We can examine how the church has succeeded in the past, however imperfectly, in providing a communal experience and to imagine what the possibilities are in a "globalized" church where the interdependence of people has become evident.

The previous chapters have described a massive change in the Roman Catholic Church. There is a widespread feeling that something important was lost. Those of us who are old enough to have lived through the period of 1945 to 1970 often say that what has been lost is a sense of community. Even people who enthusiastically approve the changes brought about by the Second Vatican Council often look back nostalgically on a sense of community that they remember from their childhood.

Is that memory of Roman Catholics faulty? Before one can judge whether there has been a loss of community, some exploration of the idea of community would be helpful in determining whether there was a Catholic community and whether it has largely disappeared.

The Nature of Community

The term community is now used with little attention to any precise meaning, but it usually has connotations that distinguish its use from that of a group, organization, or a political division. "Community" is related to "communion," a word that was coined to express a relation between human beings. The relation of communion can exist at many levels. At the most profound level, a human being has a drive to enter intimate relations with one other human being.

The physical part of a sexual union is shared with other animals, but the human experience of communion involves the whole person. The union with another person includes the hope not to lose one's own distinct existence in such a relation. Communion is the promise of a union that differentiates as it unites. Far from ceasing to exist, individuality is enhanced by communion with others. At least that is the hope and promise of communion.

"Community" at its best would be supportive of communion or a place where many communions flourish. Community requires more than two people but if it is to retain some degree of communion among all the members, there is a strict upper limit to its size. In a community everyone would know everyone else. They would know not just the names of everyone but know others with a personal depth.

For everyone to interact in a community, the upper limit to a community is about eight to ten people. The reason is simple arithmetic. In a set of x elements, the number of combinations (a to b, a to c, ab to c) is 2 to the n power plus 1 (3 elements 9 combinations; 4=15; 5=31). The number of combinations rises almost exponentially as elements increase.

The steep climb as the numbers increase is illustrated by the story of a man who wished to stay at a hotel for a month. He is offered this deal: the first night will cost one cent; then the amount will double each night; two cents the second night, four cents the third night, eight cents the fourth night, and so forth. He thinks that sounds like a good deal and readily agrees. At the end of the month, he gets a bill for thirty million dollars.

This mathematical principle when applied to a community means that the number of possible interactions among eight people is a manageable two hundred fifty-five but among twelve people it is four thousand sixty-three. There is a line in the area of eight to twelve, which when passed means that a community has become multiple communities or else the community has been replaced by a different kind of organization.

The communion between two people is properly called love. The two lovers feel as one but if the love is genuine they become more themselves. The trivialization of sexual intercourse does great harm to the beauty and special character of intimate sexual love, but real love still survives in millions of lives.

The love between members of a family, while not achieving the full depth of communion, is nonetheless one of life's greatest gifts. Every time in life that we experience community is also a gift. A demand that each person love everyone in a community is too much to ask. What a community does require is understanding, respect, concern, and care among all the members.

It can be expected but not planned that there will be friendships in a community. Friendships is a form of communion that can be of varying degrees. A colleague at work or a neighbor might be counted as a friend, although we might not know many personal details about his or her life. The deepest friendships approach the intimacy of love. Ancient authors, including Aristotle and Cicero, wrote treatises praising friendship as indispensable to human happiness.[1] Like most things valuable in life, deep friendships need care and cultivation. They take time to grow and, if not cared for, they can wither and die.

Women and men seem to maintain friends in different ways. No one can say which is the right way. Men's friendships seem to exist on a superficial level, but it has been a surprise to me that men can resume a friendship after many years. In more than a few cases I have met men whom I have not had contact with for twenty, forty or fifty years and we picked up the conversation where we had left it. I think the condition for that survival of friendship is that the friendship was developed within a genuine community.

From my limited knowledge of how women are friends, they seem to maintain a steady contact in ways that few men do. Women might talk on the phone almost daily or meet for lunch every week. Men are often content to be in touch with a friend every few months when there is a game or a movie that interests them both.

The whole human race would ideally have some of the qualities that are found in friendship and love. There would be care and respect among all people even if the deepest friendship and intimate love among everyone are not imaginable. Until very recently the human race was not confronted with the need for all its members to accept the great variety of the human. People lived in one part of the world and were unconcerned with or ignorant of how people lived somewhere else. When encounters did occur, it usually resulted in one group gaining control and treating the other group as humanly inferior. At their worst, human beings have killed each other to maintain their version of being human.

Progress was indicated by the seventeenth-century invention of the concept of tolerance. The term has a mostly negative meaning. What is tolerated is allowed to be even though it is not something that one approves of or agrees with. There is no general tolerance that a person can assume in all situations. Tolerance requires some knowledge, however superficial, of what one is tolerating. No doubt tolerating one situation is usually helpful to having that attitude in a similar situation. However, sometimes people who think of themselves as tolerant are shocked that in a new racial or religious situation they discover an intolerant streak within themselves.

That the human race is still characterized by ignorance and intolerance among its members – all its members to varying degrees – is not surprising. It takes time to get to know everyone even at a superficial level. But the time is limited before the human race could destroy itself out of ignorance, distrust, and miscalculation. Education is in a race with calamity. Many politicians, economists, and international experts work to maintain conditions of peace and cooperation. But nation-states and business corporations are not designed to enhance friendship and love.

A community is a microcosm of the human community if it embodies some of the variety in the human race. It is unrealistic to expect that a single community can be diverse in sex, gender, race, religion, age, and other characteristics. In fact, communities usually originate from a focus on one or a few such characteristics. Every community therefore confronts strangers who are "not like us." The big test of the community's genuineness is how it treats the stranger. It cannot immediately embrace the stranger as a member of the community, but it is imperative to treat the stranger with respect and care.

Jesus's teaching to love our enemies has often been ridiculed as impossible. But Jesus was very specific in saying "love to your enemies," something that included doing good to them and praying for them. The *Sermon on the Mount* proposed a revolution in ethics, but it was also a practical program. Jesus did not preach to millions of people. He mostly instructed the community of a dozen apostles whose limitations are obvious.[2] Every community is wounded by human failure, but it can nevertheless be a pointer to a greater human unity.

Roman Catholics in U.S. History

Community is a resistance to individualism in which the individual is supreme. The United States of America is known for being an individualistic country. The description applies at least to the politically and economically powerful classes. The waves of immigrants that have been a regular part of U.S. history typically gathered in their own neighborhoods and retained what community and culture they could bring from their country of origin. The culture included the group's religion and in very many cases that religion was Roman Catholicism.

The British colonies that formed the United States of America were not friendly to Roman Catholics. The nation was an uneasy alliance of secularists and Protestant Christians. Both groups viewed the Roman Catholic Church as foreign and suspect. The country needed immigrants for its development, but much of the native population worried about the fact that the religion of so many immigrants was Roman Catholic. An "American" was defined by the immigration law of 1790 as "free, white men." Each immigrant group, including the fair-skinned Irish, were originally judged to be not of the white race.

The Irish came in great numbers, especially in the 1840s when conditions in Ireland were dire. Anti-Catholicism in the United States proportionally increased in the same period. The Irish gathered in the large cities on the east coast and in the Midwestern United States. Ireland had been a stronghold of Roman Catholicism, so it is not surprising that in this foreign land the church became a central institution not only for worship but for social services.

Other immigrant groups, especially from eastern and southern Europe were also strongly Catholic. Each of these groups looked to the church for support and protection. The big difference in these later groups was that they did not speak English. They sometimes formed their own parish for speakers of French, Spanish, German, Polish, Italian, or Greek.

The priesthood and the episcopacy, however, were controlled by the Irish until the middle of the twentieth century.

Despite the cultural and linguistic differences of its members, the Roman Catholic Church became a main force in the "Americanization" of immigrants.[3] The immigrants believed in the idea of America and believed they were coming to America. They were disappointed when they found that they were in the United States. They were faced with living in terrible housing conditions and were forced to work in menial jobs. Almost half of the immigrants turned around and went back to where they had come from. The immigrants who stayed in this country believed that life would be better for their children and grandchildren. Except for blacks and native Americans, their hopes were generally fulfilled.

The Popes and the Roman curia were happy with the growth of the church in the United States, but they were wary of an American Catholic Church. There were experiments in lay ownership of church property. In the late nineteenth century, as an American Catholic Church gained strength, it took on some features of the budding progressive movement in the country. Pope Leo XIII's encyclical, *Rerum Novarum*, in 1891 gave support to the laboring class, and Bishop James Gibbons gave his backing to the Knights of Labor and labor unions.

By the end of the century Rome was fearful of "modernism," the attempt of some Catholic thinkers to come to terms with the contemporary advances in the sciences, and modern life more generally. In 1900, Pope Pius X published a condemnation of what was called Americanism, although the pope did not identify by name anyone in the United States. The condemnation reverberated for decades in the Roman Catholic Church of the United States.[4]

The U.S. American branch of Roman Catholicism did not produce many great scholars. It concentrated on building a school system that would preserve the faith of the masses. The training of the clergy in seminaries, which were separated from universities, was more concerned with orthodoxy than scholarship. Most Roman Catholics stayed in the big cities where the local parish was a center of life. The pastor of the church was a powerful figure who could command attention to the needs of the church or warn of threats from the larger society.

Roman Catholics were not welcome in the elite professional schools. Success in law or medicine was difficult to attain. They were more welcome in what one sociologist named "semi-professions" or what people in this work prefer to call "helping professions." School teaching and nursing attracted large numbers of Roman Catholics. The women were prominent in the primary schools, the men helped fill the ranks of the secondary schools. Irish Catholic women were especially prominent in nursing; the men went into the police and fire departments. Most notably, the Irish found their way into urban politics and often became powerful leaders in local politics.

Despite their large numbers and their success in some areas of work, Roman Catholics in the early twentieth century felt discriminated against. Many good jobs were not open to Catholics. There was a definite ceiling to their political ambitions, a fact that was partly responsible for the corruption in urban political machines. Discrimination against Catholics in law schools and medical schools became more subtle in the twentieth century but it remained.

Large families were a source of joy but also economic stress. Catholics strongly supported the parish, especially its parochial school. Any mixing with "non-Catholics" was frowned upon by the clergy. Participation in a Protestant service or even entering a Protestant church were forbidden. To miss Sunday Mass was a grave sin; thus, as a result the churches were overflowing every Sunday morning.

That was the Catholic Church that some of us can remember. It was the church we were born into and simply took to be a fact of life. In the wake of World War II, there were changes working their way into the church and the U.S. society around the church. It took some time, however, for these changes to become evident. Most of us were shielded from the hard times of our parents and grandparents. The nuns in the school and the clergy in the parish shaped our world view in which "the faith" provided us with strength and consolation.

Oppressed people are pressured to form a group to defend whatever their difference is that brings about oppression. A "community" can form around race, religion, or sexual difference. Some communities are formed around an interest or a hobby that strikes other people as trivial or strange. Holding meetings, gathering at conferences, dressing in a different way, and using semi-secret language are typical elements of community existence. People whose way of life is different from the surrounding society stay together as a means of survival.

The ultimate oppression in U.S. history was the slavery of black people. The slave system in this country broke up families and large numbers of slaves in any location. The slave holders knew that it would be dangerous if slaves were allowed to congregate and form communities of resistance. Slaves were forbidden to gather in large groups; preachers among the slaves were especially feared.

Until the middle of the twentieth century history books assumed that the slave holders had succeeded in destroying the family life of the slaves and the gatherings of slaves for their own worship services. When historians finally attended to the testimonies of the slaves themselves, they discovered writings that reveal that the slaves were able to maintain family connections and that they gathered for worship despite the risk of a beating for their disobedience.

The black church has remained a main support for the descendants of slaves in their struggle for equality. At present, the music and preaching in black churches is the strongest evidence of a living Christianity in the United States.

When large numbers of Catholics in the middle of the nineteenth century were struggling to attain decent living conditions, there was inevitable conflict with blacks who were engaged in the movement for their liberation. Two oppressed groups would profit by joining forces but that is seldom what occurs. The two groups are more often pitted against each other. The draft riots in New York City during the U.S. Civil War pitted black people and Irish immigrants.[5]

The Roman Catholic Church in the United States has never been welcoming to black people. There are churches today where black people are comfortable or are a majority of the congregation but that is not the main narrative. The Roman Catholic Church, to its own misfortune, remains overwhelmingly white. It has benefitted from the great influx of Hispanics who have traditionally been Catholic. Immigrants from Puerto Rico, Mexico and South America continue to enliven the present U.S. church. But the church has been in danger of losing many of these people because of a lack of attention and care.

Sexual behavior that is different from the surroundings society is a characteristic that binds people in a community. For centuries gay men formed bonds that they kept secret from the larger society. When gay men mobilized as a social force in the late twentieth century, the groups that emerged were said to be a gay community. There was support of members even beyond the nation. A distinct culture became possible when gay men were a visible force. When a rebellion of gay men against police harassment occurred in 1969 it was made possible by the concentration of gay men in Greenwich Village.

The demand of gays and lesbians for the right to live their lives like everyone else has been strikingly successful. By the fiftieth anniversary of the original uprising, there was general acceptance of gay men and lesbians, something almost unimaginable in 1969. Of course, there is not universal acceptance of such things as same-sex marriage but, the change of attitude among the general public has been surprising. The tolerance of homosexuality is not worldwide but the most severe practices of discrimination seem to be on the wane.

The paradox of such a community is that the more successful its members are in being accepted by the outside world, the greater are the forces of dissolution. If the only bond of a community is opposition to the outside world, then success can reveal that community did not exists at a deep level.

The term community has a positive meaning for most people so that calling your group a community is a way to give it protection and self-esteem. But it also trivializes and weakens the concept. Even groups that are united only by hatred and criminal activity call themselves a community. No group wishes to be known as a "bunch of thugs." The Ku Klux Klan or the mafia thinks of itself as a community, which has loyalty within the group and a mission toward the outside world.

Loyalty is not a word that is common in a community. In corrupted versions of community, there is demand for loyalty to the leader. Loyalty is a virtue when it is directed to a cause or an organization. Loyalty is not the same as friendship. The relation between friends is one of respect, care, and affection. A demand for loyalty would be suspect. In recent times, loyalty to a religious cause has largely been replaced by loyalty to the nation-state. Unless challenged by other loyalties, including that of religious communities, the nation will make dangerous demands upon its citizens.

Religious Community

Religion plays a complex role in relation to community. It often overlaps with the struggle of groups to preserve their language. That was clearly the case for immigrants to the United States from countries that had a large enough population to form a sub-culture of their own, such as Mexicans, Poles, and French Canadians. As the children became acclimated to their surroundings, especially in learning to speak English, there was inevitable tension between the generations.

Religion, like nationhood, is a glue that holds groups together but by that fact it also separates people into opposing groups. Nationhood can be divisive to the point of nations fighting wars over what may seem inconsequential issues to outsiders. Multinational groupings can show that national differences can be lived with and can even be enriching. The world is still at an early and precarious stage of nations working together and the people of many nations gathering together for peaceful objectives.

Religion, however, includes divisions of the human race, which do not seem able to be overcome. When the word religion was coined at the beginning of the Common Era it referred to the (true) worship of God. There could only be one religion; other practices were idolatrous. Any opposition to Christianity was called heresy or paganism, the rejection of the one true religion. Islam made a claim that was like Christianity's. The Islamic *umma* or community was the true religion that completed the Jewish nation and the Christian Church. Islam and Christianity inevitably clashed and the stakes were so high that the conflicts were fated to be deadly.

In the late sixteenth century, a new possibility was opened with the use of "religion" for institutions that house worship and made a claim upon a person's ultimate commitment. Henceforth, there were to be a multiplicity of religions starting with Protestant religion and Catholic religion to which were quickly added Jewish religion and Muslim religion. Catholic and Protestant were soon folded into the Christian religion as one of the world's religions.

The religious community is a small group of people who are joined by shared rituals, common beliefs, and caring individuals. Even if the religious institutions of Islam and Christianity conflict, that fact does not mean that Christian and Muslim communities within those institutions are necessarily enemies. If the religious community's beliefs include kindness and help to the stranger, then there is a meeting ground for people of different religious communities. A genuine community is intent on retaining its beliefs and rituals but not to the detriment of others. If a community is based on distrust or hatred of others, then its self-description as a religious community is of doubtful validity.

There is some danger that a religious group can think that its differences of food, dress, or speech are what constitute the community. The union of the members must be based on something deeper, but the defenders of rituals are right in their insistence on rituals that distinguish the group. The practice of such rituals when a member is separated from the group tests whether there is a community and whether the individual is one of its members.

Dietary rules are often a badge of belonging to a religious group. The rules may seem idiosyncratic and irrational but that is intrinsic to their distinguishing the community. Dietary rules are a constant reminder of the community and one's membership in it. Jews and Muslims have their dietary restrictions that orthodox members always observe.

The Second Vatican Council's elimination of Friday abstinence from meat was a bigger change than most people realized. The anthropologist Mary Douglas wrote that the bishops' attempt to replace Friday abstinence with love of neighbor showed that the traffic signals were being manned by color-blind people.[6]

Catholic Community

The Roman Catholic Church makes the claim in its name that it is already catholic. "Catholic" means universal. Why does the word universal exist? In what context does it make sense? The universal seems to be a claim that something exists everywhere and at all times. Can any finite object qualify as universal?

The meaning of a word can usually be clarified by asking what its opposite is. In the case of "universal," its opposite seems to be the particular. Everything that exists seems to be a particular thing. Even if one were to add together all the particular things, one would get a multitude of particulars but not a single universal thing.

Scientific method, as conceived in the seventeenth century, is a search for the truth by applying mathematics to the measurable aspects of experience. A minimum number of cases needs to be tested before the scientist can draw a general conclusion that – practically speaking – always holds true. Any scientist should be able to get the same conclusion by replicating the same conditions. If pressed, the scientist must admit that the conclusions are not universal truths but mathematical generalities.

A logic of art, which applies to religion, involves a process that is different from that of science. Artistic logic is not a search for a general conclusion. The arts cherish individuality. Art is likely to be the product of one person or a small group. What is surprising, sometimes even to the artist, is that millions of people may find a resonance in a particular work of art. The poetry of Shakespeare or the music of Mozart might reach people in any place and any time.

In the sciences, the process is one of going from individual cases to general conclusions. The movement of the mind is upward so as to leave below individual characteristics. In artistic and religious areas, the search is by an opposite movement, which goes deeper into particular cases. The particular cases remain while a universal – or more precisely a nearly universal effect – is realized. The universal can be approached but it is never realized.

Concerning artistic understanding, Wittgenstein wrote, "that the place I really have to get to be a place I must be at now. Anything I might reach by a ladder does not interest me."[7] Wittgenstein asks: How does someone understand a Mozart symphony? His answer: By listening to a symphony by Mozart. Then, by listening to it again. After several more listenings, one might listen to other symphonies by Mozart and after that one could compare a Mozart symphony to one by Beethoven.[8]

The Roman Catholic Church should not declare itself to be the Catholic Church. The descriptive adjective catholic is part of its mission not a present accomplishment. It is inevitable in intramural conversations that Roman Catholics refer to themselves as Catholics. But in documents addressed to the outside world it is helpful for church officials to acknowledge that the church is a religious body striving to be catholic rather than claiming that it encompasses all Christianity or all religion. Until the 1960s, Roman Catholic officials would not use the term church in referring to Protestants. The acceptance of Protestants as having a share in the universal church implies that the Catholic Church does not exist but is still a hope for the future.

The Christian Church did not begin as one organization among many similar organizations. Jesus had commanded his followers to go to all the nations of the earth. The church was to be representative of the entire human race and to be a light to all the nations.

A church was a gathering of people. The first church could have met around a table where the members enjoyed conversation and shared a meal. As in any community, there was almost no organizational structure. But the success of the Christian community meant a multiplication of communities. If there was to be a unity of the church, some beginnings of an organization were needed. There were people who had particular roles within each community and people whose job was to keep the communities linked in a single organization.

Even at the end of the second century a description of the church did not involve organizational complexity. Tertullian in addressing Romans who were suspicious of outsiders, described the church as "a body (corpus) knit together by a common confession, discipline and hope." He then described what Christians did at their gatherings: "We offer prayers for the emperor and all in authority; we read sacred writings and exhort one another to live virtuously; we place gifts in a common chest for those in need; we celebrate a common meal and lift our hands in praise and supplication."[9]

Even for so simple a gathering of people, a few roles were needed as the community identified charisms or gifts that people had received, which could serve the good of the community. Early church literature identifies three such positions: servants, elders, and overseers. "Servant" did not have the demeaning sense that it has had in modern times. The servants or deacons took care of the physical needs of the community. Elders contributed age and wisdom to the community. The last post of overseer (*episkepoi*) evolved into the role of bishop. There is no indication at least until the end of the second century that each bishop reigned over his own diocese.[10]

The success of the Christian Church in attracting new members guaranteed the emergence of a complex organization. But that fact did not determine the shape that the organization would take. One determining factor was that the church moved from the status of outsider to becoming officially sponsored by the government. An even more important factor was a belief that the church was guided by the Holy Spirit as it developed and spread. Nonetheless, the Holy Spirit had to work through human agents who were fallible in the choices they made and did not make.

The single most important organizational development was the rise of a clerical class to run the affairs of the church. The prayer leaders of the communities who read and commented on the scripture became the elite group. They could guide the many converts who lacked education. New members were only required to know the Lord's Prayer, the ten commandments, and the main elements of the story of Jesus' life, death, and resurrection. What had been fluid roles in a community now became permanent positions in the organization. The cleric or clergyman was an office holder who assumed power for decisions that affected the church's organization.

The great majority of baptized members were simply the people of the church or the laity. The word laity (*laos*) did not originally have a negative meaning, but as the underclass in a two-class structure, "laity" took on the meaning of people who were lacking in skills or knowledge. The church became composed of readers and nonreaders.

The Christian Church taught this meaning of laity to the modern world. The rising professional class in the nineteenth century found "laity" to be a useful word. Professionals are experts in their discipline and laity are clients (people who "lean on them"). Today the Christian Church is probably the only organization that keeps trying to give a positive meaning to the words lay and laity. The project has long since proved impossible. Community is obstructed by the existence of a two-class structure.

The division of the church into two classes is not in the New Testament. Neither was such a split preordained by the spread of the church and the need for organizational structure. It must be granted that the emergence of classes was seemingly inevitable because of the organizational models that were available for imitation. But if the Holy Spirit was guiding church life, one might have expected a more radical experiment in organizing large numbers of people in a way that did not run counter to the community of a dozen people.

The church did offer some resistance to the autocracies around it. But the original flaw in the church's organization was that the church was a men's club, that is, an organization in which the men became the leaders. What is amazing is that the Roman Catholic Church continues to be an organization in which all the "ordained" leaders are men. One might excuse the original flaw; there were no good models to imitate. But if it was to be "new people" for all the world to look up to, the relation between women and men should have been rethought, if not in the first centuries, then surely in modern times. No true community can exist today without a mutuality of women and men.

CHAPTER TWELVE:

Community of Communities

The title of this book, *What Happened? What Now?* contains a promise to provide the first steps for addressing the problems that affect the contemporary Roman Catholic Church. In the previous chapters that focus on a church problem I have suggested some of what needs to be done. The reform pertaining to several issues involves changing the teaching on human sexuality. I have noted, however, that the official church's attitude to sex is embedded in the structure of the church. In a more democratically structured church, with more voices that could be heard, sexual attitudes would change.

I am not so naïve to think that I or anyone else could propose an alternate structure that would be adopted by an institution that has existed for two millennia. However, that long history contains possibilities that were turned down in the past but may be worth exploring in the present and future.

I have suggested that the most important guiding principle for the church is its earliest form. Jesus of Nazareth, who is called the Christ, did not leave a blueprint for an institution that aims to continue his mission. There are documents attributed to his closest followers, which give us a picture of the earliest form of church. There are other documents that did not get the early church's approval. Some of these documents have only been discovered during the last century and are still in the process of being studied.

The earliest form of church was a group of people sitting around a table. A church that believed it had a mission to spread to all nations; obviously, it needed to develop an institutional structure to do so. Some features of that structure may have been inevitable, but others were not. I noted the remarkable fact that for more than a millennium there was no writing on the nature of the church, that is, treatises on ecclesiology. When such works did appear in the middle ages, they were influenced by the form that the church had already taken along with existing models of institutions. The adoption of the word hierarchy to mean steps upward from subdeacon to deacon to priest to bishop set a direction that has never been altered.

This four-step hierarchy was a development from a much earlier split in the church between a clergy and a laity. That division seemed necessary because the church had succeeded in attracting new members, many of whom lacked education. Those church people who could read became the instructors of those who were illiterate. It should not need pointing out that this condition no longer exists.

What is indispensable for radical change is a change of language. People often understand this demand to mean inventing clever new phrases. The main change needed is to get rid of language that obstructs thinking. The change should be in the direction of simplicity; in most cases it should be language that is borrowed from the church's own history. I have pointed out a few examples in this book, some of them are good terms that have become corrupted in the course of history.

The first step in a radical reform of the church would be to eliminate the clergy. The move is not as drastic as it may sound if one first distinguishes between "clergy" and "priesthood." The role of priest is found in many religions and the Catholic Church would not be recognizable without people exercising the function of a prayer leader. But a permanent class called the clergy is an historical development that can and should be changed.

How could such a distinction come about? It will never happen by an announcement that the church is eliminating the clergy. My suggestion has been that a step in the right direction, which could be taken immediately as a conservative move to deal with the shortage of priests, is that the church could ordain some people as temporary priests. After serving for a specified time, perhaps ten years, these priests would be replaced by others. The initial step would probably be only for men, but it might soon be apparent that women would be obvious candidates as well. What starts as a temporary move to shore up the present structure could prove itself in practice and become a permanent arrangement. A different structure for the church without "clergy" or "laity" would be on its way. The two-class structure that is a hindrance to community would be gone.

Before a further consideration of the kind of organization that the church needs, it is helpful to examine the activities that the organization should facilitate. As can happen with any institution, the press of daily events and ordinary upkeep can obscure what the institution was founded to do. A movement in the direction of a community of communities should be in service to the essential tasks of the Christian Church.

The Church's Internal Activities

Embodied in the church's mission is a sacramental principle that stems from its understanding of Jesus as the Christ. The principle has its roots in the Jewish belief in a Creator God, the Holy One who is beyond names. The material world manifests the presence of the divine. The "spiritual" in the best of Christian thinking is not at war with the body. The spiritual is found by going deep into oneself and by appreciating the beauty of the human body, the panorama of living beings, and the daily events around us.

From the beginning of its existence, the Jesus movement embodied this attitude in its basic acts of worship. The word sacrament was imported from Roman practice, and it proved to be a useful term for the church's main activities. Peter Lombard in the tenth century was probably the first person to specify that there are seven of these sacraments. The Council of Trent agreed with that number. The line that was drawn at these seven activities was somewhat arbitrary. All the liturgical uses of the material world that signify the presence of an inner grace can be called sacramental.

The genius of Trent's seven sacraments is that they form a pattern in the journey of a person from birth to death. Some of these seven are more important than others. The Reformers generally reduced the number of sacraments from seven to two: Baptism and Eucharist. These two sacraments do have a primacy.

The church has the ritual of baptism to admit a new member. It was a point of conflict in the Reformation whether baptism should be administered to babies or should be restricted to a person who was choosing to become a church member. The Roman Catholic practice of baptizing infants was tied to removing "original sin" lest the child be in danger of going to limbo. That does not carry much weight today, but baptism as a family ritual when there is a new baby seems to make sense. Baptism of the baby can be an occasion for a family to renew its own commitment to the church's work.

The church separated Confirmation from Baptism to make it a second sacrament for teenage commitment. A ritual for commitment to being a Christian seems appropriate but locating the profession of faith in adolescence does not seem realistic today. If there is to be a ritual for someone to become a church member, it should probably be when someone is an adult. Confirmation, if it is retained, might be administered at any age.

The Eucharist, which means thanksgiving, is the central Christian prayer that recalls the past, celebrates the present, and looks forward to the end. Attendance at Sunday Mass became the main test of whether one is a Catholic Church member. Unfortunately, when the obligation to attend (under pain of mortal sin) no longer was convincing, attendance drastically declined. There was a failure to make celebration of the Eucharist a communal experience with attention to the people and to artistic performance.

The Second Vatican Council in ordering the priests to preach every Sunday made a terrible mistake. Priests should have been forbidden to preach until they became sufficiently learned in the New Testament and took lessons on how to speak effectively in a public setting. Furthermore, other people in the community could often do a better job at preaching than the priest does. There is no necessary connection between priesthood and preaching.

Celebration of marriage was included as matrimony in the seven sacraments. Perhaps that sacrament should be expanded in imaginative ways, including a ceremony for courtship and a blessing for divorce when a marriage fails. Marriage could be celebrated in several stages. Perhaps the full celebration of marriage should be reserved for after twenty-five or forty years of married life, whenever it seems certain that the marriage is permanent.

The church will eventually have to accept the reality of same-sex marriage. Its acceptance throughout much of the world challenges both church and society to reflect on the nature of marriage. Same-sex marriage in some ways echoes what the church recognized as a marriage before the Council of Trent imposed a set of ecclesiastical rules. Marriage for gays or lesbians is constituted by the consent of the two persons. The same should be true of straight marriage. The phrase "marriage equality" applies to all marriages in which men and/or women are equal partners.

The sacrament of Penance, "going to confession," seems moribund for most Catholics these days. Confessing one's faults is a good and holy practice; but the Roman Catholic Church needs a different form than the confessional box of the past. When some attempts were made to move from individual to group confession the new ritual did not make much sense to people. Groups such as Alcoholics Anonymous (AA) learned from the church the value of confession, forgiveness, and mercy. These groups might now show the church how to structure individual confession within a community setting.

The sacrament of Holy Orders needs a complete overhaul. Perhaps it is not needed for the ordaining or electing of priestly leaders. Some kind of ritual is appropriate, whether or not it is part of a sacrament. For those priestly leaders who are elected bishops a solemn ritual should no doubt continue the practices of the early church. The titles of monsignor, archbishop and cardinal could be retired with no loss.

The sacrament of the sick and dying, I noted earlier, could still have an important place in the church. Any of us could use a friend and counselor when we are nearing the end. That need not be a priest. The preparation and appointment of a community member for such a task might be a way in which the church could be of great service. I do not know whether anointing someone makes sense, but the use of oils does perpetuate rituals that go back to ancient times.

These major rites could still be meaningful for people. There are other prayers such as saying the rosary and Benediction of the Blessed Sacrament that were largely abandoned at the time of the Second Vatican Council. Many Roman Catholics found the transition too abrupt and resisted almost all liturgical change. Perhaps the split in the church was unavoidable but it is nevertheless regrettable.

The reason for the seven sacraments, and "sacramentals," may have been obscured in the struggle for appropriate reform. The church's internal life is for the interior lives of its members. There is not much point to church practices if they do not lead to lives of generosity, kindness, and love.

The Church's External Activities

The liturgical practice of sacraments and sacramentals points the way to the practices of its members that are external to the church. There are many ways one might spell out what constitutes the main outward activities of the church. One way is with the still relevant language of the corporal and spiritual works of mercy. The two lists should not be sharply separated. In a sacramental church, all these practices are corporal-spiritual. The list of corporal works has traditionally included: feed the hungry, give drink to the thirsty, clothe the naked, shelter the homeless, visit the sick, and bury the dead. The spiritual works of mercy include praying for the living and the dead, comforting the afflicted, and admonishing the sinner.

These works of mercy come directly from the Christian gospel. Followers of Jesus of Nazareth should be responsive to a call to serve, "the least of my brethren." The church at its best has been known as an institution that serves the physical as well as the spiritual needs of vulnerable populations. Millions of church people continue to engage in such activities, usually outside the glare of publicity.

At the beginning, a church was a small group of people who met weekly to remember the life, death, and resurrection of Jesus. They were also known as a group that cared for those who were in need. These many groups were strung together in a movement that aspired to be worldwide. The tireless missionary, Paul of Tarsus, travelled East and then around the Mediterranean to oversee the many churches.

Throughout its history, the Christian Church has struggled to be a social not a political group. The church, against all odds, survived. It did so not because of monarchical bishops but because there were enough Christians who cared for the young, the elders, the sick, the poor, and all who were vulnerable. In the plagues that devastated Rome in the second and third centuries, the Christians were the ones who stayed and nursed the sick and dying. Other religions in Rome did not have a founder who had taught his followers to be "merciful as your heavenly Father is merciful."

There is no lack of opportunity in today's world for anyone who wishes to engage in these works. None of these activities has become outdated. Despite the progress of modern times, there are more people than ever who need these ministries. Some people today work in organizations that serve these needs of vulnerable people. Christians who do not have these activities as part of their daily work have to find ways to make them part of their life.

It is important that some people engage in these practices in a direct, face-to-face encounter, placing the food before hungry people or handing out clothes to people who need them. People who work in large organizations can lose touch with what these practices mean in the lives of the people whom they are serving.

Someone might object that these practices of mercy do not define a church because other religious and nonreligious organizations engage in similar activities. This fact counts as an advantage rather than a drawback. It is a sign that the church is contributing to the catholic religion whose full reality is still emerging. The distinctive motivation and institutional support of the church is what makes the practices inherent to Christian activity.

The Christian church would be continuing what it learned from the 613 *mitzvot* of Judaism. Most of these practices can be found in other religious institutions, including Islam and Buddhism. The Christian is called to join with all those whose work serves the good of fellow earthlings and their relation to the Holy One.

Organizational Reform

Reforms in the Roman Catholic Church that are passionately advocated, such as ordaining women or endorsing gay marriage, would probably improve the current institution but they would not get to the radical restructuring of the church that is required.

Developments over the centuries were inevitable and there is no way to duplicate today how the church looked at the time of its beginning. Developments in the history of the church produced both good results and distortions. That history is reflected in the medieval saying *ecclesia semper reformanda est,* which translates as "the church is always in need of reform."

At the time of the Second Vatican Council, Roman Catholic scholars sounded the same cry as the Protestant reformers had used: "Return to the sources." For Christian Churches that means above all a return to and a reliance upon the New Testament. The New Testament understandably cannot provide a picture of what a worldwide church two thousand years later should look like, but the two versions of church should not be in contradiction. Roman Catholics and most Protestants also claim in different forms another ecclesiastical source called "tradition."

There is a major difference in the way Roman Catholics and Protestants use the term church. Protestants regularly call church what Roman Catholics call parish. By the term church Roman Catholics usually imply the panoply of offices and the worldwide institution. Neither Protestants nor Catholics linguistically connect the big institution and the small group of people who gather for worship. In their use of "church," Catholics leave out the small dimension, Protestants leave out the big one. This ambiguity is the source of endless confusions. Ecclesiastical reform is impossible if one cannot name clearly what needs reform.

The solution to this difference between Catholic and Protestant language is the idea of community that can carry the meaning of both a universal ideal and a particular embodiment of that ideal. Every small worshipping group has to embody qualities of a universal community. And since a universal community is an ideal not a reality, the institutional links between these particular communities has to have some of the same qualities as the particular communities. Hence, the goal of a community of communities is the closest the church can come to being the Catholic or universal community.

A serious problem of the Roman Catholic Church is that\ nearly all references to "the Catholic Church" are a reference to the pope and bishops. It makes sense when referring to an institution's position on policies that the officials speak for the institution. But a problem can arise when the members of the organization have no voice, a situation that is indicated by the linguistic conflation of the institution and its officials. The Roman Catholic Church is not the only organization in which the membership does not have a say in official pronouncements, but the problem has been especially acute there.

The earliest use of the word church as a small gathering of people echoed similar gatherings in Jewish history and assemblies in Greek political life. The distinctive Christian *ecclesia* was a gathering of followers of Jesus of Nazareth. The people were held together by a specific cause with beliefs that drew upon a long tradition to which the Christian movement gave a new shape. Protestants and Catholics can probably agree that whatever subsequent meaning that "church" has, it should not eliminate or contradict this original meaning.

A group of ten people around a table seems to be an ideal form of church. The reason that this meaning did not become permanent was largely because of the church's success. The earliest followers of Jesus understood that he commanded them to spread his message to all nations. The small community of followers set out to replicate the original community in distant places. They probably could not have imagined how difficult it would be for the small group to morph into a large organization that could retain the same care, love, and dedication as that of the small group.

The Christian Church laid claim to being "a people" that was not based on ethnic, racial, national, or geographic origin. Was it naïve to think that an organization of such a people was possible? The people were to be united by worship of the nameless God who was responded to by the Jewish people. That history was given a surprising twist by the Jewish people's greatest prophet, the man from Nazareth.

The life of Jesus conveyed the paradoxical message that power is revealed in what appears to be weakness. The death of Jesus was proclaimed to be not the final word. Somehow that message of triumph survived, and it was conveyed to future generations by a community that embodied the belief that power is best manifested in a sharing of life with other people.

Unfortunately, the Christians failed to construct an organization that could retain a sense of community and an exercise of power as mutuality. Experts in group dynamics say that the ideal size of a community is eight to eleven people. Above that number, the members of a group need rules that specify procedures and someone who applies the rules. The problem begins as soon as a group adds just a few members. As one commentator has said, "We have failed to learn what Jesus of Nazareth was at some pains to show, namely, that twelve is one too many."

The organization first feels like a family; but over time – with success in its mission – it starts to feel like a soulless machine. The people at the top still speak as if the organization is one, big happy family; the people at the bottom increasingly feel that their work is not valued. Mike Abrahov used his experience in the navy as the basis for describing most institutions as like a tree of monkeys. Looking down from the top of the tree all one sees is smiling faces; looking up from the bottom of the tree one gets a different view.[1]

Church offices developed as they were needed or seemed to be needed. As soon as communities became more than a dozen people someone is in charge, and one or several people would have tasks of ministering to the group. For keeping communities joined in a common mission, leaders had to be appointed or elected.

A Democratic Church

A truism of Roman Catholic bishops is, "of course, the church is not a democracy." One might respond: Why not? If one means by a democracy that every member has a voice and vote on every issue, then the church cannot be organized that way. But neither is any nation-state or large corporation this kind of a democracy. What is usually meant when people talk about democracy is that an organization has a set of procedures that show respect for each of its members and has provisions of voting for representatives on issues that not everyone can directly address. The Christian Church can and should have such organization if anyone is to believe its claims.

At the beginning of Pope Francis's encyclical *Laudato si* is this surprising sentence: "Not all doctrinal, moral or pastoral issues need to be settled by intervention of the magisterium."[2] What the pope seems to endorse here is that an official teaching of the Roman Catholic Church, such as its teaching on birth control, can be effectively changed by the people with no help from the bishops. The question now is how to reconcile the bishops' teaching with what has been decided by the people who are directly involved.

The clerical sex-abuse scandal is a symptom of a problem with the current structure of the church. Current proposals of reform do not go deeply enough into the way that the church is organized. A system cannot be changed easily or immediately, but there can and should be an immediate start to dealing with the problem.

Pope Francis has said: "A time limit should be established for roles in the church, which are in reality a form of service ... It would be opportune for all roles of service to have a time limit – there are no lifelong leaders in the Church."[3] That is a surprising statement from the head of the church that ordains twenty-five-year-old single men for life. If all roles in the church should have a time limit, that principle includes the papacy. Pope Francis's predecessor, Pope Benedict XVI, showed the way by resigning from the papacy.

Pope Francis and the bishops have declared that the church has a problem with "clericalism." No doubt they are right. The only sure way to get rid of clericalism is to eliminate the clerical class. For eliminating the two-class structure, the step that can be taken immediately is to ordain priestly leaders for ten years.

Almost fifty years ago the sociologist Andrew Greeley proposed a "priest corps" with renewable appointments of five to ten years.[4] In my proposal, the exception could become the rule. After serving in the role of priest, a person would return to a non-official position without undergoing the current "reduction to the lay state."

Many priests in recent years have acknowledged that clericalism is a problem and they have urged their fellow priests to get rid of the attitude and practices that make up clericalism. I sympathize with these men and do not wish to belittle their efforts. But clericalism is inherent to the present system of men who promise never to have a sexual life; who are sent for education to a segregated place called a seminary; who are ordained to be the sole leader of an organization composed of "laity;" who live from contributions from the people whom they are to serve; who dress in ornate clothes; who are addressed with a paternal title; and who live in a provided residence next to their work. A priest who might be described as non-clerical would have had to resist almost every element of this system. Miraculously, some priests seem to do so but they should not have to live with such resistance.

Several authors have proposed eliminating priesthood.[5] But that would seem to eliminate something essential to a catholic church. Priesthood is an important element of Roman Catholic life and prayer. The Reformation did not attempt to eliminate priesthood but, on the contrary, open it to everyone. That seems to me the right direction and to be more feasible now than it was at the time of the Protestant Reformation.

Priestly and prophetic are useful ways to describe aspects of a Christian community. The two functions are in some tension. The priestly side looks inward and to the past, the prophetic looks outward and toward the future. One person in a community might have the talent to be a priestly leader while another person might be more inclined to be a prophetic leader. The larger institution would try to identify people who are talented for each of these roles to serve in an office for a specified length of time.

There would likely be a need for other offices of "ad-ministering," particularly for linking all the church communities. Today's technology makes a worldwide connection of communities feasible without constant expansion of layers of bureaucracy. A person might continue in a role for more than one term, but no one would immediately be appointed for life. The principle should be that church offices are open to every member, although not everyone will serve in every role.

I described earlier the collapse of the religious order, which had been an important part of the Roman Catholic Church for many centuries. I thought it was possible to imagine the religious order and family life coalescing into a new kind of religious organization, a community of communities. In recent years, there have emerged problems with marriage and family life that have parallels with the religious order, especially the issues of community and permanence.

Religious communities of the future should have an ideal of permanence, but most individual cases will turn out to be temporary. That is true of many communities today that should not be judged failures; they may have served a good purpose for a time. A community of communities should be permanent but not all its elements need to be. The church needs a great diversity in the forms that communities take; some will be more long-lasting than others.

Throughout most of its history the church has been organized by place. These local organizations were called parishes, a word that means a local unit. The small church or parish is supposed to be the universal church in miniature. But the parish, instead of being a communal expression of the great community, tended to become just the local subdivision of the large organization. Some parishes may succeed in actually being the Christian Church in miniature but to do so requires going against the current.

Place has been and remains an important element in human existence. When the monastic order emerged, the monks took a vow that included commitment to the monastery. The world is still organized by states, that is, the place that a government controls. But in the United States and much of the rest of the world today, a person's residence is only one important characteristic for the experience of community.

Organizing the church by geographical units is not an imaginative way of creating a community of communities. The religious order began to break from being organized by place when the Order of Preachers and the Franciscans went to where the need was. The Jesuits accelerated that movement as did the "religious congregations" that followed.

The Roman Catholic Church became one of the first international organizations. It had the potential to be a mixture of communities of varying size, place, ethnicity, race, sexual orientation, and permanence. But up to the 1960s the church was composed of parishes that were described by the number of families that they contained, and the "religious community," which was composed of unmarried individuals of one sex. Anyone who did not fit into one of these categories was a church outsider. The leadership of the church is still intent on affirming only these two kinds of community, even though most leaders themselves (priests, bishops) do not live in either of those communities.

The family, meaning a unit of parents and children, still deserves a special place in the church. Children need stability and the church has rightly insisted on the sacred bond that unites father, mother, and children. But the church has yet to admit that marriage has other meanings. Many people marry for companionate love, which can have fruits other than children. Those unions include both heterosexual and homosexual couples.

A community life in the contemporary world is bound to have a certain fluidity. There are many organizations today that take account of where people work or where they play. Even before the Second Vatican Council, the Roman Catholic Church could not count on Sunday being a day of rest and prayer. Extending weekly participation in the Eucharist to Saturday evening was a good move. But church leaders did little else to encourage involvement in church practices. Saturday Mass became just a convenient way to get Sunday obligation out of the way.

Larger organizations can do what an individual community cannot. For example, there is a need in the United States for an organized protest against unjust policies of the government. The joining of many smaller communities is needed to have a significant effect. Unity should be achieved by the joining of communities but not under a monarchical bishop.

Experiments must be tried to find what succeeds and what fails. Today's world of instant communication and educational possibilities offers a different challenge and greater possibilities than was true a thousand years ago or even fifty years ago when the Roman Catholic Church began its aborted reform.

The church as a worldwide organization needs to be a model of how a "people" on a great lifelong mission is organized for the long journey. The feeling of support and enthusiasm one can get in a community of eight or ten people should be enhanced, not smothered, by belonging to an organization of millions.

Authority in the early church was vested in the church as a whole. There were overseers or bishops from the beginning of the church, but their mission was to serve the inner life of the members and maintain the sacramental unity of the church. A fundamental change was signaled by the adoption in the seventh century of the term "jurisdiction," which was a political term for the exercise of control over people's lives. "Office" that had signified a duty to serve the people became a property to which money was attached. This power of governance was always in danger of becoming corrupted, but a bishop could still be seen as a representative of the people and to some degree limited by them.

A need for more order seemed apparent and a few popes of the tenth and eleventh centuries took charge by concentrating power in the papal office. The pope was not only the first among the bishops but now claimed to be the source of the bishops' power.[6]

Latin authors borrowed the term "hierarchy" from Greek mystical writings. Dionysius had coined the term hierarchy, meaning a "sacred order," to describe the movement of the angelic choirs around God. In contrast, the ecclesiologists used "hierarchy" as an organizational term. Church offices were imagined as steps upward in a holy order.

The church was organized not as a circular movement around a center, as the term hierarchy suggested. Instead, authority was imagined as located in an organization that had the form of a pyramid. "Hierarchy" became central to a Roman Catholic description of church offices. And in the nineteenth century Roman Catholic bishops themselves began to be called "the hierarchy," which makes no logical or historical sense. One cannot begin to imagine a different structure for a hierarchical organization if one group is called "the hierarchy."

Modern organizations inherited the term hierarchy from the church and equated its meaning with bureaucracy. That form of organization can be efficient for doing some kinds of work, especially work that can be divided into pieces and does not require imagination or novelty. In bureaucratic organizations power runs from top to bottom. Each individual is responsible for doing his or her job in accordance with instructions from the office that is immediately above. The man (usually) who is at the top of the pyramid speaks for the whole organization.

The more successful an organization is, the more confining is the pyramid of authority. Facebook has two billion clients; is the man at the top supposed to manage all the uses of Facebook? Can a Pope in Rome rule more than a billion Roman Catholics? At one point, Pope Francis said that he took on the responsibility for all the sexual sins of the priests. That is not the way responsibility works.

If the church is to be hierarchical, that term should be distinguished from bureaucracy. Some church organizations may function well as bureaucratic in form, but the overall pattern of church authority should be of hierarchy imagined as circular rather than as layers of a pyramid. Power would move in and out rather than up and down. At the center would be the life of Jesus as revelatory of the divine. Circling that holy order would be a community of communities that would continue the mission of divine incarnation in history.

An image that is not heard much these days, the "mystical body of Christ," is much more appropriate for the church than is a pyramid. The human body is testimony that millions of cells can function as a unity. The Roman Catholic Church claims that Jesus assigned a special role to the apostle Peter. For much of its history, there was no dispute within this church that the pope is the head of the church. But there are contrasting ways that he (or she) could be the head or the final authority of the church. The pope could be seen as a king with no limits on his power. The pope could also be a constitutional monarch with powers specified by a constitution. Or the pope might be understood as always acting within a consort of advisers whose authority must be respected. In this last image, the ultimate authority for the church is a general council within which the pope is head of the body.

From the first days of his papacy Pope Francis caught the attention of the world with his moves to get rid of the pope's monarchical trappings. He has continued to do things with the seeming purpose of de-absolutizing the papacy. Personal style includes how you dress, how you are addressed and how you address other people, how you travel in your daily journeys, what, where and with whom you eat, what your residence is, how you acquire and spend money, what you laugh at, and other details of ordinary life. Pope Francis has been attentive to such details.

The Pope managed to change the attitude of millions of people toward the Roman Catholic Church. Pope Francis has already had a longer papacy than Pope John, but he seems acutely aware that his time is short and that he wishes to establish a direction that will be difficult for a successor to reverse. The pope's success depends not merely in divesting himself of the personal symbols of a monarch but of eliminating the Vatican bureaucracy's stranglehold on church affairs and his appointing of new bishops who might carry on the work of reform.

A question that was raised in the twelfth century was what should be done if the pope is an obvious heretic or is otherwise unfit for office. The absence of an effective head was the situation in which the church found itself in 1378 when there were two (and eventually, three) claimants to the papacy. The church was divided between factions in Rome and in Avignon, France. This "great schism" lasted for forty years before a gathering of church leaders at Constance acted to appoint one legitimate pope. Beyond solving that immediate problem, the Council of Constance tried to create constitutional principles for the better functioning of the church. Central to its concerns was the meeting of general councils at least every ten years, even if not called by the pope.

On what authority did the Council of Constance act? It appealed to the original organization of the church and to the experience of the church in its first millennium. This "conciliar theory stressed the corporate association of the members of the church as the principle of ecclesiastical unity and envisaged the exercise of corporate authority by the members of the church even in the absence of an effective head."[7]

What may once have seemed to be a medieval dispute over some obscure theological point is actually central to the question of the nature of the Christian Church? A dispute between "high papalists" and conciliarists existed until the Council of Trent. In fact, the agonizing delay in calling that council was related to the concern of having to grapple with this dispute. The Council of Trent was able to affirm the pope's supreme power although it was not until the First Vatican Council that the regal pope as the form of church government was finalized. During the nineteenth and early twentieth centuries, the conciliar theory of church governance was consigned in history books to the fourteenth century.

Histories of the church often explain the conciliar theory as an ad hoc necessity, which was used once and then quickly put aside. But some twentieth-century historians saw the conciliar movement as reaching back to the early church and offering for today's church a theory for a different governance than rule by an absolutist pope. The leading historian on this issue, Brian Tierney, writes that conciliar theory was "a logical culmination of ideas that were embedded in the law and doctrine of the church itself."[8] The regal pope is a form of church government that was finalized only in the nineteenth and twentieth centuries. It is not an appropriate form of government for the twenty-first century.

The point of recounting this history is to show that quite radical changes in the way that the church operates can be compatible with tradition. People who call themselves conservative often seem to take the nineteenth century as the standard of the past. A conservative Roman Catholic should presumably be interested in the whole history of the church. Sometimes the fourteenth century or the fourth century may be more relevant for today than the sixteenth or nineteenth centuries.

The long history of the church makes it a unique organization for saving some of the pomp and ritual of the past while combining that with experiments in democratic procedures for all its members. A church of the future could be a new kind of organization that learns from past mistakes in both the church and secular society.

Pope John XXIII's Second Vatican Council almost inadvertently revealed the need for the church to open discussion about the nature of the church itself. The Council's document on the church, *Lumen Gentium*, was a start on reform. Like what happened in the fifteenth century, a 1970s reaction reasserted the pope as absolute, even though Pope Paul VI's encyclical on birth control had undermined papal authority and split the church.

Not until Pope Francis began divesting himself of the trappings of a monarch did the possibility of a democratic constitution reemerge. Francis tried to re-invigorate episcopal synods but bishops talking to each other will never get very far. Their mishandling of the clergy sex-scandal is indicative of the need for the church to have systems of accountability. The pope should long ago have called a general council that might be more ecumenical than any prior councils.

The Second Vatican Council had "experts" who assisted each bishop, something that was a move in the right direction. The Synod of 2014–2015 had the bishops on their own and the results showed why that was a bad idea. The "Third Vatican Council," or a council with a more appropriate name, should look more like the gathering in Constance in 1411 than councils since then. If the church were to use its own talent it could organize a cross-section of people from every walk of life to begin thinking about the organization of the church. It would be only a first step in a long journey that will require regular councils at different levels of the church.

The main principle of governance should be that community should be the structure at every level. The church should usually be composed of about ten people, although some parish churches of fifty or a hundred people might sometimes be appropriate. Organizations larger than that are not a community. The hundreds of thousands of churches would need to maintain a unity using electronic media, visiting between churches, and gatherings of many churches for some events. At the most inclusive level, the general or ecumenical council including the pope, would embody the final church authority.

A genuinely ecumenical gathering would include more than bishops and their advisers. It should be representative of all baptized members. The governing of the church by a general council may be more realistic now than at any time in the past. In such a government, official teaching would not be by majority rule, but members should have their experience drawn upon through forums and regular channels of communication. Not all decisions need to be based on voting by all members, but representation and voting should guarantee a voice for members.

Education in Religion and Religions

No reform can succeed without education. The religious order is a warning to the larger church. As members become better educated, some of them are likely to leave or have already left the organization. The solution is not to restrict education but instead to use the talents of everyone for creating a better organization.

The church's future depends on the education that it provides. Throughout most of modern history that statement was understood to mean that the adults should pass on their beliefs to their children. The work was done in schools presided over by a teacher. In advanced societies, schools have become complex institutions in which young people spend most of their time.

In a community of communities, education would differ greatly from today's picture. Unfortunately, the language of education is stuck in the nineteenth century. The church is an appropriate institution for challenging the assumption that "education" is equivalent to schools and that schools are normally places for children.

For teaching a religious way of life the teachers have never been confined to schools and the learning has not been restricted to the school's kind of learning. Parents were the main teachers of the young whether or not they realized that they were teaching, that is, showing someone how to do something. Religious learning needs to continue throughout the whole of life; otherwise, one's religion is likely to become a burden and a source of guilt. Or some men who are prominent in public life have acquired a fixed worldview in their Catholic high school years and are certain that they know the way that things should be. This problem has a distinctly male bias.

Education in the first few years of life is the most crucial part of anyone's education, even though most textbooks on education do not even recognize education as extending to infancy. Someone who has been lovingly cared for as an infant has a powerful advantage in life. Parents teach by "parenting," a recent and useful verb. Mother and father can make their distinct contributions to the child's openness to the world, including openness to a reality greater than what is in the infant's immediate surroundings. Christian doctrines are not the stuff of childhood, but mythical tales, invisible companions, and daily rituals enrich a child's religious experience.

On the other side, a person who has a narrow or abusive experience in childhood might find remedies later in life, but life is difficult enough without adults suppressing the natural exuberance of children.

When it is time for instruction in religion, an intelligent practicing of the catholic religion today requires knowledge of one's own religion and some grasp of the many religions in the world. The first form of religious education – teaching to be religious – occurs in the practice itself as guided by what the Roman Catholic Church calls catechetical instruction.

This education in religious practice, was never a good fit for school and classroom. The worshipping community is the appropriate setting for teaching by the performance of liturgy. Not only the one who presides at the liturgy but others who perform roles such as homilist or music director are also religious teachers.

The second kind of teaching – teaching religions – finds its appropriate setting in the classroom. Many secular universities as well as religiously affiliated colleges have departments of religion. Adults who have not been to college may not get much exposure to this kind of teaching, but every citizen needs some knowledge of how religions affect the world. In this kind of course, the stance of the teacher is a neutral observer; all religions are given a fair hearing.

A complement to this study of religions is the study of the religion of Roman Catholicism. A parish today or a gathering of communities in the future has a responsibility to provide some courses or structured discussions of the Roman Catholic religion. This kind of teaching is clearly distinguishable from catechetical formation.

The aim of the teaching of the Roman Catholic religion is to understand the religious elements of the church and to criticize what does not seem to make sense. The structure of the church, the philosophical assumptions of its doctrines, and the relation between Catholic moral teaching and contemporary science, should be critically examined.

Is it naïve to think that an institution would sponsor courses critical of itself? Most institutions may not be willing to do that but a large, powerful, and intelligently directed institution would recognize the value of the strategy.

Unless Roman Catholic Church officials allow criticism of their teaching by loyal members of the church, the field will be left to those who wish to destroy the teaching. The equating of education in religion with catechetical-theological instruction in approved doctrine will cause the intellectually curious to drift away from the church. The Roman Catholic Church needs orthodoxy and authority, but these ideas cannot be developed and rethought without the teaching of religion.

If this kind of teaching were to occur in the church of today, it would lead to radical but well-grounded changes in the structure of the church. Resistance to these changes is inevitable but radical change is already occurring. The choice is whether to oppose all change or attempt to develop a well-educated church membership for whatever the church may look like in the future.

ENDNOTES

Chapter One

1   Alan Jacobs, *In the Year of Our Lord 1943* (New York: Oxford University Press, 2018), 16.

2   John Blum, *From the Morgenthau Diaries* (Boston: Houghton Mifflin, 1959), 38.

3   Thomas Merton, *Seven Storey Mountain* (New York: Mariner, 1999).

4   Bruce Cumings, *The Korean War: A History* (New York: Modern Library, 2010), 241.

5   Garry Wills, "Shallow Calls to Shallow," *Harper's Magazine,* April 2019, 78.

6   John Tracy Ellis, *American Catholics and the Intellectual Life* (New York: Heritage Foundation, 1956).

7   *Everson v. Board of Education*, 1947; *McCollum v. Board of Education*, 1948.

8   Gregory Black, *Hollywood Censored: Morality Codes, Catholics and the Movies* (Cambridge: Cambridge University Press, 1996).

Chapter Two

1   Martin Luther King, Jr., Interview on *Meet the Press,* April 17, 1960.

2   Martin Luther King, Jr., *I Have a Dream: Writings and Speeches that Changed the World* (New York: Harper One, 1992).

3   Dieter Hessel and Maggie Kuhn, *Maggie Kuhn on Aging: A Dialogue* (Louisville, KY: Westminster/John Know, 1977).

4   One of the influential writers at that time was Vine Deloria, Jr., *We Talk, You Listen* (New York: Macmillan, 1970); *Custer Died for Your Sins* (New York: Scribner, 2018).

5   "Conservatives were for it. Liberals were for it. Democrats, Republicans, and Independents were for it. So were the ins and outs, the executive and legislative branches of the government" – *New York Times,* April 23, 1970, 1.

6   Pope John XXIII, *Pacem in Terris* (Peace on Earth) (New York: St. Paul, 1963).

7   John O'Malley, *What Happened at Vatican II?* (Cambridge, MA: Harvard University Press, 2018), 141.

8   Gabriel Moran, *Theology of Revelation* (New York: Herder and Herder, 1966).

9   Xavier Rynne, *Letters from Vatican City* (New York: Farrar, Strauss, 1963). Eventually, the Xavier Rynne books became a small library.

10   "Nostra Aetate," in *Vatican II: The Conciliar and Postconciliar Documents,* Edited by Austin Flannery (Collegeville, MN: Liturgical Press, 1996).

11   Franz Rosenzweig, *The Star of Redemption* (Notre Dame, IN: University of Notre Dame Press, 1985).

Chapter Three

1   Peter Baker, "Nixon tried to Spoil Johnson's Vietnam Peace Talks," *The New York Times,* January 2, 2017.

2   John Finnis, *Moral Absolutes: Tradition, Revision and Truth* (Washington, DC:: Catholic University of America Press, 1991), 86.

3   Pope Pius XII, "Apostolate of the Midwife," *Catholic Mind,* January 1952.

4   *National Catholic Reporter,* April 15, 1967.

5   Interview with Austen Ivereigh, "A Time of Great Uncertainty," *Commonweal,* May 2020, 24-28.

6   Michael Sean Winters, "In Defense of *Humanae Vitae*," *National Catholic Reporter,* July 25, 2018.

7   Robert McClory, *Turning Point: The Inside Story of the Birth Control Commission and How Humanae Vitae Changed the Life of Patty Crowley and the Future of the Church* (New York: Crossroad, 1997); Robert Blair Kaiser, *The Politics of Sex and Religion* (Kansas City MO: Leaven Press, 1985).

8   David Geiringer, *The Pope and the Pill* (Manchester: Manchester University Press, 2020).

9   Charles Curran, *Loyal Dissent: Memoir of a Catholic Theologian* (Washing-

ton, DC: Georgetown University Press, 2006).

10   Gabriel Moran, "Religious Life is Dead," *National Catholic Reporter,* December 1970.

11   Gabriel Moran and Maria Harris, *Experiences in Community* (New York: Herder and Herder, 1968).

12   Maria Harris, *Dance of the Spirit* (New York: Bantam Press, 1989); *Jubilee Time: Celebrating Women, Spirit, and the Advent of Age* (New York: Bantam Press, 1995).

13   Her books include *Fashion Me a People* (Louisville, KY: Westminster John Knox, 1989); *Teaching and Religious Imagination* (New York: Harper and Row, 1987); *Proclaim Jubilee: A Spirituality for the Twenty-First Century* (Louisville, KY: Westminster John Knox, 1996).

14   *New York Times,* "Church finally Listens on Abuse by Priests, February 12, 1995; *Boston Globe,* "Spotlight" articles beginning on January 6, 2002.

15   *Commonweal,* January 4, 2019, 10.

16   Pennsylvania Grand Jury, A Report; Peter Steinfels, "Vehemently Misleading: The Pennsylvania Grand-Jury Report is Not What It Seems," *Commonweal,* January 25, 2019, 13-26.

17   Peter Steinfels was the main author of the *New York Times* report in 1995.

18   Thomas Doyle and Richard Sipe, *Sex, Priests, and Sacred Codes: The Catholic Church's 2000 Year Paper Trail of Sexual Abuse* (London: Crux, 2016). The quotation is from a lecture by Doyle at Gonzaga University in 2019.

19   Peggy Orenstein, *Boys and Sex: Young Men on Hookups, Love, Porn, Consent and Navigating the New Masculinity* (New York: Harper, 2020).

20   *The Production Code of the Motion Picture Industry* (1930–1967) at www.productioncode.dhwriting.com.

21   William Alcott, *A Young Man's Guide* (New York: American Medical Association, 1913; reprinted 1940).

22   *Declaration on Certain Questions concerning Sexual Ethics* (Rome: Congregation for the Doctrine of the Faith, 1975), section 9.

23   Betty Friedan, *The Feminine Mystique* (New York: Dell, 1964).

24   Pope Pius, "Address to International Congress of Hematology," *The Pope Speaks,* September 12, 1958.

25   Pope Francis, in a press conference aboard a plane, July 22, 2013. Robert McClory, "Pope Francis and Women's Ordination," *National Catholic Reporter,* September 16, 2013.

26   *Dutch Catechism* (New York: Herder and Herder, 1969).

27   Gabriel Moran, *Present Revelation: The Search for Religious Foundations* (New York: Herder and Herder, 1972).

Chapter Four

1   Nicholas Lash, "Teaching or Commanding," *Commonweal*, December 13, 2010, 17-20.

2   Gabriel Moran, *Scripture and Tradition: A Survey of the Controversy* (New York: Herder and Herder, 1963), 99.

3   Gabriel Moran: *Theology of Revelation* (New York: Herder and Herder, 1966).

4   Gabriel Moran, *Catechesis of Revelation* (New York: Herder and Herder, 1966).

5   Gabriel Moran, *Present Revelation: The Search for Religious Foundations* (New York: McGraw Hill, 1972).

6   Gabriel Moran, *Both Sides: The Story of Revelation* (New York: Paulist Press, 2001).

7   The Latin translation of Paul with a form of *revelatio* is found in in Rom. 8:19, ICor 1:7, Gal 1:12, Gal 2:2, Eph 3:3. The term was also used for Lk 2:32 when the gospel was translated into Greek.

8   Rev. 20:1-6.

9   Augustine, *City of God* (New York: Penguin Books, 2003), Book 20:6.

10 Thomas Aquinas, *Summa theologiae* (New York: McGraw Hill, 1964), 1.1.1

11 Thomas Aquinas, *Summa theologiae*, 1.12.13.1

12 Thomas Aquinas, *Summa theologiae*, 1.1.8

13 M.D. Chenu, *Nature, Man and Society in the Twelfth Century* (Toronto, ON: University of Toronto Press, 1997).

14 The work of Karl Rahner was especially influential in transforming the method of theology. Rahner begins from the human condition. He then employs Thomas Aquinas and modern thinkers, such as Immanuel Kant and Martin Heidegger, to interpret Catholic tradition.

15 John Rist, *Plotinus: The Road to Reality* (Cambridge: Cambridge University Press, 1967); Plotinus, *Enneads* (London: Faber and Faber, 1969); Paul Rorem, "The Uplifting Spirituality of Pseudo Dionysius," in *Christianity and Spirituality*, ed. Bernard McGinn and John Meyerdorff (New York: Crossroad, 1985, I, 147-48).

16 Joachim of Fiore, *Enchiridion Super Apocalypsim* (Toronto, ON: Pontifical Institute of Medieval Studies, 1986). Marjorie Reeves, *Joachim of Fiore* (New York: Harper, 1977).

17 Ernest Bloch, *The Principle of Hope* (Cambridge, MA: MIT Press, 1986), 127.

18 *Meister Eckhart: Teacher and Preacher, ed. Bernard McGinn* (New York: Paulist Press, 1987; Hildegard of Bingen, *Scivias* (New York: Paulist Press,

1990)

19   The wood carvings were largely the work of Albrecht Durer. The drawings
      in the Bible were by Michael Beal, *The Book of Revelation: A Biography*
      (Princeton, NJ: Princeton University Press, 2018),

20   Etienne Gilson, *Reason and Revelation in the Middle Ages* (New York: Scrib-
      ner, 1966).

21   John O'Malley, *When Bishops Meet: An Essay Comparing Trent, Vatican I
      and Vatican II* (Cambridge, MA: Harvard University Press, 2019).

22   Pope Francis, *Laudato si: On Care for our Common Home* (Washington,
      DC: USCB, 2015), par. 85.

Chapter Five

1   Aristotle, *Physics*, 192b.

2   Arthur Lovejoy and Franz Boaz, *Primitivism and Related Ideas in Antiquity*
     (Baltimore, MD: Johns Hopkins University Press, 1935).

3   St Paul refers to women not wearing hats in church as unnatural. Subse-
     quent Christians writers would declare many things to be "unnatural" such
     as, shaving, lending at interest, sexual intercourse during menstruation,
     wearing wigs, eating kosher foods, and circumcision. John Boswell, *Chris-
     tianity, Social Tolerance and Homosexuality: Gay People in Western Europe
     from the Beginning of Christianity to the Fourteenth Century* (Chicago, IL:
     University of Chicago Press, 2015), 166.

4   Plato, *Republic*, 5:27.

5   Gregory Lopez and Massimo Pigliucci, *A Handbook for New Stoics: How to
     Thrive in a World out of Control* (New York: The Experiment, 2019).

6   Francis Bacon, *The Organon and Related Writings* (Indianapolis, IN:
     Bobbs-Merrill, 1960).

7   G. K. Chesterton, *Saint Francis of Assisi* (Garden City, NY: Image Books,
     1959), 87.

8   Marcus Tullius Cicero, *On Moral Ends* (Cambridge: Cambridge University
     Press, 2001), 3:31. *The Republic* and *The Laws* (New York: Oxford Universi-
     ty Press, 1998).

9   Pamela Hall, *Narrative and the Natural Law* (Notre Dame: University of
     Notre Dame Press, 1994). Thomas Aquinas *Summa theologiae* 1.3.94.2

10   Thomas Aquinas, *Summa* 1.2.94.

11   Plato, *Republic*, 471a

12   Augustine, *City of God* (Baltimore, MD: Penguin Books, 1972), 1:21, 4:15,
     19:7; R.A. Marcus, *St. Augustine's View on the Just War* (Oxford: Blackwell,

1983).

13 Henry Shue, *Basic Rights: Substance, Affluence and U.S. Foreign Policy* (Princeton, NJ: Princeton University Press, 1996).

14 New natural law theory began with the writing of Germain Grisez in the 1960s. *Contraception and the Natural* Law (Milwaukee, WI: Bruce, 1964). Prominent writers today include Robert George, *Conscience and its Enemies: Confronting the Dogmas of Secular Liberalism* (Wilmington, DE: Intercollegiate Studies), 2016.

15 John Finnis, *Natural Law and Natural Rights* (New York: Oxford University Press, 2011).

Chapter Six

1 Gabriel Moran, *America in the United States and the United States in America* (Indianapolis, IN: iUniverse, 2018).

2 "Pope Francis Declares Death Penalty Unacceptable in All Cases," *New York Times,* August 2, 2018, A1.

3 U.S. Catholic Bishops, *The Challenge of Peace,* (Washington, DC: U.S. Catholic Conference, 1983).

4 Konrad Lorenz, *On Aggression* (New York: Mariner Books, 1974) is often misunderstood to have claimed that violence is inherent to human nature.

5 Gordon Allport, *The Individual and his Religion* (New York: Macmillan, 1967).

6 Amy-Jill Levine, *The Misunderstood Jew: The Scandal of the Church and the Jewish Jesus* (New York: Harper, 2001), 47.

7 Martin Buber, *Two Types of Faith* (New York: Harper Torch, 1961), 69.

8 Walter Wink, *Jesus and Nonviolence* (Philadelphia, PA: Fortress Press, 2003), 10 -11.

9 Flavius Josephus, *The Jewish War,* rev.ed. (New York: Penguin Classics, 1984), II, 92.

10 Quoted in Pinchas Lapide, *The Sermon on the Mount* (Maryknoll, NY: Orbis Books, 1986), 96; Christopher Hitchens, commenting on the text to love your enemies, says: "I think the enemies of civilization should be beaten and killed and defeated. And I think it is sickly and stupid and suicidal to say that we should love those who hate us." Quoted in Chris Hedges, *I Don't' Believe in Atheists* (New York: Free Press, 2008). 23.

11 George W. Bush, October 11, 2002: "Though Congress has now authorized the use of force, I have not ordered the use of force. I hope the use of force will not be necessary."

12   Jacques Maritain quoted in Mary Ann Glendon, *A World Made New: El-eanor Roosevelt and the Universal Declaration of Human Rights* (New York: Random House, 2001), 77.

13   Tom Holland, *Dominance: How the Christian Revolution Remade the World* (New York: Basic Books, 2019), 401.

14   Brian Tierney, *The Idea of Natural Rights* (Grand Rapids, MI: Eerdmans, 2001), 65-66.

15   Garry Wills, *Inventing America: Jefferson's Declaration of Independence* (New York: Vintage Books, 2018).

16   *Code of Canon Law.*

17   The controversy over property already existed as early as Gratian's *Decretum* in the twelfth century that became the basis of canon law. Tierney, *The Idea of Natural Rights*, Chapter 2.

18   John Locke, *The Second Treatise on Civil Government* (New York: Prometheus, 1986), Chapter 9.

19   Locke, *Second Treatise,* Section 124.

20   Frederick Douglass, "The Inhumanity of Slavery," in *Autobiographies.* (New York: Library of America, 1994), 427.

21   Mary Ann Glendon, *A World Made New: Eleanor Roosevelt and the Universal Declaration of Human Rights* (New York: Random House, 2001).

22   Glendon, *A World Made New,* 67.

23   Gabriel Moran, *Uniquely Human: The Basis of Human Rights* (Indianapolis, IN: iUniverse, 2016).

24   Augustine's conditions for going to war (*jus ad bellum*) are: a just cause, competent authority, right intention, limited objective, last resort, reasonable hope of success; conditions for fighting a just war: discrimination and proportionality. John Langan, "The Elements of St. Augustine's Just War Theory," *The Journal of Religious Ethics,* (Spring, 1984), 19-38.

25   Pope John XXIII, *Peace on Earth* (New York: Paulist Press, 1963).

Chapter Seven

1   Emily Matchar, "In Liberal Europe, Abortion Laws Come with their own Restrictions," *The Atlantic,* August 5, 2013.

2   The World Health Organization estimates that 80 percent of women having abortion do not have ready access to contraceptives. See *Lancet,* May 2016.

3   Barbara Ehrenreich and Deidre English, *For Her Own Good* (New York: Anchor Books, 2005), 30.

4   Kristin Luker, *Abortion and the Politics of Motherhood* (Berkeley, CA: Uni-

versity of California Press, 1985), 60.

5   Luker, *Abortion*, 46-47.

6   For the best surveys of the practice of abortion before and after the Supreme Court decision, see Mary Ann Glendon, *Abortion and Divorce in Western Law* (Cambridge MA: Harvard University Press, 1987), 41. The especially important study she cites is: *General Social Surveys* 1972–1987 (Chicago IL: National Opinion Research Center, 1987).

7   Guttmacher Institute, "Characteristics of U.S. Abortion Patients in 2014 and Changes since 2008," May 2016; Pew Research Center in 2014 found 22 percent of abortion patients were Catholic women and about one fourth of them were married. Patrick Brown, "Catholics are just as likely to get an Abortion as other U.S. Women. Why?" *America*, January 24, 2018.

8   Congregation for the Doctrine of the Faith, *Declaration on Procured Abortion* (Rome: Vatican Press, 1974), Section 7.

9   John Noonan, ed., *The Morality of Abortion: An Almost Absolute Value in History* (Cambridge MA: Harvard University Press, 1970).

10   John Noonan, *An Almost Absolute*, 54.

11   Jerome, *On Ecclesiastes*, 2:5; Augustine, *De Originae animae*, 4.4.

12   *Treatise on Laws with the Ordinary Gloss* (Washington, DC: Catholic University of America Press, 1993); John Noonan, *The Morality of Abortion*, 20.

13   I refer here to church officials. There is also a small industry of conservative Roman Catholic philosophers and theologians dedicated to reconciling Thomas Aquinas with current church teaching on abortion. A good example is Germain Grisez, *Abortion: The Myths, the Realities and the Arguments* (Washington DC: Corpus Books, 1970). For a list of such works, see John Haldane and Patrick Lee, "Aquinas on Human Ensoulment, Abortion and the Value of Life," *Philosophy*, 78(2003), Footnote 5.

14   For a careful study of Thomas Aquinas's texts, see Fabrizio Amerini, *Aquinas on the Beginning and End of Life* (Cambridge, MA: Harvard University Press, 2013), especially Chapter 5.

15   John Noonan, *The Morality of Abortion*, 23

16   Congregation for the Doctrine of the Faith, *Declaration on Procured Abortions*, Footnote 19.

17   Thomas Aquinas, *Summa theologiae*, Ia, q. 19, art 2: "Person signifies what is noblest in the whole of nature."

18   Bernard Häring, *The Law of Christ* (Westminster, MD: Newman Press, 1963).

19   "Pope Francis Broaches a Rare Topic: Abortion," *National Catholic Reporter*, May 9, 2014, 11.

20   Kelefa Sanneh, "The Intensity Gap," *New Yorker*, October 27, 2014, 39.

21　Robert George, *Conscience and its Enemies: Confronting the Dogmas of Secular Liberalism* (Wilmington, DE: Intercollegiate Studies Institute, 2016)

22　Edward O. Wilson, *The Meaning of Human Existence* (New York: Liveright, 2014) is an example of a leading biologist declaring what human existence means. Not surprisingly, religious questions are simply unintelligible to him.

23　A split of the bishops on this point surfaced in 2021 when Cardinal Blase Cupich of Chicago objected to a statement put out by Bishop José Gomez, acting as head of the bishops' conference. Some bishops, like Cupich, would acknowledge that Catholic politicians are bound by their office to uphold the law of land even if they have some personal opposition to abortion.

24　W. Barry Garrett, "High Court holds Abortion to be a 'Right of privacy,'" *Baptist Press*, January 31, 1973.

25　Randall Balmer, "The Real Origin of the Religious Right," *Politico*, May 27, 2014.

26　David French, *National Review*, March, 2019.

27　The statistics are from the Alan Guttmacher Institute: *Abortion and Women's Health: A Turning Point for America* (New York: Guttmacher Institute, 1990).

28　The U.S. Supreme Court has been ridiculed for saying that corporations are people. The Court was not inventing the idea. The blind spot in the *Citizens United v. Federal Elections Commission* decision was not to recognize that the money of (artificial) persons can overwhelm the political process.

Chapter Eight

1　Alfred Kinsey, *Sexual Behavior in the Human Male* (Bloomington. IN: Indiana University Press, 1998).

2　Kinsey, *Sexual Behavior.*

3　John Finnis, *Moral Absolutes: Tradition, Revision and Truth* (Washington, DC: Catholic University of America Press, 1991).

4　*Declaration on Certain Questions concerning Sexual Ethics* (Rome: Congregation for the Doctrine of the Faith, 1975), Section 8.

5　*Declaration on Certain Questions*, Section 8.

6　Congregation for the Doctrine of the Faith, *On the Pastoral Care of Homosexual Persons* (Rome: Vatican Press, 1986), 3.

7　U.S. Catholic Bishops, *Ministry to Persons with a Homosexual Inclination*: Guidelines for Pastoral Care (Washington, DC: U.S. Catholic Conference, 2006).

8   U.S. Catholic Bishops, *Ministry to Persons*, 10-11.

9   Pamela Hall, *Narrative and the Natural Law: An Interpretation of Thomistic Ethics* (Notre Dame, IN: University of Notre Dame Press, 2017), 28. She is commenting mainly on q. 92 of Thomas's *Summa theologiae*.

10 International Theological Commission: *A New Look at Natural Law* (Rome Vatican Press, 2012), II:52.

11 Edward Pentin, *The Rigging of a Vatican Synod* (San Francisco, CA: St. Ignatius Press, 2015).

12 James Porterfield, *Obergefell v. Hodges* (New York: Enslow Publishing, 2017).

13 William Baude. "Is Polygamy Next?" *New York Times*, July 21, 2015, A27.

14 Congregation for the Doctrine of the Faith, *Considerations regarding Proposals to Give Legal Recognition to Unions between Homosexual Persons* (Rome: Vatican Press, 2003), 7.

15 Interim Report of the Synod 2014.

Chapter Nine

1   Ronald Dworkin, *Life's Dominion: An Argument about Abortion, Euthanasia, and Individual Freedom* (New York: Random House, 2011), 195: "The Roman Catholic Church is the sternest, most vigilant, and no doubt most effective opponent of euthanasia as it is of abortion."

2   Pope Benedict XVI, *Let God's Light Shine Forth: The Spiritual Vision of Pope Benedict XVI*, ed. Robert Moynihan (New York: Doubleday), 155; on the meaning of euthanasia, see: James Rachels, "Active and Passive Euthanasia," *New England Journal of Medicine*, 292 (January 9, 1975), 78-80; William May, *Testing the Medical Covenant: Active Euthanasia and Health Care Reform* (Grand Rapids, MI: Eerdmans, 1996), 14.

3   Plato, especially in *Phaedrus* (New York: Penguin Books, 2005).

4   Aristotle, *Rhetoric* (New York: Random House, 1954), 123.

5   Simone de Beauvoir, *The Coming of Age* (New York: W.W. Norton, 1996), 380.

6   Leslie Stahl, *Becoming Grandma: The Joys and Science of the New Grandparenting* (New York: Blue Rider Press), 2017.

7   Bert Smith, *Aging in America* (Boston, MA: Beacon Press, 1974)

8   Quoted in Gail Sheehy, *Predictable Crises of Adult Life*, (New York: Ballantine, 2006), 279.

9   CS Lewis, quoting George McDonald in C.S. Lewis, *George MacDonald: An Anthology: 365 Readings* (New York: Harper Collins, 2015).

10   Norman Cousins, *Anatomy of an Illness as Perceived by the Patient* (New York: W.W. Norton, 2005).

11   Aristotle, *Nicomachean Ethics*, Books 8, 1155a3.

12   Ronald Blythe, *The View in Winter: Reflections on Old Age*, (London: Hymns Ancient and Modern Ltd, 2005)

13   Gary Laderman, *Rest in Peace: A Cultural History of Death and the Funeral Industry in the Twentieth Century* (New York: Oxford University Press, 2003).

14   Benen Ling, "These Death Stocks are barely clinging to Life," *Seeking Alpha*, June 20, 2019.

15   Kay Redfield Jamison, *Night Falls Fast: Understanding Suicide* (New York: Vintage, 2000), 21.

16   Michael Redinger, "'Futility' and End of Life Care," *Commonweal*, Feb. 2020), 38-43.

17   Susan Jacoby, "We're Aging Fast and Not Doing Anything about It," *New York Times*, December 26, 2019, A27.

18   *Declaration on Euthanasia* (Rome: Congregation for the Doctrine of the Faith, 1980).

19   Pope Pius XII, "The Prolongation of Life," *The Pope Speaks*, 4(1958), 303-98.

20   Daniel Callahan, The Troubled Dream of Life: *In Search of a Peaceful Death* (Washington, DC: Georgetown University Press, 2000), 81.

21   *The Tablet*, January 4, 2020, 25

22   *Catechism of the Catholic Church*, 2nd ed. (New York: Random House, 2012), 608.

Chapter Ten

1   *National Catholic Reporter*, September 6-19, 8.

2   Brett Salkeld, *Transubstantiation: Theology, History and Christian Unity* (Grand Rapids, MI: Baker Publishing Co., 2019).

3   Flannery O'Connor, *The Habit of Being* (New York: Farrar, Straus and Giroux, 1979), 125.

4   Richard Rohr, *The Universal Christ*, (New York: Crown, 2018), 131.

5   Robert Orsi, *History and Presence* (Cambridge, MA: Harvard University Press, 2016).

6   William Faulkner, *Requiem for a Nun* (New York: Vintage, 2011).

7   Thich Nhat Hanh, *The Pocket Thich Nhat Hanh* (Boulder, CO.: Shambhala, 2012), 122.

8   Matthew Fox, *Breakthrough: Meister Eckhart's Creation Spirituality* (New York: Image Books, 1980), 48.

9   Mary Midgley, *Beast and Man: The Roots of Human Nature* (New York: Routledge, 2002), 324; see the similar view of Konrad Lorenz, *On Aggression* (New York, Mariner Books, 1974), 294-95.

10   Hans Boersma, *Heavenly Participation: The Weaving of Sacramental Tapestry* (Grand Rapids, MI: Eerdmans, 2010).

11   Giles Emery, "Ecclesiastical Fruits of the Eucharist in St. Thomas Aquinas," *Nova et Vetera* 2, no.1 (2004), 60.

12   Rohr, *Universal Christ*, 133.

Chapter Eleven

1   Aristotle, *Nicomachean Ethics*; Book 8; Cicero, *On Old Age, On Friendship, On Divination* (Cambridge, MA: Harvard University, 1923).

2   Mt, Chapters 5,6,7.

3   Andrew Greeley, *Religious Change in America* (Cambridge, MA: Harvard University Press, 1996); *American Catholics: A Social Portrait* (New York: Basic Books, 1978).

4   Pope Pius X, *On the Doctrine of the Modernists and the Syllabus of Modern Errors* (Charlotte, NC: Create Space, 2014).

5   David Oshinsky, *Bellevue: Medicine and Mayhem at America's Most Storied Hospital* (New York: Doubleday, 2016), Chapter 5.

6   Mary Douglas, *Natural Symbols* (New York: Routledge, 2003).

7   Ludwig Wittgenstein, *Culture and Value* (London: Wiley-Blackwell, 1998), 7.

8   Ludwig Wittgenstein, *Lectures and Conversations on Aesthetics, Psychology, and Religious Belief*, ed. Cyril Barrett (Oxford: Blackwell, 1966).

9   Tertullian, *Apology* (Cambridge, MA: Harvard University Press, 1931), 24.

10   Garry Wills, *Why Priests? A Failed Tradition* (New York: Viking, 2013), 12.

Chapter Twelve

1   Mike Abrahoff, *It's Your Ship*, quoted in William Maxwell, *Ethics 101: What Every Leader Needs to Know* (New York: Center Street, 2015), 83.

2   Pope Francis, *Amoris Laetitia* (Rome: Vatican Press, 2016), par. 3.

3   Pope Francis, "Address to Renewal in the Holy Spirit," July 4, 2015 in *Na-*

tional Catholic Reporter, April 25, 2016.

4   Andrew Greeley, *Priests: A Calling in Crisis* (Chicago: University of Chicago Press, 2004), Chapter 9.

5   Garry Wills, *Why Priests? A Failed Tradition*: James Carrol, "How to Save the Catholic Church. Dismantle the Priesthood," *The Atlantic*, April 2019; not surprisingly, priests did not agree with the proposal. Francis Clooney, "Don't Abolish the Priesthood: Redeem It," *America*, June 19, 2019.

6   Francis Oakley, *The Conciliarist Tradition: Constitutionalism in the Catholic Tradition 1300-1870* (New York: Oxford University Press, 2008), 13.

7   Brian Tierney, *Foundations of Conciliar Theory* (New York: Brill, 1998), 140.

8   Brian Tierney, *Foundations*, 13.